eFieldnotes

HANEY FOUNDATION SERIES

A volume in the Haney Foundation Series, established in 1961
with the generous support of Dr. John Louis Haney

eFIELDNOTES

The Makings of Anthropology in the Digital World

Edited by

Roger Sanjek and Susan W. Tratner

PENN

UNIVERSITY OF PENNSYLVANIA PRESS

PHILADELPHIA

Published by
University of Pennsylvania Press
Philadelphia, Pennsylvania 19104-4112
www.upenn.edu/pennpress

Printed in the United States of America
on acid-free paper

10 9 8 7 6 5 4 3 2 1

Library of Congress Cataloging-in-Publication Data

eFieldnotes : the makings of anthropology in the digital world / edited by Roger Sanjek and Susan W. Tratner.
    pages cm. — (Haney Foundation series)
    Examines how anthropological fieldwork has been affected by technological shifts in the 25 years since the 1990 publication of Fieldnotes : the makings of anthropology, edited by Roger Sanjek, published by Cornell University Press.
    Includes bibliographical references and index.
    ISBN 978-0-8122-4778-7 (alk. paper)
    1. Ethnology—Fieldwork—Technological innovations. 2. Anthropology—Fieldwork—Technological innovations. 3. Ethnologists—Effect of technological innovations on. 4. Anthropologists—Effect of technological innovations on. 5. Ethnology—Methodology—Technological innovations. 6. Anthropology—Methodology—Technological innovations. 7. Computers and civilization—Research. 8. Cyperspace—Social aspects—Research. 9. Anthropological archives. I. Sanjek, Roger, editor. II. Tratner, Susan W., editor.
GN346.E45 2016
301.0285—dc23

                                                                2015014682

Contents

Preface

Susan W. Tratner and Roger Sanjek

This volume has its roots in the predigital era. Roger's edited volume *Field-notes: The Makings of Anthropology*, published in 1990, focused attention on how anthropologists record their experiences when doing ethnographic fieldwork. On its cover are Margaret Mead and Gregory Bateson working in their "mosquito room" in an Iatmul village with the technology of 1938, namely notepads, two manual typewriters, and film cameras. The volume provided an array of perspectives on fieldnotes and fieldwork, introduced useful vocabulary (such as "headnotes" and "scratchnotes"), offered critical guidance to researchers, and has circulated widely and been cited frequently. In the intervening years, technology has changed not only how anthropologists conduct their fieldwork but also how they record, process, analyze, and communicate their findings. These changes present new technical, ethical, and theoretical challenges fieldworkers face that could not have been addressed or anticipated two and a half decades ago.

Roger had begun contemplating a successor volume to *Fieldnotes* when Susan and he happened to meet at a small restaurant in their New York City neighborhood in May 2011. Susan was an anthropologist studying anonymous discussion boards where parents of toddlers and young children post information and express opinions. Our discussions about the impact of new digital technologies on ethnography continued through a score of meetings during 2011–2014. We shared and commented on readings, Susan helped Roger decode and translate digital terminology, and we agreed to co-organize and coedit a volume on "efieldnotes." In 2012, we invited the contributors to this volume to participate in panels we chaired at the 2013 Society for Applied Anthropology (SfAA) meetings in Denver and the American Anthropological Association (AAA) meetings in Chicago (all but three could and did); we also circulated a reading list on Internet ethnography, including work by our coauthors, and hosted overlapping groups of efieldnotes participants at dinner discussions during the 2012 AAA meetings in San Francisco, 2013 SfAA and AAA meetings in Denver and Chicago, and 2014 AAA meetings in Washington, D.C. In an interesting twist on the online versus IRL (in real life) question, the SfAA panel has existed as a podcast (http://sfaapodcasts.net/2013/03/25/efieldnotes -makings-of-anthropology-in-a-digital-world/) since 2013, with presentations by Roger, Jenna Burrell, Martin Slama, and Lisa Cliggett followed by a lively audience discussion.

As the wheels of anthropology have turned over the past two and a half decades, so have the wheels of the world and the wheels of our lives during the period in which this book was conceived and produced. In places our readers will visit in chapters that follow, the aftermath of the March 11, 2011, disasters in Japan; the continued violence affecting Kurdistan and Kurds; and the 2014 devastation of Ebola in Liberia have shaped the work and personal lives of many anthropologists, including William Kelly, Diane King, and Mary Moran. More joyfully, seven babies entered the lives of six of our *eFieldnotes* coauthors: Kenzo Douglas Kubo (Burrell), August and Maurice Jones, Jesus Andrew (King), Julian Channing Kraemer Moore, Luuk Verheijen (Schrooten), and Miles Tratner.

Susan would like to express her gratitude to Roger, a true gentleman, for inviting her to be part of this project—none of this would have happened without his confidence and support. She also thanks her SUNY Empire State colleagues for their inspiration and camaraderie, and Dean Cynthia Ward for release time to work on this volume. And she remains grateful for her parents Alan and Irene Warshauer, her families by birth and marriage, and her friends the Baias, Lewin/Matthews, and Meyers, who are like family. Finally, home is where the heart is, and her heart belongs to Matthew, Ian, and Miles: thank you for filling my life with music, laughter, and joy.

Roger would like to acknowledge his sister-in-law Mary Morioka, who told him to "go for it" following William Kelly's 2010 email (see Chapter 1, this volume). And we both acknowledge the supportive appraisal and sage advice of our University of Pennsylvania Press reader Don Brenneis, as well as the gracious and welcome assistance of Peter Agree, Amanda Ruffner, Elizabeth Glover, Jeremy Lane, Will Boehm, John Hubbard, Eric Halpern, Erica Ginsburg, and Catherine Chilton at the press.

PART I

TRANSFORMATIONS AND CONTINUITIES

Chapter 1

From Fieldnotes to eFieldnotes

Roger Sanjek

In 1979, the eminent social anthropologist Fei Xiaotong visited the United States for a month, the first return of this Malinowski student and Chinese public intellectual since the early 1940s (see Arkush 1981; Fei 1939). His "fleeting glimpses," as he called them, were prescient. One of the first things he described was how, when he and a companion asked to move their airplane seat reservations so they could sit together, the airline desk attendant "instantly typed up some symbols on a fluorescent screen right next to her, and on the screen the answer needed came glowing out, and she took my seat number back and gave us two seats together." He noted electronic devices "reorganizing the activity of men and of things" in stores, hotels, transportation terminals, universities, and libraries nationwide. Telephonic communication and computers, "living treasures" of American life, as he put it, "allow people dispersed in widely separated places to organize collective activity in an instant, and these collective activities can be begun and completed, without having to gather them in a designated place or continue them for a long time. A new kind of social collectivity has appeared. . . . If you follow this direction of development through," Fei wrote, "it can have such an influence on the organization of the collective activity of mankind, that it really makes you ponder" (1979–1980: 6–7).[1]

It would take another two decades before such pondering by anthropologists, or sustained ethnographic fieldwork concerning the impact and use of these new digital technologies, would emerge in earnest.[2] Meanwhile, in the early 1990s, the Internet, originally created by "a partnership among three groups: the [U.S.] military, universities, and private corporations . . . fused together into an iron triangle . . . during and after World War II," was made publically accessible to a few million users, and, in 1993–1994, the World Wide Web (of URL addresses), developed by the European Organization for Nuclear Research (CERN), became widely available (Isaacson 2014: 217–261, 405–419, 482–483). By 2004, there were six hundred million Internet users, and by 2015, 2.9 billion, some 40 percent of the world's population.[3] During this same period, cell (or mobile) phone networks expanded, and in 2010, there were more than four and a half billion subscriptions worldwide (Ling and Horst 2011: 363–364). Even more recently, Facebook since 2004, YouTube since 2005, Twitter since 2006, and other new platforms have reshaped the digital environment.

A few years after Fei's visit, at the 1985 American Anthropological Association annual meeting, I chaired a session on fieldnotes, the anthropological writings that precede the writing of ethnography. In the resulting volume, *Fieldnotes: The Makings of Anthropology* (Sanjek 1990a), my coauthors and I considered the forms, history, use, destinations, meanings, and resonances of fieldnotes over the one hundred–year history of ethnographic fieldwork. We identified the widespread disciplinary practice of transforming handwritten scratchnotes (inscriptions) into typed fieldnotes (descriptions) and their subsequent use in constructing ethnographic articles and books, a process developed and consolidated by founding figures Frank Cushing, Franz Boas, W. H. R. Rivers, Bronislaw Malinowski, and Margaret Mead. Much within anthropology has changed since our 1985 session, both theoretically and methodologically, but perhaps most significant is the impact of new technologies and modes of communication on our choice of fieldwork methods, sites, and issues. The perspectives on fieldnotes in our 1990 volume are not obsolete, but today they need rethinking and expansion.[4]

Digital Arrivals and Anthropological Fieldnotes

A sizable portion of the "vast and increasing corpus of [fieldwork] literature" (Parkin 2000: 259) published since 1990 contains little or no mention of fieldnotes[5] or, at most, provides further elaboration of the processes of producing and using them and other field-based writings (such as diaries, letters, records, local documentation, previous researchers' fieldnotes, and writings by assistants and collaborators) examined in *Fieldnotes*.[6] Much of this discussion, moreover, refers retrospectively to the pre–personal computer and pre-Internet fieldwork eras.

The introduction of new digital technologies for analyzing, producing, circulating, and enhancing fieldnotes began in the 1970s, and early developments were acknowledged in *Fieldnotes* (Johnson and Johnson 1990; Sanjek 1990b: 38, 1990c: 389). At that time, the tedious coding of fieldwork results on IBM punch cards; running piles of them through data analysis programs on mainframe computers; and working with large, unwieldy, accordion-folded paper printouts, was still a fresh memory.[7] Some digital databases for long-term fieldwork projects were started in this way during the 1970s and maintained and updated in later decades as digital technology improved (Black-Rogers 2001; Johansen and White 2002; Kemper 2002).

In the early 1980s, the major innovations were the home or personal computer (PC), and word processing software, and they revolutionized the writing of ethnography. As Harry Wolcott put it, "My typing has always been slow and riddled with errors. My dependence on others to type and retype my drafts slowed the . . . process immeasurably. . . . With my manuscript on the screen in front of me or quickly transformed to hard copy, I now edit continuously, rather than having to wait until someone finishes retyping a corrected draft" (1999: 267). For those conducting fieldwork "at home" or in settings abroad where desktop computers were available, the word processing of fieldnotes in digital text files quickly became the norm (see De Walt and DeWalt 2011: 175; Shore 1999: 26). Others continued to work in locales where this was not possible, such as Katy Gardner, who wrote her fieldnotes on a typewriter in Bangladesh during 1988 and 1989 (1999: 54), and Monique Skidmore, who produced hers manually in Burma during 1996 (2006: 49).

In the 1990s, portable laptop computers (and, later, notebooks and other devices) made word processing of fieldnotes in the field more common and less exceptional (Kemper 2002: 301). Joshua Hotaka Roth used a laptop during his 1994 fieldwork among Brazilian Nikkei in Japan (2003: 338)[8]; and by the early 2000s, this was practicable even in relatively remote fieldwork settings, such as Niger (Greenough 2006: 147) and, using a solar panel energy source, Soqotra Island in Yemen (Peutz 2006: 85; compare Bernard 2011: 297).

PCs and laptops also made data analysis "packages" readily available at home, in the field, or anywhere (Kemper 2002: 300–301; Royce and

Kemper 2002: xxviii–xxix). Although such tools continue to play valuable roles in dealing with ethnographers' (and team projects') own "big data" sets (Bernard 2011; Kemper and Royce 2002), the allure of some imagined perfect text analysis software to do the hard work of coding, indexing, and turning fieldnotes into ethnography vanished during the 1990s (Stewart 1998: 52–56; Wolcott 1990: 32–35, 1999: 267–269) and remains a will-o'-the-wisp (DeWalt and DeWalt 2011: 175, 179–210; Heath and Street 2008: 94–95). As Alex Stewart put it then: "From beginning to end, inquiry [in ethnography] is characterized by non-linear cycles of comparisons between units of data and a range of other mental activities, including observation, labeling, indexing, reflections on various literatures and cases, memoing, and incipient theorization" (1998: 52).[9] And as Tom Boellstorff, Bonnie Nardi, Celia Pearce, and T. L. Taylor put it now:

> We could in principle use a range of qualitative data analysis programs [yet] it is striking that none of us ever used them. Our experience has been that they typically require a steep learning curve and are frequently constrained by analytic assumptions built into the software. . . . Instead, we opt for the flexibility of standard word processing, data-base, and spreadsheet programs—and even paper and pen—to comment on, highlight, move, and search for data. Thus, while not in any way discouraging the use of [such] programs, we emphasize . . . the key to data analysis is to interact with the dataset: read it, study it, immerse oneself within it. (2012: 165–166, and see 167–181)

In my reading of the fieldwork literature, the earliest mention of "the Internet" (Des Chene 1997: 82) occurs in Gupta and Ferguson's *Anthropological Locations* (1997), which derives from a conference held in February 1994. The first actual use of the Internet while doing fieldwork that I have discovered is the student-advisor email correspondence, beginning in November 1994, between Allaine Cerwonka, who was conducting urban research in Melbourne, Australia, and Liisa Malkki, at the University of California, Irvine, an exchange that forms the basis of their book *Improvising Theory* (Cerwonka and Malkki 2007).[10] Email quickly afforded an increasingly utilized communication channel—not only between fieldworkers and advisors but also with family and colleagues at home and to make opening contacts and maintain communication during and after fieldwork with those we study.[11] Using email, initially, and perhaps still for some of us, replaced sending handwritten or typed letters by postal services, thus rendering an established form of communication simpler and quicker to accomplish. (I have wondered, however, whether, while doing fieldwork during 1970–1971 in Accra, Ghana, the time and deliberation it took to compose each "monthly report" I mailed to my advisor in New York presented an "affordance" value that more frequent email exchange might obviate.[12])

The next use of the Internet noted in the fieldwork literature was, by the later 1990s, visiting websites, many of which provided instantly the kinds of information ethnographers were accustomed to consult in published form or ferret out. Soon, the proliferating universe of URLs offered much more than this, and the Internet became a research medium utilized before, during, and after fieldwork (as well as in other professional activities) by all anthropologists (see Bestor 2003; Skidmore 2006: 55; Steinhoff 2003: 37). As Internet-enabled communication became more complex, ethnographers encountered and made use of web posts and responses, bulletin boards, chat rooms, listservs, blogs, text messaging, embedded videos, and social network sites (E. Coleman 2010).

In their introduction to *Anthropologists in a Wider World: Essays on Field Research*, derived from seminars at the Oxford Institute of Social and Cultural Anthropology in 1997 and 1998, two editors of the collection pronounced that "to understand forms of human life is to grasp connections [within] those settings in which people build some enduring sense of shared position" and that "until one engages with people closely, one does not know what those connections are," whether the people are "clustered in a village, or spread across the internet" (Dresch and James 2000: 7). Nowhere in the volume was "the internet" mentioned again, but it was now an acknowledged component of the twenty-first century world that anthropologists confront.[13]

This was even more evident in Merry White's reflection on her fieldwork in the 1980s and 1990s among Japanese teenagers.

> This study was conducted before the widespread use in Japan of the Internet, cell phones, and beepers. . . . Now, most teens have access to a cell phone. . . . and email and chat rooms make access to friends, virtual and otherwise, an easy matter. . . . These new media . . . provide . . . vehicles for future research, both in themselves as

objects of inquiry and as mediating devices for communication with informants. [Still,] the full "sociography" . . . must also include the street wisdom, the smell of the coffee shops, and the parade of fashion and styles teens will continue to experience. (2003: 33–35; see also Ito, Okabe, and Matsuda 2005)

Even as White's words were published, anthropologists conducting dissertation research worldwide were using digital technologies "to keep in contact with home and up to speed with regional and global processes that impact the communities they study." Moreover, "today's informants and collaborators are also able to employ these technologies to inform themselves about the world and global political economy," and the way in which anthropologists may be "received by community members [is] based on images and stereotypes produced by globalized communication media" (Hoffman and Gardner 2006: 11; see also Hoffman 2006: 25–27).

Nonetheless, digital connection is not universal and certainly not equal.[14] As Gabriella Coleman reminds us, "With the exception of cell phones . . . many digital technologies are still not in reach of most of the world's population" (2010: 488). Furthermore, the limited-feature or recycled hardware used by many of the world's masses and underclasses would be considered inadequate by the tech savvy of the San Francisco Bay area, or Tokyo, or Berlin, or upscale Beijing. Rather than a digital divide, it is digital slopes that prevail, along lines of wealth, class, market penetration, education, age, gender, North-South and urban-rural inequalities, and world language literacy and facility.[15]

An Ethnographer's Digital Arrivals Story

Trained in the 1960s, my fieldwork in Brazil, Ghana, and with the Gray Panther movement in that decade and the next utilized the standard fieldnote process: a small notebook for scratchnotes and a manual or electric typewriter for fieldnotes and ethnographic writing. Then, in 1984, as my fieldwork in Queens, New York, began, I moved to a personal computer (with a twenty megabyte hard drive!), a laserjet printer, and a word processing program (Multimate) for fieldnotes and other writing. This research project involved a team, and we coordinated our activities and meetings by telephone, U.S. mail, and Xerox photocopying (I also acquired a home copier in 1984). U.S. Census and other government documentary resources were purchased or, like journal articles, photocopied in libraries. I continued to work at this technological level through completion of my fieldwork in 1996 and my book, *The Future of Us All: Race and Neighborhood Politics in New York City* (Sanjek 1998a).

A late adopter, I did not go online or begin using email until 2000. I acquired my first cell phone in 2002, primarily to keep in touch with family members about my mother's and parents-in-law's declining health conditions.

In 2003, I inaugurated an undergraduate fieldwork class focused on Flushing, Queens, a diverse neighborhood with a growing Chinese presence, adjacent to Queens College, where I taught. I offered the course four times between 2003 and 2007, with groups of from four to eight students. Although these numbers were similar in size to my Elmhurst-Corona team two decades earlier, and the range of fieldwork sites—shopping strips, houses of worship, a senior center, libraries, parks, and district-level politics—was also similar, digital technologies afforded efficiencies and opportunities that were new.

After our first meeting, we coordinated each week by email and cell phone, deciding the day before class, according to the weather forecast, whether to meet in the field or in the college computer lab. In Flushing, we sometimes dispersed and used cell phones to regather. After the first week, students emailed their initial fieldnotes to each other, and the following week's discussion of what to include, in how much detail, made further teaching about fieldnote technique by me superfluous. The students read and critiqued and self-critiqued each other's and their own notes and learned together how they could improve them (compare Boellstorff et al. 2012: 86; DeWalt and DeWalt 2011: 89). They continued to share their fieldnotes weekly, and each student drew on the entire class corpus of notes in writing his or her final fieldwork reports. On computer lab days, we together visited websites of community organizations, city government agencies, and the local press, and I supplied commentary and led discussions. We also accessed U.S. Census data for the tracts we studied, and we were able to do online analyses of population and housing patterns in our fieldwork area. These technological tools and resources enabled us to do much more in a single semester than was possible in the pre-Internet 1980s.

Concurrent with my Flushing fieldwork experience, I returned to my Gray Panther activism and research of 1977–1987 to update and complete my book *Gray Panthers* (2009b). From 2004 to 2010, I participated in the New York City group, which had reactivated in 2003; I attended national conventions in Seattle and Detroit, and national board meetings in Washington, D.C.; and Lani Sanjek and I revisited Berkeley, California, where our involvement had begun thirty years earlier.[16]

In 2004, when I began, communication among national Gray Panther board members, as within the local groups, was half by email, half by U.S. mail. By 2006, email predominated, with all national board members and local group leaders using it. In 2004, a San Francisco member began a Yahoo listserv connecting forty-one active members nationwide. It was used most intensely during 2005 by members of eleven Panther groups for sharing plans and information as they participated in demonstrations, forums, and radio and television programs to oppose President George W. Bush's campaign to privatize Social Security. A national Gray Panther website was established in 1998, later revamped, and, unlike the listserv, continued until the national Gray Panthers disbanded in 2015. It had been created to replace the national newspaper (later newsletter) begun in 1972 and discontinued in 2000. By 2010, the website served primarily to post email-blast issue updates accompanying requests for donations. During the 2000s, the membership and number of local Gray Panther groups declined considerably, but the few such groups remaining in 2015 still maintained local websites and utilized email. During 2004–2010, I was editor of fourteen issues of the New York Gray Panthers newsletter, all of which were posted online as well as delivered to members by U.S. mail (Sanjek 2015a). Overall, the membership losses the Gray Panthers faced in these years could not have been reversed through digital technology alone.

These two fieldwork engagements in the 2000s made plain to me that both how we conduct fieldwork and what we study now involve digital dimensions that must be embraced. This was evident as well in the publications of colleagues, of my own and later generations, whose work I followed. James Watson (2004), for example, wrote about the digitally connected global network of four thousand Man lineage members whom he had begun studying in their Hong Kong New Territories home village in 1969. Mary Moran, in her book *Liberia: The Violence of Democracy* (2006), described the digital news sources, cell phone links, and diaspora websites and blogs that emerged in that country's decade of extended civil war.[17] And Lanita Jacobs analyzed online discussions about hair on AFROAM-L, a listserv for African American topics, in a chapter of her book *From the*

Kitchen to the Parlor: Language and Becoming in African American Women's Hair Care (2006).

As I began to learn of this new (to me) world of research about new technologies in the lives of people globally, my own life continued to change via digital technology. In 2009, a hitherto unknown Croatian double second cousin, residing in Copenhagen, found me through Google. Her and my Ceboci grandmothers had been sisters, and our Šanjek grandfathers brothers; her grandparents remained in Croatia while mine migrated to New York. We began an extended email correspondence, and, in 2012, Lani Sanjek and I traveled to Denmark to meet my cousin and her husband. While there, we visited the Croatian consul, who told us he had located a possible relative in Kansas City with whom he was corresponding by email. "There is a lot of this going on in Europe now," he added.

In 2011, following my youngest brother David's death, his friends and colleagues posted scores of remembrances and tributes on a message board, Facebook, websites, and blogs. My brother Rick and I consequently learned much about his social network, a source of solace for us (compare Miller 2011: 191–192; Ryan 2012). And in 2012, I attended my fiftieth high school reunion, an event organized by email. Although the planning and the day itself conformed closely to anthropologist Keiko Ikeda's study *A Room Full of Mirrors: High School Reunions in Middle America* (1998), a third of those attending had previously posted personal details on a reunion message board and had thus already introduced themselves electronically to each other, smoothing considerably our actual, face-to-face reconnections (compare Miller 2011: 165–166).

I continue to use email every day in my personal life and anthropological work life, and to me, Daniel Miller's description of some of his Trinidad informants hits home: "These days, quite a few people act as though their true brain—in the sense of remembering what they are supposed to do and when—exists only on hard disc" (Miller 2011: 114). When Lani Sanjek or I encounter a blue screen, and possible hard disk failure, we become agitated and freeze up until the problem is resolved.

Genesis of *eFieldnotes*

At some point in the early 2000s, a Cornell University Press editor approached me about a new edition of *Fieldnotes* that would take this changing infrastructure of ethnographic research into account by adding some new essays and discarding some old ones. He offered to locate a coeditor to help with this, but that did not sit right. I felt *Fieldnotes* stood on its own: each year it added a couple of hundred copies in sales to the eleven thousand to date.[18] But then, late in 2010, William Kelly wrote me: "I still regard 'Fieldnotes' as one of the lasting accomplishments of recent decades and I still require it of all first-year [Yale] doctoral students. Perhaps in a few years you should consider an update to get people to talk about the same issues as we grapple with them in the digital age with a new cohort of ethnographers. It could be a very lively and productive project."[19] I responded: "I am deeply touched by your regard for *Fieldnotes*. . . . You have really got me thinking . . . about an *eFieldnotes: Makings of Anthropology in [the] Digital World* successor volume."

After beginning with Gabriella Coleman's impressive 2010 *Annual Review of Anthropology* piece "Ethnographic Approaches to Digital Media" and her papers on hackers and Anonymous,[20] and although I was still more a digital immigrant than a native (no smartphone, not on Facebook, no Twitter account), during 2012, I plunged into reading what I discovered to be a rich and fascinating new ethnographic literature. This included several informative ethnographies—Daniel Miller and Don Slater's *The Internet* (2000), Jan English-Lueck's *Cultures@Siliconvalley* (2002, see also 2010), Nicole Constable's *Romance on a Global Stage* (2003), Heather Horst and Daniel Miller's *The Cell Phone* (2006), Tom Boellstorff's *Coming of Age in Second Life* (2008), Mizuko Ito and colleagues' *Hanging Out, Messing Around, and Geeking Out* (2010), Bonnie Nardi's *My Life as a Night Elf Priest* (2010), Daniel Miller's *Tales from Facebook* (2011), John Postill's *Localizing the Internet* (2011), Jenna Burrell's *Invisible Users: Youth in the Internet Cafes of Urban Ghana* (2012), and Cara Wallis's *Technomobility in China: Young Migrant Women and Mobile Phones* (2013) (see also Kraemer 2012; Wang 2013). (Burrell's ethnography was especially enjoyable because, during the early 1970s, I did fieldwork in an Accra neighborhood not far from where she worked.)

At the 2011 and 2012 AAA meetings, I attended digital anthropology sessions where I heard a range of younger scholars, including Jordan Kraemer, who had organized two of the panels and studied young Germans' online and offline lives in Berlin (2012, 2013). Susan Tratner also recommended to me key work in journals by post–Internet generation anthropologists, including Mieke Schrooten (2010, 2012) and Martin Slama (2010, 2011).

In planning the projected volume, Dr. Tratner and I invited anthropologists we hoped might be interested: Moran, Kelly, Horst, Nardi, Burrell, Kraemer, Schrooten, and Slama. We also turned to Jean Jackson and Rena Lederman, who were contributors to the original *Fieldnotes*, and Lisa Cliggett, whose writings on Zambia and on the Gwembe Tonga Research Project archives I admired and who participated in an AAA session on aging I organized in 2008 (Cliggett 2002, 2005, 2010). Jackson and Lederman in turn introduced us to Graham Jones and Bambi Schieffelin's writings on online language (2009a, 2009b; Jones, Schieffelin, and Smith 2011), and Cliggett to Diane King's work on the Kurdish diaspora, including its digital life (2008, 2014).[21]

Computers, digital archives, the Internet, and mobile devices are changing both our lives and anthropology in significant ways. The consequences for fieldwork are emerging daily, and they already affect interactions with informants, definitions of data, and ethnography's disciplinary future. How do these new topics and methods of research result in, even necessitate, new ways of recording, utilizing, storing, living with, and feeling about both traditional and new forms of ethnographic fieldnotes?

Read on.

Notes

1. Compare Hart 2004, 2010; and see E. Coleman 2010; Horst and Miller 2012; Isaacson 2014; Leonardi, Nardi, and Kallinikos 2012; Pertierra 2010; Turkle 2011. On "the organization of collective activity" via digital media in Fei's contemporary homeland, see Wallis 2013; Wang 2013.

2. As discussed by Wilson and Peterson 2002, and E. Coleman 2010.

3. Hart 2004: 22; Vara 2014. On the physical materiality and geography of Internet fibers, cables, and connections, see Blum 2012; Lewis 2014.

4. For further related writings by contributors to the original *Fieldnotes* volume, see Bond 2000; Clifford 2003; Jackson 1990, 1997a, 1997b, 1997c, 1997d; Johnson 2003; Johnson and Sackett 1998; Lederman 2006a, 2006b, 2006c, 2007; Lutkehaus 1995; Obbo 2006; Ottenberg 1994; Sanjek 1991, 1993, 1996, 1997, 1998b, 1999, 2001, 2009a, 2009b, 2009c, 2014; Smith 2003; Wolf 1992, 2013. See as well Rofel 2003, and three documentary videos featuring Ella Lury Wiswell, Robert J. Smith, and David Plath (Plath 1996a, 1996b, 1996c).

5. Amit 2000; Bell, Caplan, and Karim 1993; Burawoy 2009; Faubion and Marcus 2009; Fowler and Hardesty 1994; Geertz 1995: 88; Kumar 1992; Sanford and Angel-Ajani 2006; Sluka and Robben 2012; Vogt 1994: 113–115, 303.

6. Anderson 1990: vii–viii, 48, 60, 73, 86, 149; Cerwonka and Malkki 2007:67, 76, 80–84, 98–99, 102, 103, 143; Fabian 2010; Fenton 2002: 92, 94, 97; Goodale

1996: 3, 50, 69–70, 80, 124, 186; Hendry 1999: 48, 65, 143, 147–148; Hoffman 2006; James 2000; Kan 2002: 200–202, 204; Kemper and Royce 2002: 11, 19–21, 26–27, 66, 69, 83, 84, 271–272, 320–321; Lave 2011: 119–146; Macintyre 1993: 46, 51, 55–58; Okely 2012; Panini 1991: 11, 18, 33, 48, 57, 77; Perry 1989: 12–16, 29–30, 56, 119, 130; Steinhoff 2003: 38–39; Ward 1989: 3–4, 8, 22, 65, 87, 194, 106, 116, 124, 138.

7. In 1977, I worked with two quantitative data sets in this manner (Sanjek 1977, 1987; Sanjek, Forman, and McDaniel 1979) while I was a postdoctoral fellow in Quantitative Anthropology with Public Policy Emphasis at the University of California, Berkeley (Sanjek 2015b: 300–301).

8. See also Lutkehaus 1995: 25n.14. Diane King used a laptop even earlier, in 1989 in Malaysia; see Chapter 15, this volume, note 1.

9. An argument reprised in Burawoy 2009; Cerwonka and Malkki 2007; and Lave 2011. See also Lederman 1986 and Sanjek 1990d: 213–215.

10. This volume might be compared with Kimball and Partridge's similar *The Craft of Community Study* (1979), which was based on letters ("snail mail") between a mentor in Florida and a graduate student conducting fieldwork in Colombia during 1972–1973.

11. Cahn 2002: 321–322; S. Coleman 2010: 175; Hoffman 2006: 22; Jones 2006: 169; Marcus 2010: 75; Ogawa 2006: 210; Peterson 2009: 46; Pink 2000; Roberts 2003: 305–306; Wulff 2000: 155, 158.

12. See also Heath and Street (2008: 79–81, 108, 128) on composing periodic "conceptual memos," and Anderson (1990) and Ward (1989) for examples of the value of letters written while in the field. On "affordances" more generally, see Faraj and Azad 2012.

13. Yet note the acknowledgment by Constable of suspicion about Internet research among her anthropological colleagues (2003: 33). See also Tratner, Chapter 10, this volume, citing Forte 2002.

14. E. Coleman 2010: 492; Hoffman 2006: 26; Miller 2011: 191; Miller and Horst 2012: 20; Vara 2014.

15. See Barendregt 2012; Burrell 2012; Constable 2003; Cook 2004; Horst and Miller 2006; Madianou and Miller 2012; Moran, Chapter 4, this volume; Rosenberg 2011; Stokes 2011; Wallis 2013; Wang and Brown 2011.

16. The Gray Panthers during these years, and to a considerable degree in earlier decades as well (Sanjek 2009b), exemplified Bonnie Nardi's (2007) model of a "placeless organization."

17. National and ethnic diaspora websites and blogs have sparked a fascinating body of ethnographic work: for example, Bernal 2005; Graham and Khosravi 2002; Longboan 2011; see also Nardi et al. 2004.

18. It has been widely used in classes and frequently cited and discussed in the fieldwork literature—see, for example, DeWalt and DeWalt 1998, 2011; Erickson and Stull 1998; Fabian 2010; Fischer 1994; Gupta and Ferguson 1997; Heath and Street

2008; Kelly 2005; LeCompte and Schensul 2012; Okely 2012; Parkin 2000; Schensul and LeCompte 2010; Stewart 1998; Wolcott 1995, 1999.

19. I had attended a warmly appreciative, full-room session honoring Kelly at the AAA annual meeting in 2010. Although we had never met, I wrote to congratulate him and explained that I had long admired his work (for example, Kelly 1991, 2004), and, now that I was retired, I was looking forwarding to reading more (on which, see his website: http://wwkelly.commons.yale.edu/; see also Ikeda 1992).

20. These writings are available on her website: http://gabriellacoleman.org/. See also Coleman 2013a, 2013b.

21. Burrell directed me to the blog "Ethnography Matters" (http://ethnography matters.net/) and to the innovative work of Tricia Wang (2012, 2013; Wang and Brown 2011) on digital technology use and fieldwork methods.

Bibliography

Amit, Vered, editor. 2000. *Constructing the Field: Ethnographic Fieldwork in the Contemporary World*. London: Routledge.

Anderson, Barbara Gallatin. 1990. *First Fieldwork: The Misadventures of an Anthropologist*. Prospect Heights, Ill.: Waveland.

Arkush, R. David. 1981. *Fei Xiaotong and Sociology in Revolutionary China*. Cambridge, Mass.: Harvard University Press.

Barendregt, Bart. 2012. Diverse Digital Worlds. In *Digital Anthropology*. Edited by Heather A. Horst and Daniel Miller, 203–224. New York: Berg.

Bell, Diane, Pat Caplan, and Wazir Jahan Karim, editors. 1993. *Gendered Fields: Women, Men and Ethnography*. London: Routledge.

Bernal, Victoria. 2005. Eritrea On-Line: Disapora, Cyberspace, and the Public Sphere. *American Ethnologist* 32 (4): 660–675.

Bernard, H. Russell. 2011. *Research Methods in Anthropology: Qualitative and Quantitative Approaches*. 5th edition. Lanham, Md.: AltaMira.

Bestor, Victoria Lyon. 2003. Appendix: Digital Resources and Fieldwork. In *Doing Fieldwork in Japan*, edited by Theodore C. Bestor, Patricia G. Steinhoff, and Victoria Lyon Bestor, 367–373. Honolulu: University of Hawai'i Press.

Black-Rogers, Mary. 2001. Effects of Adoption on the Round Lake Study. In *Strangers to Relatives: The Adoption and Naming of Anthropologists in Native North America*, edited by Sergei Kan, 99–117. Lincoln: University of Nebraska Press.

Blum, Andrew. 2012. *Tubes: A Journey to the Center of the Internet*. New York: HarperCollins.

Boellstorff, Tom. 2008. *Coming of Age in Second Life: An Anthropologist Explores the Virtually Human*. Princeton, N.J.: Princeton University Press.

———, Bonnie Nardi, Celia Pearce, and T. L. Taylor. 2012. *Ethnography and Virtual Worlds: A Handbook of Method*. Princeton, N.J.: Princeton University Press.

Bond, George Clement. 2000. Historical Fragments and Social Constructions in Northern Zambia: A Personal Journey. *Journal of African Cultural Studies* 13 (1): 76–93.

Burawoy, Michael. 2009. *The Extended Case Method: Four Countries, Four Decades, Four Great Transformations, and One Theoretical Tradition*. Berkeley: University of California Press.

Burrell, Jenna. 2012. *Invisible Users: Youth in the Internet Cafes of Urban Ghana*. Cambridge, Mass.: MIT Press.

Cahn, Peter S. 2002. Being the Third Generation in Tzintzuntzan. In *Chronicling Cultures: Long-Term Field Research in Anthropology*, edited by Robert Van Kemper and Anya Peterson Royce, 313–328. Walnut Creek, Calif.: AltaMira Press.

Cerwonka, Allaine, and Liisa H. Malkki. 2007. *Improvising Theory: Process and Temporality in Ethnographic Fieldwork*. Chicago: University of Chicago Press.

Clifford, James. 2003. *On the Edges of Anthropology (Interviews)*. Chicago: Prickly Paradigm Press.

Cliggett, Lisa. 2002. Multigenerations and Multidisciplines: Inheriting Fifty Years of Gwembe Tonga Research. In *Chronicling Cultures: Long-Term Field Research in Anthropology*, edited by Robert Van Kemper and Anya Peterson Royce, 239–251. Walnut Creek, Calif.: AltaMira Press.

———. 2005. *Grains from Grass: Aging, Gender, and Famine in Rural Africa*. Ithaca, N.Y.: Cornell University Press.

———. 2010. Aging, Agency, and Gwembe Tonga Getting By. *Journal of Aging, Humanities, and the Arts* 4 (2): 98–109.

Coleman, E. Gabriella. 2010. Ethnographic Approaches to Digital Media. *Annual Review of Anthropology* 39: 487–505.

———. 2013a. *Anonymous in Context: The Politics and Power behind the Mask*. Internet Governance Paper no. 3. Waterloo, Ontario: Centre for International Governance Innovation. Accessed March 13, 2015. https://www.cigionline.org/publications/2013/9/anonymous-context-politics-and-power-behind-mask.

———. 2013b. *Coding Freedom: The Ethics and Aesthetics of Hacking*. Princeton, N.J.: Princeton University Press.

Coleman, Simon. 2010. Re-presenting Anthropology. In *Ethnographic Practice in the Present*, edited by Marit Melhuus, Jon P. Mitchell, and Helena Wulff, 169–175. New York: Berghahn.

Constable, Nicole. 2003. *Romance on a Global Stage: Pen Pals, Virtual Ethnography, and "Mail Order" Marriages*. Berkeley: University of California Press.

Cook, Susan E. 2004. New Technologies and Language Change: Toward an Anthropology of Linguistic Frontiers. *Annual Review of Anthropology* 33: 103–115.

Des Chene, Mary. 1997. Locating the Past. In *Anthropological Locations: Boundaries and Grounds of a Field Science*, edited by Akhil Gupta and James Ferguson, 66–85. Berkeley: University of California Press.

DeWalt, Kathleen M., and Billie R. DeWalt. 2011. *Participant Observation: A Guide for Fieldworkers*. Walnut Creek, Calif.: AltaMira.

DeWalt, Kathleen M., and Billie R. DeWalt, with Coral B. Wayland. 1998. Participant Observation. In *Handbook of Methods in Cultural Anthropology*, edited by H. Russell Bernard, 259–299. Walnut Creek, Calif.: AltaMira.

Dresch, Paul, and Wendy James. 2000. Introduction: Fieldwork and the Passage of Time. In *Anthropologists in a Wider World: Essays on Field Research*, edited by Paul Dresch, Wendy James, and David Parkin, 1–25. New York: Berghahn.

English-Lueck, J. A. 2002. *Cultures@SiliconValley*. Stanford, Calif.: Stanford University Press.

———. 2010. *Being and Well-Being: Health and the Working Bodies of Silicon Valley*. Stanford, Calif.: Stanford University Press.

Erickson, Ken, and Donald Stull. 1998. *Doing Team Ethnography: Warnings and Advice*. Thousand Oaks, Calif.: Sage.

Fabian, Johannes. 2010. Ethnography and Memory. In *Ethnographic Practice in the Present*, edited by Marit Melhuus, Jon P. Mitchell, and Helena Wulff, 16–27. New York: Berghahn.

Faraj, Samer, and Bijan Azad. 2012. The Materiality of Technology: An Affordance Perspective. In *Materiality and Organizing: Social Interaction in a Technological World*, edited by Paul M. Leonardi, Bonnie A. Nardi, and Jannis Kallinikos, 237–258. Oxford: Oxford University Press.

Faubion, James D., and George E. Marcus, editors. 2009. *Fieldwork Is Not What It Used to Be: Learning Anthropology's Method in a Time of Transition*. Ithaca, N.Y.: Cornell University Press.

Fei Xiaotong [Fei Hsiao-Tung]. 1939. *Peasant Life in China: A Field Study of Country Life in the Yangtze Valley*. London: Routledge & Kegan Paul.

———. 1979–1980. Fleeting Glimpses of America. *Dagonbao* (October–November), Hong Kong; *Wen Hui Bao* (January), Shanghai. Typescript. Translated by Martin Whyte.

Fenton, William N. 2001. He-Lost-a-Bet (Howanʔneyao) of the Seneca Hawk Clan. In *Strangers to Relatives: The Adoption and Naming of Anthropologists in Native North America*, edited by Sergei Kan, 81–98. Lincoln: University of Nebraska Press.

Fischer, Michael. 1994. *Applications in Computing for Social Anthropologists*. London: Routledge.

Forte, Maximilian. 2002. Another Revolution Missed: Anthropology of Cyberspace. *Anthropology News* 43 (9): 20–21.

Fowler, Don D., and Donald L. Hardesty, editors. 1994. *Others Knowing Others: Perspectives on Ethnographic Careers*. Washington, D.C.: Smithsonian Institution Press.

Gardner, Katy. 1999. Location and Relocation: Home, "the Field" and Anthropological Ethics (Sylhet, Bangladesh). In *Being There: Fieldwork in Anthropology*, edited by C. W. Watson, 49–73. London: Pluto Press.

Geertz, Clifford. 1995. *After the Fact: Two Countries, Four Decades, One Anthropologist*. Cambridge, Mass.: Harvard University Press.

Goodale, Jane C., with Ann Chowning. 1996. *The Two-Party Line: Conversations in the Field*. Lanham, Md.: Rowman & Littlefield.

Graham, Mark, and Shahram Khosravi. 2002. Reordering Public and Private in Iranian Cyberspace: Identity, Politics, and Mobilization. *Identities: Global Studies in Culture and Power* 9: 219–246.

Greenough, Karen Marie. 2006. Dispatch from the Sahelian Range: Renegotiating Expectations and Relationships Among the Woodaabe of Niger. In *Dispatches From the Field: Neophyte Ethnographers in a Changing World*, edited by Andrew Gardner and David M. Hoffman, 137–151. Long Grove, Ill.: Waveland.

Gupta, Akhil, and James Ferguson. 1997. Discipline and Practice: "The Field" as Site, Method, and Location in Anthropology. In *Anthropological Locations: Boundaries and Grounds of a Field Science*, edited by Akhil Gupta and James Ferguson, 1–46. Berkeley: University of California Press.

Hart, Keith. 2004. Notes Toward an Anthropology of the Internet. *Horizontes Antropologicos* 10 (2): 15–40. Accessed September 1, 2014. http://www.uclouvain.be/cps/ucl/doc/pols/documents/Hart_-_notes_towards_an_anthropo_of_the_internet.pdf.

———. 2010. The Digital Revolution and Me. "The Memory Bank: A New Commonwealth—Ver. 5.0." Accessed September 1, 2014. http://thememorybank.co.uk/2010/01/08/the-digital-revolution-and-me/.

Heath, Shirley Brice, and Brian W. Street. 2008. *On Ethnography: Approaches To Language and Literacy Research*. New York: Teachers College Press.

Hendry, Joy. 1999. *An Anthropologist in Japan: Glimpses of Life in the Field*. London: Routledge.

Hoffman, David M. 2006. Swimming Through Fieldwork: Constructing Trust in the Mexican Caribbean. In *Dispatches from the Field: Neophyte Ethnographers in a Changing World*, edited by Andrew Gardner and David M. Hoffman, 15–31. Long Grove, Ill.: Waveland.

———, and Andrew Gardner. 2006. Fieldwork and Writing from the Field. In *Dispatches from the Field: Neophyte Ethnographers in a Changing World*, edited by Andrew Gardner and David M. Hoffman, 1–13. Long Grove, Ill.: Waveland.

Horst, Heather, and Daniel Miller. 2006. *The Cell Phone: An Anthropology of Communication*. London: Berg.

———, editors. 2012. *Digital Anthropology*. London: Berg.

Ikeda, Hajime, producer. 1992. *William Kelly*. Video. Urbana, Ill.: Media Production Group.

Ikeda, Keiko. 1998. *A Room Full of Mirrors: High School Reunions in Middle America*. Stanford, Calif.: Stanford University Press.

Isaacson, Walter. 2014. *The Innovators: How a Group of Hackers, Geniuses, and Geeks Created the Digital Revolution*. New York: Simon & Schuster.

Ito, Mizuko, Sonja Baumer, Matteo Bittanti, danah boyd, Rachel Cody, Rebecca Herr-Stephenson, Heather A. Horst, Patricia G. Lange, Dilan Mahendran, Katynka Z. Martinez, C. J. Pascoe, Dan Perkel, Laura Robinson, Christo Sims, and Lisa Tripp.

2010. *Hanging Out, Messing Around, and Geeking Out: Kids Living and Learning with New Media*. Cambridge, Mass.: MIT Press.

Ito, Mizuko, Daisuke Okabe, and Misa Matsuda, editors. 2005. *Personal, Portable, Pedestrian: Mobile Phones in Japanese Life*. Cambridge, Mass.: MIT Press.

Jackson, Jean E. 1990. "Déjà Entendu": The Liminal Qualities of Anthropological Fieldnotes. *Journal of Contemporary Ethnography* 13 (1): 8–43. Reprinted in 1995 in *Representation in Ethnography*, edited by John Van Maanen. London: Sage; and in 2008 in *Representing Ethnography*. Vol. 3. Edited by Paul Atkinson and Sara Delamont, 22–51. Los Angeles: Sage.

————. 1997a. Fieldnotes. In *The Dictionary of Anthropology*, edited by Thomas Barfield, 188. Malden, Mass.: Blackwell Publishers.

————. 1997b. Fieldwork. In *The Dictionary of Anthropology*, edited by Thomas Barfield, 188–190. Malden, Mass.: Blackwell Publishers.

————. 1997c. Informants. In *The Dictionary of Anthropology*, edited by Thomas Barfield, 262. Malden, Mass.: Blackwell Publishers.

————. 1997d. Participant-observation. In *The Dictionary of Anthropology*, edited by Thomas Barfield, 348. Malden, Mass.: Blackwell Publishers.

Jacobs-Huey, Lanita. 2006. *From the Kitchen to the Parlor: Language and Becoming in African American Women's Hair Care*. New York: Oxford University Press.

James, Wendy. 2000. Beyond the First Encounter: Transformations of "the Field" in North East Africa. In *Anthropologists in a Wider World: Essays on Field Research*, edited by Paul Dresch, Wendy James, and David Parkin, 69–90. New York: Berghahn.

Johansen, Ulla C., and Douglas R. White. 2002. Collaborative Long-Term Ethnography and Longitudinal Social Analysis of a Nomadic Clan in Southeastern Turkey. In *Chronicling Cultures: Long-Term Field Research in Anthropology*, edited by Robert Van Kemper and Anya Peterson Royce, 34–58. Walnut Creek, Calif.: AltaMira Press.

Johnson, Allen. 2003. *Families of the Forest: The Matsigenka Indians of the Peruvian Amazon*. Berkeley: University of California Press.

————, and Orna Johnson. 1990. Quality into Quantity: On the Measurement Potential of Ethnographic Fieldnotes. In *Fieldnotes: The Makings of Anthropology*, edited by Roger Sanjek, 161–186. Ithaca, N.Y.: Cornell University Press.

————, and Ross Sackett. 1998. Direct Systematic Observation of Behavior. In *Handbook of Methods in Cultural Anthropology*, edited by H. Russell Bernard, 301–331. Walnut Creek, Calif.: AltaMira.

Jones, Graham. 2006. Laboring Under Illusionism: Notes from the Study of French Magic. In *Dispatches from the Field: Neophyte Ethnographers in a Changing World*, edited by Andrew Gardner and David M. Hoffman, 167–178. Long Grove, Ill.: Waveland.

————, and Bambi Schieffelin. 2009a. Enquoting Voices, Accomplishing Talk: Uses of be + like in Instant Messaging. *Language and Communication* 20: 77–113.

————, and Bambi Schieffelin. 2009b. Talking Text and Talking Back: "My BFF Jill" from Boob Tube to YouTube. *Journal of Computer-Mediated Communication* 14: 1050–1079.

————, Bambi Schieffelin, and Rachel E. Smith. 2011. When Friends Who Talk Together Stalk Together: Online Gossip as Metacommunication. In *Digital Discourse: Language in the New Media*, edited by Crispin Thurlow and Kristine Mroczek, 26–47. New York: Oxford University Press.

Kan, Sergei. 2001. Friendship, Family, and Fieldwork: One Anthropologist's Adoption by Two Tlingit Families. In *Strangers to Relatives: The Adoption and Naming of Anthropologists in Native North America*, edited by Sergei Kan, 185–217. Lincoln: University of Nebraska Press.

Kelly, William W. 1991. Directions in the Anthropology of Contemporary Japan. *Annual Review of Anthropology* 20: 395–431.

————. 1999. Caught in the Spin Cycle: An Anthropological Observer at the Sites of Japanese Professional Baseball. In *Lives in Motion: Composing Circles of Self and Community in Japan*, edited by Susan Orpett Long, 137–149. Ithaca, N.Y.: East Asia Program, Cornell University.

————. 2005. Review of Theodore C. Bestor, Patricia G. Steinhoff, and Victoria Lyon Bestor, editors, *Doing Fieldwork in Japan*. *Journal of Japanese Studies* 31 (1): 141–145.

Kelty, Christopher. 2009. Collaboration, Coordination, and Composition: Fieldwork After the Internet. In *Fieldwork Is Not What It Used to Be: Learning Anthropology's Method in a Time of Transition*, edited by James D. Faubion and George E. Marcus, 184–206. Ithaca, N.Y.: Cornell University Press.

Kemper, Robert V. 2002. From Student to Steward: Tzintzuntzan as Extended Community. In *Chronicling Cultures: Long-Term Field Research in Anthropology*, edited by Robert Van Kemper and Anya Peterson Royce, 284–312. Walnut Creek, Calif.: AltaMira Press.

————, and Anya Peterson Royce, editors. 2002. *Chronicling Cultures: Long-Term Field Research in Anthropology*. Walnut Creek, Calif.: AltaMira Press.

Kimball, Solon T., and William L. Partridge. 1979. *The Craft of Community Study: Fieldwork Dialogues*. Gainesville: University Presses of Florida.

King, Diane. 2008. Back from the "Outside": Returnees and Diasporic Imagining in Iraqi Kurdistan. *International Journal on Multicultural Societies* 10 (2): 208–222.

————. 2014. *Kurdistan on the Global Stage: Kinship, Land, and Community in Iraq*. New Brunswick, N.J.: Rutgers University Press.

Kraemer, Jordan. 2012. Mobile Berlin: Social Media and the New Europe. Ph.D. dissertation, University of California, Irvine.

————. 2013. Friend or *Freund*: Social Media and Transnational Connections in Berlin. *Human-Computer Interaction* 29 (1): 53–77. Accessed September 4, 2014. http://www.tandfonline.com/doi/abs/10.1080/07370024.2013.823821.

Kumar, Nita. 1992. *Friends, Brothers, and Informants: Fieldwork Memoirs of Banaras.* Berkeley: University of California Press.

Lave, Jean. 2011. *Apprenticeship in Critical Ethnographic Practice.* Chicago: University of Chicago Press.

LeCompte, Margaret D., and Jean J. Schensul. 2012. *Analysis and Interpretation of Ethnographic Data: A Mixed Methods Approach.* 2nd edition. Walnut Creek, Calif.: AltaMira.

Lederman, Rena. 1986. The Return of Redwoman: Field Work in Highland New Guinea. In *Women in the Field: Anthropological Experiences*, edited by Peggy Golde, 361–388. Berkeley: University of California Press.

———. 2006a. The Ethical Is Political. *American Ethnologist* 33: 545–548.

———. 2006b. Introduction: Anxious Borders Between Work and Life in a Time of Bureaucratic Ethics Regulation. *American Ethnologist* 33: 477–481.

———. 2006c. The Perils of Working at Home: IRB "Mission Creep" as Context and Content for an Ethnography of Disciplinary Knowledges. *American Ethnologist* 33: 482–491.

———. 2007. Comparative "Research": A Modest Proposal Concerning the Object of Ethics Regulation. *PoLAR* 30: 305–327.

Leonardi, Paul M., Bonnie A. Nardi, and Jannis Kallinikos, editors. 2012. *Materiality and Organizing: Social Interaction in a Technological World.* Oxford: Oxford University Press.

Lewis, Michael. 2014. The Wolf Hunters of Wall Street. *New York Times Magazine*, March 31. Accessed February 4, 2015. http://www.nytimes.com/2014/04/06/maga zine/flash-boys-michael-lewis.html?module = Search&mabReward = relbias%3Aw %2C%7B%222%22%3A%22RI%3A18%22%7D&_r = 0.

Ling, Rich, and Heather Horst. 2011. Introduction: Mobile Communication in the Global South. *New Media & Society* 13 (3): 363–374.

Longboan, Liezel. 2011. E-gorots: Exploring Indigenous Identity in Translocal Spaces. *South East Asia Research* 19 (2): 319–341.

Lutkehaus, Nancy C. 1995. *Zaria's Fire: Engendered Moments in Manam Ethnography.* Durham, N.C.: Carolina Academic Press.

Macintyre, Martha. 1993. Fictive Kinship or Mistaken Identity? Fieldwork on Tube-tube Island, Papua New Guinea. In *Gendered Fields: Women, Men and Ethnography*, edited by Diane Bell, Pat Caplan, and Wazir Jahan Karim, 44–62. London: Routledge.

Madianou, Mirca, and Daniel Miller. 2012. *Migration and New Media: Transnational Families and Polymedia.* London: Routledge.

Marcus, George E. 2009. Introduction: Notes Toward an Ethnographic Memoir of Supervising Graduate Research Through Anthropology's Decades of Transition. In *Fieldwork Is Not What It Used to Be: Learning Anthropology's Method in a Time of Transition*, edited by James D. Faubion and George E. Marcus, 1–34. Ithaca, N.Y.: Cornell University Press.

————. 2010. Notes from Within a Laboratory for the Reinvention of Anthropological Method. In *Ethnographic Practice in the Present*, edited by Marit Melhuus, Jon P. Mitchell, and Helena Wulff, 69–79. New York: Berghahn.

Miller, Daniel. 2011. *Tales from Facebook*. Malden, Mass.: Polity Press.

————, and Heather Horst. 2012. The Digital and the Human: A Prospectus for Digital Anthropology. In *Digital Anthropology*, edited by Heather A. Horst and Daniel Miller, 3–35. New York: Berg.

————, and Don Slater. 2000. *The Internet: An Ethnographic Approach*. London: Berg.

Moran, Mary. 2006. *Liberia: The Violence of Democracy*. Philadelphia: University of Pennsylvania Press.

Nardi, Bonnie A. 2007. Placeless Organizations: Collaborating for Transformation. *Mind, Culture, and Activity* 14 (1–2): 5–22.

————. 2010. *My Life as a Night Elf Priest: An Anthropological Account of World of Warcraft*. Ann Arbor: University of Michigan Press.

————, Diane J. Schiano, Michelle Gumbrecht, and Luke Swartz. 2004. Why We Blog. *Communications of the ACM* 47 (12): 41–46.

Obbo, Christine. 2006. But We Know It All! African Perspectives on African Knowledge. In *African Anthropologies: History, Critique and Practice*, edited by Mwenda Ntarangwi, David Mills, and Mustafa Babiker, 154–169. London: Zed.

Ogawa, Akihiro. 2006. Initiating Change: Doing Action Research in Japan. In *Dispatches from the Field: Neophyte Ethnographers in a Changing World*, edited by Andrew Gardner and David M. Hoffman, 207–221. Long Grove, Ill.: Waveland.

Okely, Judith. 2012. *Anthropological Practice: Fieldwork and the Ethnographic Imagination*. London: Berg.

Ottenberg, Simon. 1994. Changes over Time in an African Culture and in an Anthropologist. In *Others Knowing Others: Perspectives on Ethnographic Careers*, edited by Don D. Fowler and Donald L. Hardesty, 91–118. Washington, D.C.: Smithsonian Institution Press.

Panini, M. N., editor. 1991. *From the Female Eye: Accounts of Women Fieldworkers Studying Their Own Communities*. Delhi: Hindustan Publishing Corporation.

Parkin, David. 2000. Fieldwork Unfolding. In *Anthropologists in a Wider World*, edited by Paul Dresch, Wendy James, and David Parkin, 259–273. New York: Berghahn.

Perry, John, editor. 1989. *Doing Fieldwork: Eight Personal Accounts of Social Research*. Geelong, Victoria, Australia: Deakin University Press.

Pertierra, Raul. 2010. *The Anthropology of New Media in the Philippines*. Quezon City: Institute of Philippine Culture, Ateneo de Manila University.

Peterson, Kristin. 2009. Phantom Epistemologies. In *Fieldwork Is Not What It Used to Be: Learning Anthropology's Method in a Time of Transition*, edited by James D. Faubion and George E. Marcus, 37–51. Ithaca, N.Y.: Cornell University Press.

Peutz, Nathalie. 2006. Of Goats and Foreigners: Research Lessons on Soqotra Island, Yemen. In *Dispatches from the Field: Neophyte Ethnographers in a Changing World*, edited by Andrew Gardner and David M. Hoffman, 83–103. Long Grove, Ill.: Waveland.

Pink, Sarah. 2000. "Informants" Who Come "Home." In *Constructing the Field: Ethnographic Fieldwork in the Contemporary World*, edited by Vered Amit, 96–119. London: Routledge.

Plath, David W., producer. 1996a. *Ella's Journal.* Video. Urbana, Ill.: Media Production Group.

———. 1996b. *The Language of My Teachers.* Video. Urbana, Ill.: Media Production Group.

———. 1996c. *Times of Witness: Fieldwork in Japan.* Video. Urbana, Ill.: Media Production Group.

Postill, John. 2011. *Localizing the Internet: An Anthropological Account.* New York: Berghahn.

Roberts, Glenda S. 2003. Bottom Up, Top Down, and Sideways: Studying Corporations, Government Programs, and NPOs. In *Doing Fieldwork in Japan*, edited by Theodore C. Bestor, Patricia G. Steinhoff, and Victoria Lyon Bestor, 294–314. Honolulu: University of Hawai'i Press.

Rofel, Lisa. 2003. The Outsider Within: Margery Wolf and Feminist Anthropology. *American Anthropologist* 105 (3): 596–604.

Rosenberg, Tina. 2011. Everyone Speaks Text Message. *New York Times Magazine*, 20–24, December 9. Accessed February 4, 2015. http://www.nytimes.com/2011/12/11/magazine/everyone-speaks-text-m essage.html?pagewanted = all&_r = 0.

Roth, Joshua Hotaka. 2003. Responsibility and the Limits of Identification: Fieldwork Among Japanese and Japanese Brazilian Workers in Japan. In *Doing Fieldwork in Japan*, edited by Theodore C. Bestor, Patricia G. Steinhoff, and Victoria Lyon Bestor, 335–351. Honolulu: University of Hawai'i Press.

Royce, Anya Peterson, and Robert V. Kemper. 2002. Long-Term Field Research Metaphors, Paradigms, and Themes. In *Chronicling Cultures: Long-Term Field Research in Anthropology*, edited by Robert V. Kemper and Anya Peterson Royce, xiii–xxxviii. Walnut Creek, Calif.: AltaMira Press.

Ryan, Jenny. 2012. The Digital Graveyard: Online Social Networking Sites as Vehicles of Remembrance. In *Human No More: Digital Subjectivities, Unhuman Subjects, and the End of Anthropology*, edited by Neil L. Whitehead and Michael Wesch, 71–87. Boulder, Colo.: University Press of Colorado.

Sanford, Victoria, and Asale Angel-Ajani, editors. 2006. *Engaged Observer: Anthropology, Advocacy, and Activism.* New Brunswick, N.J.: Rutgers University Press.

Sanjek, Roger. 1977. *A Profile of Over 60 Health Services Users: A Report and Recommendations.* Berkeley, Calif.: Over 60 Health Clinic Geriatric Health Services Program.

———. 1987. Anthropological Work at a Gray Panther Health Clinic: Academic, Applied, and Advocacy Goals. In *Cities of the United States: Studies in Urban*

Anthropology, edited by Leith Mullings, 148–175. New York: Columbia University Press.

———, ed. 1990a. *Fieldnotes: The Makings of Anthropology*. Ithaca, N.Y.: Cornell University Press.

———. 1990b. Fire, Loss, and the Sorcerer's Apprentice. In *Fieldnotes: The Makings of Anthropology*, edited by Roger Sanjek, 34–44. Ithaca, N.Y.: Cornell University Press.

———. 1990c. On Ethnographic Validity. In *Fieldnotes: The Makings of Anthropology*, edited by Roger Sanjek, 385–418. Ithaca, N.Y.: Cornell University Press.

———. 1990d. The Secret Life of Fieldnotes. In *Fieldnotes: The Makings of Anthropology*, edited by Roger Sanjek, 187–270. Ithaca, N.Y.: Cornell University Press.

———. 1990e. A Vocabulary for Fieldnotes. In *Fieldnotes: The Makings of Anthropology*, edited by Roger Sanjek, 92–121. Ithaca, N.Y.: Cornell University Press.

———. 1991. The Ethnographic Present. *Man* 26: 609–628. Revised version published in 2014 in Roger Sanjek, *Ethnography in Today's World: Color Full Before Color Blind*. Philadelphia: University of Pennsylvania Press.

———. 1993. Anthropology's Hidden Colonialism: Assistants and Their Ethnographers. *Anthropology Today* 9 (2): 13–18. Revised version published in 2014 in Roger Sanjek, *Ethnography in Today's World: Color Full Before Color Blind*. Philadelphia: University of Pennsylvania Press.

———. 1996. Ethnography. In *Encyclopedia of Social and Cultural Anthropology*, edited by Alan Barnard and Jonathan Spencer, 193–198. London: Routledge. Revised version published in 2014 in Roger Sanjek, *Ethnography in Today's World: Color Full Before Color Blind*. Philadelphia: University of Pennsylvania Press.

———. 1997. Review of Robert Emerson, Rachel Fretz, and Linda Shaw, *Writing Ethnographic Fieldnotes*. *American Anthropologist* 99: 195.

———. 1998a. *The Future of Us All: Race and Neighborhood Politics in New York City*. Ithaca, N.Y.: Cornell University Press.

———. 1998b. What Ethnographies Leave Out. *Xcp: Cross-Cultural Poetics* 3: 103–115. Revised version published in 2014 in Roger Sanjek, *Ethnography in Today's World: Color Full Before Color Blind*. Philadelphia: University of Pennsylvania Press.

———. 1999. Review of Martin Orans, *Not Even Wrong: Margaret Mead, Derek Freeman, and the Samoans*. *Oceania* 69: 309–310.

———. 2001. Field Observational Research in Anthropology and Sociology. *International Encyclopedia of the Social and Behavioral Sciences*, edited by Neil Smelser and Paul Baltes, 8: 5620–5625. Amsterdam: Elsevier. Revised version published in 2014 in Roger Sanjek, *Ethnography in Today's World: Color Full Before Color Blind*. Philadelphia: University of Pennsylvania Press.

———. 2009a. The Book That Wrote Me. In *Anthropology Off the Shelf: Anthropologists on Writing*, edited by Alisse Waterston and Maria Vesperi, 172–181. Malden, Mass.: Blackwell.

————. 2009b. *Gray Panthers*. Philadelphia: University of Pennsylvania Press.

————. 2009c. St. Vincent, the Thunder God, and the Ethnographer. *Philippine Quarterly Journal of Culture & Society* 37: 253–258.

————. 2014. *Ethnography in Today's World: Color Full Before Color Blind*. Philadelphia: University of Pennsylvania Press.

————, editor. 2015a. Archive: Newsletters. Gray Panthers: Age and Youth in Action. Accessed February 3, 2015. http://www.graypanthersnyc.org/archive/newsletters/index.html.

————. 2015b. Mutuality and Anthropology: Terms and Modes of Engagement. In *Mutuality: Anthropology's Changing Terms of Engagement*, edited by Roger Sanjek, 285–310. Philadelphia: University of Pennsylvania Press.

————, Sylvia H. Forman, and Chad McDaniel. 1979. Employment and Hiring of Women in American Departments of Anthropology: The Five-Year Record, 1972–1977. *Anthropology Newsletter* 20 (1): 6–19.

Schensul, Jean J., and Margaret D. LeCompte. 2010. *Essential Ethnographic Methods: A Mixed Methods Approach*. 2nd edition. Walnut Creek, Calif.: AltaMira.

Schrooten, Mieke. 2010. Virtual Migrant Communities: "Orkut" and the Brazilian Case. COMCAD Working Papers no. 80. Bielefeld, Germany: Centre on Migration, Citizenship and Development. Accessed February 4, 2015. http://www.uni-bielefeld.de/tdrc/ag_comcad/downloads/workingpaper_80_Schrooten.pdf.

————. 2012. Moving Ethnography Online: Researching Brazilian Migrants' Online Togetherness. *Ethnic and Racial Studies* 35: 1794–1809.

Shore, Chris. 1999. Fictions of Fieldwork: Depicting the "Self" in Ethnographic Writing (Italy). In *Being There: Fieldwork in Anthropology*, edited by C. W. Watson, 25–48. London: Pluto Press.

Skidmore, Monique. 2006. Scholarship, Advocacy, and the Politics of Engagement in Burma (Myanmar). In *Engaged Observer: Anthropology, Advocacy, and Activism*, edited by Victoria Sanford and Asale Angel-Ajani, 42–59. New Brunswick, N.J.: Rutgers University Press.

Slama, Martin. 2010. The Agency of the Heart: Internet Chatting as Youth Culture in Indonesia. *Social Anthropology/Anthropologie Sociale* 18: 316–330.

————. 2011. Translocal Networks and Globalisation Within Indonesia: Exploring the Hadhrami Diaspora from the Archipelago's North-East. *Asian Journal of Social Sciences* 39: 238–257.

Sluka, Jeffrey A., and Antonious C. G. M. Robben. 2012. Fieldwork in Cultural Anthropology: An Introduction. In *Ethnographic Fieldwork: An Anthropological Reader*. 2nd edition. Edited by Antonious C. G. M. Robben and Jeffrey A. Sluka, 1–47. Chichester, U.K.: Wiley-Blackwell.

Smith, Robert J. 2003. Time and Ethnology: Long-Term Field Research. In *Doing Fieldwork in Japan*, edited by Theodore C. Bestor, Patricia G. Steinhoff, and Victoria Lyon Bestor, 352–366. Honolulu: University of Hawai'i Press.

Steinhoff, Patricia G. 2003. New Notes from the Underground: Doing Fieldwork Without a Site. In *Doing Fieldwork in Japan*, edited by Theodore C. Bestor, Patricia G. Steinhoff, and Victoria Lyon Bestor, 36–54. Honolulu: University of Hawai'i Press.

Stewart, Alex. 1998. *The Ethnographer's Method*. Thousand Oaks, Calif.: Sage.

Stokes, Abby. 2011. *"Is This Thing on?" A Computer Handbook for Late Bloomers, Technophobes, and the Kicking & Screaming*. New York: Workman.

Turkle, Sherry. 2011. *Alone Together: Why We Expect More from Technology and Less from Each Other*. New York: Basic Books.

Vara, Vauhini. 2014. Four Charts That Defined the World in 2014. *The New Yorker*, December 20. Accessed February 4, 2015. http://www.newyorker.com/business/currency/four-charts-defined-global-economy-2014?intcid = mod-latest.

Vogt, Evon Z. 1994. *Fieldwork Among the Maya: Reflections on the Harvard Chiapas Project*. Albuquerque: University of New Mexico Press.

Wallis, Cara. 2013. *Technomobility in China: Young Migrant Women and Mobile Phones*. New York: New York University Press.

Wang, Tricia. 2012. Writing Live Fieldnotes: Towards a More Open Ethnography. *Ethnography Matters*, August 2. Accessed February 4, 2015. http://ethnographymatters.net/2012/08/02/writing-live-fieldnotes-towards-a-more-open-ethnography/.

———. 2013. Talking to Strangers: Chinese Youth and Social Media. Ph.D. diss., University of California, San Diego.

———, and Barry Brown. 2011. Ethnography of the Telephone: Changing Uses of Communication Technology in Village Life. *MobileHCI (2011)*, August 30–September 2: 37–46. Accessed February 4, 2015. http://triciawang.com/storage/papers/wang_brown.pdf.

Ward, Martha. 1989. *Nest in the Wind: Adventures in Anthropology on a Tropical Island*. Prospect Heights, Ill.: Waveland.

Watson, C. W. 1999. A Diminishment: A Death in the Field (Kerinci, Indonesia). In *Being There: Fieldwork in Anthropology*, edited by C. W. Watson, 142–163. London: Pluto Press.

Watson, James L. 2004. Presidential Address: Virtual Kinship, Real Estate, and Diaspora Formation—the Man Lineage Revisited. *Journal of Asian Studies* 63: 893–910.

White, Merry Isaacs. 2003. Taking Note of Teen Culture in Japan: Dear Diary, Dear Fieldworker. In *Doing Fieldwork in Japan*, edited by Theodore C. Bestor, Patricia G. Steinhoff, and Victoria Lyon Bestor, 21–35. Honolulu: University of Hawai'i Press.

Wilson, Samuel, and Leighton Peterson. 2002. The Anthropology of Online Communities. *Annual Review of Anthropology* 31: 449–467.

Wolcott, Harry F. 1990. *Writing up Qualitative Research*. Newbury Park, Calif.: Sage.

———. 1995. *The Art of Fieldwork*. Walnut Creek, Calif.: AltaMira.

———. 1999. *Ethnography: A Way of Seeing*. Walnut Creek, Calif.: AltaMira.

Wolf, Margery. 1992. *A Thrice-Told Tale: Feminism, Postmodernism, and Ethnographic Responsibility.* Stanford, Calif.: Stanford University Press.

———. 2013. *What the Water Buffalo Wrought.* Victoria, B.C.: Trafford.

Wulff, Helena. 2000. Access to a Closed World: Methods for a Multilocale Study on Ballet as a Career. In *Constructing the Field: Ethnographic Fieldwork in the Contemporary World*, edited by Vered Amit, 147–161. London: Routledge.

Chapter 2

Digital Technologies, Virtual Communities, Electronic Fieldwork: The Slow Social Science Adapts to High-Tech Japan

William W. Kelly

The first edition of *Fieldnotes* (1990) is that rare collection that has been consistently instructive and thought provoking throughout the decades since its publication. It remains relevant and enlightening to me, both in guiding my own field research practices and for introducing my students to the central significance of fieldnotes for our research and writing. Even this year (2014), it is required summer reading for students entering our Ph.D. program in sociocultural anthropology here at Yale.

The volume was not the first to discuss fieldnotes, but it was the first to bring into the discipline's awareness their manifold forms and functions and the disparate practices of note-taking, from the early ethnographers like Malinowski, Boas, and Mead to the volume contributors' generation. In particular, it demonstrated three crucial qualities of fieldnotes and note-taking over the history of our discipline. First, the collective lesson of the sixteen chapters was that anthropologists' use of the broad term "field-notes" actually covers a wide mental and material life cycle, from the chrysalis of headnotes and scratchnotes, jotted quickly in the midst of daily activities, to the full bloom of notebooks, cards, and files, written out in nightly sessions or less frequent binges. The actual practices of note-taking—our forms of notation; our preferences for techniques of writing down, typing up, speaking into, or keyboarding; and our complex feelings about notes—these and other features of fieldnotes have always varied widely.

However, and this is the second and perhaps most crucial lesson of the volume, whatever the forms of or feelings about fieldnotes, they generally play a more central role in the field research process than we frequently realize. In the midst of fieldwork, we must often gird ourselves to sit down at the moment in the day—late at night or first thing in the morning—to remember and record what we have done since the last time we "wrote up" our notes. However, what *Fieldnotes* brought out was the crucial significance of what we might call the "three R's" of note-taking—recording, reviewing, and reflecting. Over and over, the chapters document how the routine (a fourth R!) of remembering and recording continually prompts reflections on lines of inquiry, inspires connections among who and what is happening, exposes gaps, and generally heightens one's sensitivity to the research setting. I will return to this later in the chapter because it remains germane to the argument I will make.

Finally, the contributors to the original volume also drew attention to the multiple and freighted "afterlives" of our fieldnotes. We may return from the field, but the notes and other materials that we return with keep that experience present and palpable for years and often decades. They have material substance; they sit on our shelves or rest in file cabinets (or now in hard drives and cloud storage). They have intellectual force, as contemplative stimulus and reference for our writing. And they exert a powerful emotional charge as sources of pride and anxiety, possession and obsession.

Thus it is an intriguing challenge to consider what a quarter of a century of technological change and disciplinary transformation has meant to our field research practices since the publication of *Fieldnotes*. This is especially true given the digital revolution we have experienced over that period. In 1989, as Sanjek and his authors were finishing their chapters, the World Wide Web did not exist. I was just replacing $5\frac{1}{4}$ inch floppy disks with the new hard-cased $3\frac{1}{2}$ inch disks; my brand-new IBM desktop computer took up my entire desk top. Amazon was a culture area, not a corporate behemoth; "social media" was an oxymoron; institutional research boards did not exist; George Marcus had not yet uttered his fateful phrase, "multisited research"! It is bracing to think about what the past quarter of a century has brought to our methods and analytical priorities and theoretical orientations. Memory is a form of time-space compression.

My approach to this challenge has been to examine the large body of English-language ethnographic research publications about Japan that have appeared since the original *Fieldnotes*. I chose this point of entry not (just) from lazy self-interest—I am a Japan anthropologist—but also because I believe that Japan anthropology is a useful diagnostic for other regional anthropologies and for other topical zones of the discipline. There are several reasons for this.

Japan anthropology has produced quite a rich corpus of regional ethnography. Since our first Ph.D. dissertation, filed by John Embree at the University of Chicago in 1937 ("Suye Mura: A Changing Economic Order"), there have been more than 350 English-language dissertations in anthropology on Japan, largely done at U.S. universities but with others filed at British, Canadian, European, Australian, Singaporean, and, recently, Japanese universities. The growth of Japan anthropology has been particularly explosive since the publication of *Fieldnotes*, with just over 200 of the 350 dissertations filed after 1989. To this, we can add some 140 ethnographic monographs and many hundreds of articles and volume chapters. The anthropology of Japan may well be the largest single-country corpus of field research in the discipline, historically deep and topically broad.

Equally important, Japan anthropology pioneered many topics that have since become popular and productive in the broader discipline. From the 1960s, for instance, often well in advance of the discipline elsewhere, Japan anthropologists started producing studies of business corporations (white- and pink-collar offices and blue-collar assembly lines), government bureaucracies, high-rise apartment complexes, old-age homes, urban day laborer exchanges, formal schooling from kindergarten to college, television studios, urban train stations, and more. Since 1990, as Table 2.1 indicates, the scope of field research in and of Japan has expanded exponentially, well beyond even this earlier range to topics distant, digital, and distributed.

So I undertook as broad a review as I could manage from this outpouring of dissertations and monographs since the original *Fieldnotes*, paying special attention to the accounts of methods given by the authors themselves, in sometimes full and frank detail. I have not had access to actual fieldnotes beyond my own and those of several of my students, but I have talked with some Japan colleagues about their fieldnote practices, and I believe that a review of 200 or so of the dissertations and most of the 140 monographs does offer an instructive perspective on field methodology.

Table 2.1. Field Research in and About Japan, 1990–2013: A Sample of People and Places from 200 Ph.D. Dissertations and 140 Ethnographic Monographs

Women's production cooperatives	Elderly resident Koreans
Deaf political organizations	Widows and single mothers
Anime production studios	Overseas housewife circles
Manga publishing houses	Whaling hamlets and fishing ports
Broadcast television newsrooms	Female abalone divers
Pop idol agencies	Organic agriculture communes
Robotics laboratories	Department store sales floors
Second Life sites	Financial derivative trading groups
Gamers and cosplayers	Japanese corporate subsidiaries in France
Iranian migrants in Tokyo	Japanese avant-garde fashion designers
Osaka day laborers	Alcoholic spouse support groups
Urban homeless camps	HIV/AIDS clinics and activists
Osaka Burakumin neighborhood	Right-wing political groups
Japanese-Filipina marriages	Shinto shrines
Japanese-Brazilian workers	Mountain pilgrimages
Karaoke boxes and bars	Volunteer social organizations
Rap music clubs and recording studios	Nonprofit organizations (NPOs) and
Reggae clubs	nongovernmental organizations
"Noise" performance spaces	(NGOs)
Funeral companies	Overseas tour groups
Commercial wedding halls	Child protection agencies
Childbirth "back home"	Maid cafes and otaku spaces
Psychiatric clinics	Domestic violence shelters
Addict support groups	High school sex education classes
Feminist activist circles	Working-class high schools
Waste treatment facilities	"Freeter" bars
Antipollution social movements	Sumo wrestling stables
Earthquake research laboratory	Company sports teams
Exam preparatory schools	Fitness clubs
Advertising agencies	Recreational marathon clubs
Universities and junior colleges	Professional baseball clubs
Host clubs and hostess bars	Martial arts dojos
Convenience stores	Tokyo Disneyland and other theme parks
Okinawan women's war memories	Japanese supermarket chain in Hong
Deep-rural elderly	Kong

What did I discover? Is a radical revision of *Fieldnotes* required to reflect a radical change in our research practices? The short answer—which shocked me—is that there seems to have been far less change in fieldnote taking and wider fieldwork practices than I was led to expect from the digital revolution and the expansion of research topics and sites. To put it more precisely, *what* we now study has indeed expanded immensely—our topics, our questions, and our sites—and the *concepts* we use to analyze what we study have broadened impressively; the palette of theories that color our work runs the full spectrum of the social sciences and humanities. However, for many more cases than not, my argument in this chapter is that our actual research practices bear a striking resemblance to the practices that *Fieldnotes* V-1 examined so thoroughly and so discomfortingly. By practices, I mean the thick nexus of project design, fieldwork (in its deceptively multiple forms and among those forms, fieldnotes), and the subsequent process that formulates our field research through reasoning and writing to final representations as dissertations, books, and articles. In other words, fieldnotes, from head to foot.

I was left puzzled by this general methodological continuity and much disappointed (I had wanted to bring readers a message of dramatic change!). To be sure, the mobilities and modalities of communication have multiplied beyond what any of us could have imagined in 1990. The quality, density, and duration of field contact have proliferated. Fieldnote-taking itself has changed for many anthropologists, who are now armed with smartphones, digital pens, voice recognition software, mapping programs, and other recording techniques.

Much has been made of multisited research (Marcus 1995), but equally importantly, we have become multisited *researchers*. Whatever distance between home and fields existed in the past has collapsed. When I first went to rural northeast Japan for my dissertation research in 1976, I would write a thin, one-page aerogramme every couple of weeks to my parents and friends back in the United States, but in two years, I never made a single international phone call. Now, from the same rural location, with 24/7 Internet, smartphones, and social media, I have daily Skype conversations with my daughter and others back home, instantaneous communications with my students and colleagues in my home department, and, if I choose, every university library journal, streaming Netflix movie, and online newspaper I want from home. The long-standing immiscibility of home and field has been thoroughly disrupted.

We are still inquisitively observing—be it homeless tent shelters, national fisheries bureaucracies, global financial services firms, shellfish diver routines, early morning sumo wrestler practices, or anime script conferences. We are still constantly interviewing and incessantly talking and furiously scribbling and obsessively recording. We are still, more occasionally, participating—as assembly line workers in auto factories, as clerks in convenience stores, as feminist circle archivists, as disaster relief volunteers, as Rakugo performers and teen idol judges, and in many other roles.

The following is quite typical of the accounts of field methods that still characterize almost all of the dissertations. It is from a study of several religious and ethics-training associations in Tokyo:

> My fieldwork consisted of: 1) attendance at daily and weekly meetings and social gatherings, and at monthly and annual ceremonies; 2) participation in study sessions, training retreats, workshops and conferences; and 3) formal and informal interviews with individual members. In order to gain a broader understanding of individual members in and beyond their organizations I also met with informants outside of official institutional contexts. In addition to participant-observation, among the 46 individuals I conducted interviews with I followed up with 25 informants for more personalized in-depth interviews at their homes and at my apartment. I also stayed overnight with their families to join morning meetings and followed informants throughout a typical day. When I returned for follow-up fieldwork in late 2011, I visited these informants to follow-up on the continuous changes in their lives, especially after the March 11, 2011 disaster. (Gagné 2013: 17)

Because I had the opportunity to work with Gagné through his dissertation project, I know well how thorough was his note-taking and how integral that practice was to the evolving analysis. It might be argued that small-scale religious movements are an anthropological staple and reliance on such a conventional field strategy is hardly surprising. To be sure, strikingly "contemporary" research sites and topics have provoked experimentation and innovation, but even where we might surely expect radical methodological shifts, methodological continuities still prevail.

For instance, in the aftermath of the earthquake, tsunami, and nuclear plant disasters that befell Japan on March 11, 2011, anthropologist Theodore Bestor, historian Andrew Gordon, and their colleagues at Harvard's Reischauer Institute of Japanese Studies began assembling what has become perhaps the largest digital archive of a human/natural disasterscape, data-vacuuming the digital world for material and links, maintaining open access, and inviting all users, including anthropologists, to explore, research, and curate this "big-data" base, facilitating a kind of post hoc, distributed digital fieldwork.[1] The possibilities for creative research and analysis are immense, and there are some fascinating projects at the database website that scholars, students, and others have done with its primary documents, interviews, photographs, and other resources.

Nonetheless, for all the big data–mining possibilities of the Digital Archive of Japan's 2011 Disasters, the anthropologists now doing active field research in the Tohoku region on postdisaster issues have almost all eschewed big data for small worlds. A striking example of ongoing research is the recent volume *Japan Copes with Calamity* (Gill, Steger, and Slater 2013), five of whose contributors are anthropologists developing separate post-3.11 ethnographic monographs: Tom Gill, with angry farmers in the Fukushima nuclear zone; Brigitte Steger, with the dispirited elderly in the temporary shelters; Alyne Delaney, with the coastal fisherfolk whose livelihood was devastated; Tuukka Toivonen, with the surges of youthful volunteers from Tokyo; and David Slater, with the resolute survivors in the mud-clogged houses along the Sanriku coast. Slater's account is quite representative of their common fieldwork pattern:

> The data for this paper comes from more than 50 volunteer trips I made during the 18 months after the disaster in March, to places ranging from Otsuchi in Iwate to Chiba City and even Tokyo. My duties ranged from handing out food and blankets in emergency shelters in March and April to winterizing the temporary housing units when it got cold again. Most of the work was manual labour, with digging mud out of houses being the most common form, but this gradually gave way to beautification of the grounds around the units and then to more complex community care, sometimes referred to as "care of the heart." I also led groups of students and business executives, both Japanese and foreign, in an effort to increase CSR (Corporate Social Responsibility) giving among larger companies. We are now engaged in an oral narrative project on the construction of local story repositories, referred to as "Archives of Hope," at 8 different sites in Tohoku. (Slater 2013: 267–268)

We may draw another example from the very different but equally "contemporary" topic of robotics. Japan has the largest production and largest population of robots in the world, and Hirofumi Katsuno, among a half dozen other anthropologists, has been exploring the "techno-animism" among humans and robots as they enter into shared worlds of intimate sociality. How? By joining a robot-building circle, crafting a robot, and competing with it, all the while pondering this mixed sociality of human-human, human-robot, and robot-robot through interviews and note-taking.

> These amateur robot-builders form local groups to have weekly meetings for exchanging information in such large cities as Tokyo, Nagoya, Osaka, and Fukuoka. I conducted fieldwork in two such groups from September 2005 to August 2007: one based in Akihabara, Tokyo, the center of Japanese consumer technology, and the other at a robot museum in Fukuoka called Robosquare. I participated as a neophyte robot-builder and experienced the processes of learning robot-making, joining the robot-builders' community, building a robot, and taking part in the competitions held at public venues such as industrial expositions, theme parks, local festivals, and hospitals. . . . Along with other local robot-builders, including some from my program, I met amateur robot-builders from all over Japan. Based on this common experience, six of us formed a group to develop our robots collaboratively and started to meet at Robosquare on a weekly basis. (Katsuno 2010: 37–38)

Another recent dissertation, by Chiho Inoue (2012), explored how the digital space of linked Japanese households over transnational distance (between Texas and Tokyo) was sustained by regular domestic camcording—using the recursive method of camcording the camcording, eventually enlisting the families in their own autorecording and analysis of the sessions on both sides of the Texas-Tokyo divide—but he found that the process of analytical discovery and methodological refinement still required the mediation of fieldnotes.

> The focus of my dissertation is to investigate the intersection of two domestic spaces that diasporic families overlap by way of webcam. . . . I conducted interviews and made videotapes of webcam interactions in participants' homes [in Texas] . . . I traveled to Japan four times . . . I interviewed families and videotaped webcam interactions

based in Japan. . . . Once the family became accustomed to the recording device, I invited the family to participate in the data collection process. I left the video recorder at the house, taught the family when and how to press the record button, and how to change a cassette. Every week I visited the family, collected the recorded tapes, and gave them a new set of blank tapes. As soon as I obtained the tapes, I watched them, took notes, and made a list of questions that I would bring to the family the following week. Sometimes a webcam conversation started while I was visiting the families. In that case, I joined the conversation. . . . While webcam conversation data allowed for direct analysis of interactional coordination in webcam-mediated spaces, interviews provided me with ethnographic data on participants' habitual ways of using a webcam and other tools to interact with their extended family members. (Inoue 2012: 24, 27, 30, 37)

Ian Condry's recent monograph on the production of anime was also an ingenious analysis of a diffuse world of material, economic, aesthetic, and social dimensions and global reach that was grounded in interactions, interviews, and immersion that crossed the real and digital divide:

> My research centers on ethnographic fieldwork, primarily in several anime studios in Tokyo . . . attending script meetings, voice recordings, and editing sessions, and I conducted interviews with dozens of creators . . . I attended anime conventions . . . and I follow many aspects of online anime fandom in both Japan and the United States. (Condry 2013: 5)

What these and many other (almost all other!) examples from the corpus I have examined demonstrate is that our methods, including the mundane acts of note-taking, remain, by and large, *recognizable* to any of the contributors to the 1990 *Fieldnotes*. In dissertation after dissertation, in monograph after monograph, there is a strong family resemblance in the inevitable "methods" section about an ensemble of activities and practices that provide the evidentiary base of the analysis. A thousand analytical flowers may be blooming in riotous color, but they still seem to be growing from familiar methodological soil.

Why Is This?

If indeed this is a fair assessment, why is it so? Perhaps there are some readers who are thinking (even smugly!), well, that is just Japan anthropology for you, isn't it? It confirms their lurking suspicion that Japan anthropology is a hopelessly anachronistic backwater of the discipline, and if we would only turn to other ethnographic regions, we would find far more evidence of new methods, innovative strategies, transformational field logics, and creative appropriations to the new worlds (digital and real) around us. Maybe so, but I will leave that to others to demonstrate—while holding to my own suspicion that such readers will not reach a different conclusion.[2]

Indeed, in many respects, my finding here about the contemporary corpus of Japan anthropology is consonant with arguments and experience of four of our most accomplished ethnographers of virtual life worlds. Tom Boellstorff, Bonnie Nardi, Celia Pearce, and T. L. Taylor recently produced a most stimulating "handbook of method" for *Ethnography and Virtual Worlds* (2012). One of their strongest conclusions was about the continuing salience of our regulative fiction, "participant observation," as *reflective* method as well as reflexive experience in digital lifeworlds that were unimaginable back in 1990. Their fieldwork in virtual domains and social gaming is still rooted in participant observation; indeed, participation, as gamer or as digital-double avatar, may be even more necessary than real-world fieldwork, and they assert forcefully that the technologies of the virtual multiply rather than replace the demands of note-taking:

> Participant observation is the embodied emplacement of the researching self in a fieldsite as a consequential social actor. . . . Through participant observation, ethnographers step into the social frame in which activity takes place. . . .
>
> In addition to fieldnotes, virtual worlds provide unique data collection possibilities based on the software that underpins them. . . . These include chatlogs, screenshots, and audio and video recording. None of these data sources should be construed as a substitute for fieldnotes, but fieldnotes need to take them into account. (Boellstorff et al. 2012: 65, 84)

The lesson of their work, together with those following similar Japan-centered virtual worlds, is that, more often than not, our move into new dimensions of experience, with new technological means, allows—perhaps demands—that we do *more* of what we have been doing, rather than *less* of what we were doing.

Beyond this, however, I think there are at least three other reasons why actual research practices have been changing noticeably more slowly than the questions that drive the research, the sites of research, the theories that inspire that research, and the analyses that we fashion from that research. The first is that "fieldwork" has always been a forgiving cover term for an adaptive mélange of methods (and I mean "cover" in the double sense of an umbrella term and an effective disguise). As the cases cited above illustrate, even the most recent projects still rely upon the serendipity of encounters, the nimbleness and resourcefulness of the researcher, and this supple mix of methods. Direct engagement, sustained encounter, an intellectual and emotional openness—these remain the rather underspecified research qualities that we expect in ourselves, our colleagues, and our students.

To put it in other terms, the discipline still assesses our work much more at the level of "doing" fieldwork rather than in the details of what precisely was done. Situated analytical reasoning is generally valued over demonstrated statistical significance. We do not demand publication (even citation) of fieldnotes or other field materials, and we do not require ethnographic writing and reasoning to conform to a standard set of protocols that will measure results against replication, as in other social sciences.

Second, it remains true of our modes of inquiry that we may begin our projects with a place or begin with a topic or a question or even a hypothesis, but field research by most of us is open-ended in the literal sense of the term. It is iterative, reflexive, generative—we incant a litany of descriptors for the emergent quality of ethnographic analysis that continues to put a premium on grounded discovery.

Journalism may be history's first draft; surely, fieldnotes are ethnography's first draft. But they have a more profoundly immediate place. Wherever we go, before we ask about local lifeways, we must "learn to ask" in Charles Briggs's apposite phrase (Briggs 1986). Our best questions are *following* questions, not *leading* questions. And those questions get sharper, our engagement deepens, and our conversations become more focused through the routine of note-taking, which, we all know, is as essential to the *reasoning process* as to the *recording project*. It is not the variable forms of notation but the regular practice of notation that moves our inquiries into focus and toward understanding, and this helps to explain the persistence of the practice.

A third reason why most of us remain bound to a methodological conservatism is the inertia of our location in the academy. It is our home work as much as our fieldwork that keeps us cautious. By this, I mean that although our research fields and questions are expanding continuously, even exponentially, our writing conventions and publishing platforms change much more slowly. The fieldwork-based, solo dissertation for the doctoral degree; the "dissertation book" based on that dissertation for tenure; reliance on ranked disciplinary journals for promotion and advancement still constitute the demands and standards of our university workplaces, promotion committees, and academic colleagues. Despite the casualization of academic employment, the nervous experiments with digital publishing, the insidious infiltration of corporate audit logics into university assessment, and more, the academy's standards and practices, enunciated and implicit, continue to dominate the discipline, and these have been slow to change.

And I do not think they will change significantly until the center of disciplinary gravity shifts from the academy or at least until we are more broadly distributed across locations beyond the academy. There have always been important practitioners of anthropology outside universities and colleges, but they remain underacknowledged, and they often must emulate academic forms of research and writing rather than pioneer new styles. Perhaps the recent expansion of anthropologists in corporate settings will precipitate experimentation. Consider, for example, the example that Dawn Nafus and ken anderson give of corporate ethnographic research groups that literally write on the walls of the project rooms:

> Project rooms [provide] a physical, three dimensional space to write, display artifacts and media, and draw. Though used differently in different places, the practice of writing on the walls has become an everyday part of life as an anthropologist in industrial contexts. Walls have become materials to think with, think through, and perform what it is researchers are thinking about. Our main claim is that these are not just simple mnemonic devices, a record of what happened while doing fieldwork or while thinking through business problems, but that these materials make a certain social configuration possible. Social relations happen in the process of

people moving between text, visual material, and orality. (Nafus and anderson 2009: 138)

Such methods are still, however, on the horizon of possibility, and I have used the very large archive of Japan anthropology, 1990–2013, to argue that the methodological currents run slowly in the mainstream.

If so, the skeptical reader might ask, do we really need this new version of *Fieldnotes* after all? Of course we do—without a doubt, as one can see when reading through the other chapters of this book that offer a new generation of best practices, exemplary cases, and cautionary tales with new technologies of field research. Here, though, I have tried to draw attention not to the novel but to what remains conventional and why such conventions remain so. As long as our research problem orientation is toward grounded inquiry and emergent understanding, our research practices, whatever new technologies and socialities they may employ, will require an ongoing routine of recording, reviewing, and reflecting.

This is a case, then, in which a V-2 does not replace its V-1 but rather augments and extends it. The 1990 volume will not be rendered obsolete. It remains relevant for enlightening us about issues of form and function, of privacy and responsibility, of sentiment and surveillance, of diligence and negligence that still surround our core methodological practices. We are indeed the slow social science, but we have also long been the self-contentious rather than the self-confident social science. This new edition will only serve to sustain our healthy level of constructive anxiety and self-improvement.

Notes

1. The portal for the "Digital Archive of Japan's 2011 Disasters" is http://www.jd archive.org/en/home.

2. For instance, no recent and thoughtful reviews of regional ethnography have remarked on field research and recording innovations. See, for instance, Albera 2006; Chernela 2005; Lederman 2005, 2008.

Bibliography

Albera, Dionigi. 2006. Re-visioning the Mediterranean. *History and Anthropology* 17 (2): 109–133.

Boellstorff, Tom, Bonnie Nardi, Celia Pearce, and T. L. Taylor. 2012. *Ethnography and Virtual Worlds: A Handbook of Method*. Princeton, N.J.: Princeton University Press.

Briggs, Charles. 1986. *Learning How to Ask: A Sociolinguistic Appraisal of the Role of the Interview in Social Science Research*. New York: Cambridge University Press.

Chernela, Janet M. 2005. Anthropology of Amazonia. In *Envisioning Brazil: A Guide to Brazilian Studies in the United States*, edited by Marshall C. Eakin and Paulo Roberto de Almeida, 203–240. Madison: University of Wisconsin Press.

Condry, Ian. 2013. *The Soul of Anime: Collaborative Creativity and Japan's Media Success Story*. Durham, N.C.: Duke University Press.

Embree, John Fee. 1937. Suye Mura: A Changing Economic Order. Ph.D. diss. University of Chicago.

Gagné, Isaac Thomas. 2013. Private Religion and Public Morality: Understanding Cultural Secularism in Late Capitalist Japan. Ph.D. diss., Yale University.

Gill, Tom, Brigitte Steger, and David H. Slater. 2013. *Japan Copes with Calamity: Ethnographies of the Earthquake, Tsunami and Nuclear Disasters of March 2011*. Oxford: Peter Lang.

Inoue Chiho Sunakawa. 2012. Virtual "Ie" Household: Transnational Family Interactions in Japan and the United States. Ph.D. diss., University of Texas, Austin.

Katsuno Hirofumi. 2010. Materializing Dreams: Humanity, Masculinity, and the Nation in Contemporary Japanese Robot Culture. Ph.D. diss., University of Hawai'i at Manoa.

Lederman, Rena. 2005. Challenging Audiences: Critical Ethnography in/for Oceania. *Anthropological Forum* 15 (3): 319–328.

———. 2008. Anthropological Regionalism. In *A New History of Anthropology*, edited by Henrika Kuklick, 310–325. New York: Blackwell.

Marcus, George E. 1995. Ethnography In/of the World System: The Emergence of Multi-sited Ethnography. *Annual Review of Anthropology* 24: 95–117.

Nafus, Dawn, and ken anderson. 2009. Writing on Walls: The Materiality of Social Memory in Corporate Research. In *Ethnography and the Corporate Encounter: Reflections on Research in and of Corporations*, edited by Melissa Cefkin, 137–157. New York: Berghahn.

Slater, David H. 2013. Moralities of Volunteer Aid: The Permutations of Gifts and Their Reciprocals. In *Japan Copes with Calamity: Ethnographies of the Earthquake, Tsunami and Nuclear Disasters of March 2011*, edited by Tom Gill, Brigitte Steger, and David H. Slater, 267–292. Oxford: Peter Lang.

Chapter 3

Changes in Fieldnotes Practice over the Past Thirty Years in U.S. Anthropology

Jean E. Jackson

This chapter reports on eighteen interviews I conducted with anthropologists in 2013 about their fieldnote practices and concerns. I compare them with seventy interviews I carried out in 1984–1985 (Jackson 1990a, 1990b) using the same questions:

What is your definition of fieldnotes?

What was your training in fieldnotes practice—preparation and mentoring, formal and informal?

Have you shared your fieldnotes with anyone?

What can you tell me about your *feelings* about your fieldnotes—the actual, physical notes—during fieldwork and afterwards?

Is there a mystique about fieldnotes within the profession?

Do you believe that fieldnotes are connected in some way to an anthropologist's identity? If so, in what way?

What is your response to the assertion that "unlike historians, anthropologists create their own documents"?

It became clear while doing the earlier interviews that fieldnotes were an entry point to a number of topics in anthropology—and not only methodological and epistemological ones. Many wide-ranging and thorny issues emerged, most of which reappeared during the 2013 interviews. In presenting my findings from this recent set, I look first at observations about the effects of changes in technology on fieldnote-taking. I then turn to the topics I asked about directly and to several problematic issues I have consolidated under the rubric "the perversities of fieldnotes." Finally, I offer some general reflections on how anthropological fieldwork has changed over the past thirty years, paying particular attention to changes in fieldnotes practice.

New Technologies

One of the 2013 interviewees mentioned sending fieldnotes as text messages, which made the activity invisible—no one nearby noticed anything out of the ordinary. Two others used software programs for notes, for example, Scrivener, and another told me she scanned her handwritten notes. One interviewee said she found herself taking fieldnotes on her smartphone when she did not have her notebook, and still another mentioned using her phone's recorder function for interviews. We may note, however, that sixteen of the eighteen 2013 interviewees reported that they took handwritten notes at least some of the time (compare Kelly, Chapter 2, this volume). The reasons offered for this included the freedom this permitted ("I draw diagrams"; "I draw arrows") and the obtrusiveness of computers or devices.

Almost all interviewees mentioned keeping in touch electronically with informants after returning home. "Staying in touch with them through social media is the only reason I stay in Facebook. I have an ongoing chronicle through this on-line community. Even though I haven't been back in two and a half years, they don't see me as someone who just came and left." With email, Facebook, and Skype chats, several interviewees reported asking themselves: "Where does the field end?" One told me, "I'm not rigorously doing fieldwork [now], but the fieldwork didn't end when I left." Another added, "Given the technology, like Facebook, I can easily call someone on the phone, or email them. So where does the field end? I could access more fieldnotes, and I still continue taking fieldnotes, not in the manner of a [traditional] notebook but [through] Facebook correspondence."

Some interviewees expanded on the impact of electronic communication for research as a whole. One mentioned that Gupta and Ferguson's comment that "notes are taken in the field, and write-up occurs at home" (perhaps referring to 1997: 42–43) no longer applies: "How do we think of the practice of anthropology and ethnography when you can constantly update, [and] when you can continue learning as if you were present? It's difficult to . . . think of it in the same way as before."

Two interviewees complained that certain older technologies made typed notes less accessible later on—for example: "They're on floppies." The new technologies can produce other problems, however. As one interviewee commented about the many ongoing email exchanges she had with informants, "They're in my Inbox. I've got to deal with it. I get a note every two days that I'm at quota."

Many interviewees responded to my question about the definition of fieldnotes by commenting on the consequences of doing fieldwork in an age of electronic communications. One, studying election campaigns, explained that because she had "boxes and boxes" and many computer files of blog posts and similar materials, her notes were basically an index telling her where to look for a given subject. "The fieldnotes included surveys, research data from companies, videos, printed PR material for the candidates, advertisements."

Several responses implied that the new technologies decreased the "precious" nature of fieldnotes when compared to earlier periods, in part because electronic fieldnotes could be copied and shared much more easily. The well-known concern about protecting notes from loss has greatly lessened. "You can send them to your mom to hold." Another interviewee explained that she sent a compact disk of what she had written so far back home with everyone who visited her.

A related issue concerns changes in institutional oversight, in particular, institutional review boards (IRBs). IRBs now can basically dictate how one takes notes as well as their ultimate disposition. One interviewee said that her university IRB wanted her to store her fieldnotes on a separate, locked, non-networked computer. This was "logistically impossible," as she had only one computer in the field. Two interviewees brought up their use of encryption software, which had been an IRB requirement and was mentioned in the consent forms used in their fieldwork.

The Definition of Fieldnotes

The seventy interviews I carried out thirty years ago provided much thoughtful and engaged reflection on fieldnotes. Even the seemingly straightforward question "What is a fieldnote?" was answered in surprisingly varied ways. Conventional notes in a notebook, entries in a diary, letters sent home, and audiotapes were often mentioned, but not all interviewees classified these as fieldnotes. Some, for example, distinguished "data" from fieldnotes; others offered more inclusive definitions.

Similarly, the 2013 interviewees interpreted my request for a definition of fieldnotes in a variety of ways. One marked difference, however, concerned which field writings are to be considered "fieldnotes." Everyone saw them as a record of observations, but for many, preliminary analysis and interpretation now counted as well. One interviewee, for example, stated that fieldnotes should be thought of as "a place to put reflections and interpretations" and that the "data is not kept separate from my thoughts about it, although I keep them separated [in my mind]."

Fieldnotes' physicality was readily commented on—as one interviewee asserted, "I savor the materiality of this pile of documents." Another stated that although she could now search within her fieldnotes by computer, "There was something [I missed] about going physically through them, looking through them." Another said that for her, "They are a kind of archive, tangible. I'm thinking in terms of, like, a fetish, they represent something else [apart from information] and are in and of themselves an artifact." Yet another commented that she was holding on to her old fieldnotes, keeping them in her office, even though "you can't access what's on the floppies." Another observed that "all these binders" at home in her study brought her pleasure when she looked through them, adding, "not that I go to them often." And one interviewee noted that because his "jottings" were chronological, he could readily recall, "Oh, that was the week when this happened." Still another simply said that because her fieldnotes were taken during the early to mid-1990s, they had become artifacts of that time.

In my earlier writings (Jackson 1990a, 1990b), I concluded that fieldnotes are liminal, and my recent interviews contain more comments about this "betwixt and between" characteristic.

> Fieldnotes are the way station between the fieldwork and the ethnography. [They constitute a kind of] gap between the doing and being there and the written published analysis.

> I know that I write things in my fieldnotes that I would never publish. Sometimes I'm extremely rude when writing them because it's

quicker to describe things in that way. The way that I do them, I'm just trying to get it all down, before I fall asleep usually.

Fieldnote Training and Sharing

Mysterious, invisible, taken for granted—these and similar descriptors for fieldnote practice appeared during the 1984–1985 interviews and in the 2013 round as well. One person said that people usually "don't understand . . . how ethnographies come about. Students . . . don't understand the process, how it is constructed. The process is often like a mystery." Another admitted she had no idea what her colleagues' fieldnotes were like nor how writing them allowed these colleagues to come to the conclusions they did. "If they are difficult personalities, well, what kind of data did they record?" Another commented, "The relationship between what people see and write [in the field], and then what they write [later], it's a mystery."

In the earlier interviews, several anthropologists said that one needed to actually take fieldnotes in order to learn how to do it. A consequence of this "idea that you learn through experience," according to one interviewee, "makes it a mystifying process." As another put it, "Yeah, definitely; it seems like there's kind of an art about fieldnotes." Once one becomes comfortable with fieldnote-taking, moreover, it can reassure the investigator. "It's more like real work when I'm getting down to the fieldnotes."

Various interviewees pondered over the somewhat contradictory observations that fieldnotes are "core" and "fundamental" yet also "invisible" in some ways and that fieldnotes are absolutely central but "not necessarily thought about so much." One observed that anthropologists "convert the buzzing world into something manageable" without talking about it very much and that although "[the decades-old guidebook] Notes and Queries is very systematic, we don't discuss it much, how you do it."

A number of interviewees also touched on the notion of invisibility in response to my questions about anthropological identity and mystique. One replied that the questions made him "grapple [with] this taken-for-granted aspect. It's so fundamental to who we are and what we do." Still, he said, although he talks about fieldnotes to his students, he does not tell them how to take them. "It's a basic part of our practice. I guess I assume people know how to do it." When he sends students out to study neighborhoods he gives them guidelines and detailed instructions about other aspects of fieldwork—"How you talk to people, [that] you should look at posters, etc." But, he said, "I never said to them what kinds of notes to take."

One interviewee commented on a project involving a team of researchers, all of whom took notes.

> We gave them long instructions about ethnography but we didn't talk about fieldnotes and certainly didn't talk about them giving us their fieldnotes, which they used to write their chapters. I wanted to produce a book, but we didn't take advantage of all these available notes. In retrospect that was a big mistake. I'm wondering that maybe we didn't do it because fieldnotes are kind of taken for granted.

When asked about sharing fieldnotes, most interviewees acknowledged that fieldnotes were seldom shared, in part because they would not be of any value to someone else. "They wouldn't be useful." "The really raw fieldnotes wouldn't make much sense to people." "Who would be interested in them anyway?"

Feelings About Fieldnotes

As in my 1980s interviews, several of the 2013 interviewees mentioned that all materials transported back from the field were valuable for that reason alone. One noted the sense of attachment she felt to her notes "because they're worn." Another said "encountering these notebooks is very evocative. They are a material object that was there with me, so it shows I was there. . . . Here, this was very leisurely writing. There not. Here, I killed a bug. It's on the page." Another observed that several pages in her notebook were stained, "maybe with [chili] paste. They're wrinkled, they get dirty in your backpack. They bring you back." One interviewee related that his advisor carried copies of a famous anthropologist's fieldnotes with him to the field, and in spite of the fact that they were copies, the visible accumulated stains confirmed their value.

Fieldnotes establish and represent interfaces with authorities such as one's advisor, department, or university IRB. An interviewee who spoke about the way fieldnote-taking was mystified when being transmitted to graduate students speculated that this was also an indication of the power imbalance between professors and students. Another discussed the worries that can arise around the requirement for anthropological fieldworkers to obtain informed consent. He referred to two labor leaders who lived together as lesbians; everyone knew about this, "but it was [publically] unspeakable." How, then, to deal with this issue when writing up fieldnotes and, even more worrying, in publishing, even though these two women had signed consent forms?

As occurred in my earlier research, my initial request for an interview about fieldnotes sometimes elicited a negative response such as: "You don't want to talk to me." Another interviewee recalled of his initial negative response to my interest in new technologies, "I thought I might be a bad example." On the other hand, several respondents made comments during the interviews affirming that taking fieldnotes made them feel proud or gave them pleasure. "At once [they are] a real point of pride, and something that . . . it's very gratifying seeing . . . all in one place." Or, as another put it, "It's funny, there's a kind of productive feel about it, I feel really good. Gathering data is like gathering fruits and vegetables, it feels like you're accomplishing something."

Nonetheless, negative feelings about their fieldnotes from some interviewees continued to surface in the course of the interviews.

It makes me feel very sad. I'm writing my dissertation and they feel very inadequate. I didn't trust my ethnographic instinct, it's hard to write down what you were feeling at the moment, to create a fieldnote you'd be proud of, that you'd want someone to see.

It does impose some kinds of limitations. Those notes reflect disappointments, frustrations, inadequacies. They reflect all I accomplished, but also all I didn't accomplish.

And as one fieldworker involved in a team research project lamented, "We all feel that we're doing it wrong. There must be some special way, even though we know that you have to just find a way that works for you." As in the 1980s interviews, the recent interviewees frequently commented on the way fieldnotes elicit memories and feelings, at times powerful ones. "These artifacts . . . take me back to Nigeria and to the process of dissertation writing . . . to those memories, the process of writing and the analysis afterwards, and how hard it was." "They have an ability to evoke a nostalgia that at the moment you didn't appreciate because you were so focused on capturing [the ongoing events]."

One interviewee explained that rereading her fieldnotes allowed her to understand how she had changed over time and to see "when I was wrong, times when I learned from my mistakes. So . . . yes, somehow [with] the handwritten ones, it's almost like being back there again." Another stated that because she had become "like a different person," she read her fieldnotes "with a new eye. They are things that I wrote, that I did create, and now I have a different relationship [to them]." Still another spoke of being deeply attached to the fieldnotes, seeing them "as the words that expressed things that I learned, and were meaningful to the people I was working with [and] what it meant to write that."

The Mystique of Fieldnotes

Clearly, fieldnotes represent much more than, say, laboratory notes. One interviewee responded to my question about their "mystique" by using the word "fetish" and continued, "If there's a mystique to it, it feels to me that there's something intangible about this process that is more than, for instance, taking notes in class. I feel that someone is giving something to me, especially when they're sharing difficult events." Another said, "I had a special notebook, it was a gift. I think it had a Navaho design on the cover. That was where I was going to put these notes that were going to be something else someday."

Fieldnotes can possess an "aura." "There's definitely an aura about them. Why do I keep them? Not that I can imagine looking at them again, but I kind of have to keep them. Why, I don't know. It just doesn't feel like something you would dispose of." The "raw and cooked" metaphor that appeared in my earlier interviews also reappeared in the later interviews. Fieldnotes were "kind of sacred, the raw data—raw in many ways." Another interviewee used both this metaphor and the "aura" imagery. "You get a sense going through your graduate training and [learn that] the act and object of producing fieldnotes has its own aura. You want to put yourself into them, to be meticulous. From there will emerge the cooked. Without the raw, there's no cooked."

The role fieldnotes play in publications was mentioned in similar terms. "They're often deployed in direct quotes, a guarantor of authenticity, experiential authenticity. Yeah, a certain mystique and also artifice . . . surrounds them." On the practice of quoting one's fieldnotes, he explained: "That's an interesting kind of move. [My] book contains a lot of vignettes that are close to verbatim, along with preliminary interpretations. But to actually say that something was in your fieldnotes confers a simulacrum of immediacy, and an introduced element of reflexivity." He added that "laying bare . . . employing the artifice . . . reveals the artifice as well. Interesting kind of tension there."

Fieldnotes are spoken of as "core" to anthropology and are seen to stand for much about the discipline and its epistemological premises. My 2013 interviews produced many comments to this effect:

> It's certainly part of a research methodology. Lots of people describe themselves now as doing ethnography, but in ways that wouldn't fit the kind of training that you and I had, and fieldnotes are a part of that.

> Yeah, absolutely, and they're very much a product of your modes of attention in the field. And our discipline is defined by the ethnographic method.

> It's part of what Malinowski called "the ethnographer's magic."[1]

Another added, "Supposedly, with the Geertzian technique, you later pull out the details—the room, facial details—on the blank page, a listing of pieces from the scene of the ethnographic encounter." It is thus crucial, in that moment of going back "there," to be able to write, he said, to remember, "Oh, yeah, that green chair," because the chair works as a kind of mnemonic. "Getting that key quote or key sentence verbatim is important, but also [the fieldnotes help] convey everything around the ethnographic moment—smells, colors."

Fieldnotes and Anthropological Identity

An important finding that emerged from the earlier interviews was that fieldnotes are a synecdoche for the researcher—a part standing for the whole. This was strongly confirmed by the 2013 interviewees' views about how fieldnotes are connected to disciplinary identity.

> My identity as an anthropologist? I take fieldnotes. But they're also a product of my particular way of being an anthropologist.

> You know your fieldnotes are what make you an anthropologist. That's why I feel so much anxiety, so protective of them.

> They're a part of your formative experiences doing research. . . . My fieldnotes are . . . an index of my time doing research.

> It's something I'm definitely aware of, my place in the production of these documents, my training, my interactions.

> Fieldnotes serve to demonstrate the fieldworker's authenticity in the sense of verifying that they were there.

> When you first get to the field, you're searching for legitimacy. Maybe the art of taking fieldnotes confers legitimacy. You're on the outside, you want to get in on the inside.

> Before you've published anything, you don't necessarily have a lot to show other than what you've experienced. So the kind of notes that one takes, it's probably [a] kind of residue of the experience.

> Once it's written down, it proves that you've been there. A talisman, proof that something actually happens.

Another interviewee said simply that fieldnotes were the traces left from field research encounters. They are, in addition, what may outlive the anthropologist "in terms of being able to access someone's fieldnotes, say from forty years ago."

Fieldnotes may also represent research projects as a whole. As one interviewee reflected, given that anthropologists' fieldnotes were "the substance of the project in some way . . . a constitutive part of the project . . . maybe that's why I don't want to throw them away." Fieldnotes are also a synecdoche for the relationship between researcher and community. One interviewee said that "fieldnotes [are] to some extent about relationships between anthropologists and informants. . . . The places that he or she chooses to be." Another interviewee compared research in archives and ethnographic fieldwork to illustrate the relationship between fieldworker and research community. He had discovered that writing up research based on archives was "so much more pleasurable, because there's no sense of responsibility to anybody."

Several interviewees pointed to ways that they as individuals differed from other anthropologists who had worked or currently were working in the same research community. They noted identity components, like age, gender, and ethnoracial identity, which influenced what they were told and, consequently, what their fieldnotes contained, because it was they who wrote them.

Fieldnotes further were a synecdoche for anthropology in relation to other disciplines. An interviewee remarked that one of his complaints about reading history was that it often erred on the side of the idiographic. When such work is undertheorized, he said, it does not provide him with "the kind of theoretical engine that good ethnography does." Fieldnote-taking, he explained, "is a kind of theoretical praxis" that mobilizes "a certain analytic matrix." Another interviewee observed that fieldnotes were iconic markers of fieldwork encounters that may be difficult to objectify and describe in writing. So "I try to evoke the actual movement, what was the feeling, the sensorial aspects."

Several of my interviewees commented on the way fieldnote practice is explicitly linked to anthropological knowledge production. The first noted that anthropologists are "no longer invisible, and no longer absent in our ethnographies," whereas in earlier periods an anthropologist might have written in a non–self-reflexive way, simply describing situations: "this is the way it is." But, he continued, anthropological knowledge "doesn't just emerge out of nowhere. [We] are the ones producing certain kinds of knowledge," and "it's important to make these bridges that show the relationship between what we privilege in our notes and the ethnographies we produce later."

A second interviewee observed that "your own self is inevitably inextricable from the material you record. No one else could create the document that you create." A third interviewee commented that insofar as anthropology is somewhat anxious about its status as a science of interpretation, "I think that the practice of making fieldnotes also kind of buttresses the legitimacy of the qualitative research that we do."

Yet another interviewee noted that, as happens in any science, the mode of inscribing establishes the mode of legitimacy, and that "day to day, the regularity of writing and reflecting, becomes an indistinguishable part of the experience of doing fieldwork. Notes are the handmaiden of the research." The last of this set of interviewees commented that reading Margery Wolf's *A Thrice-Told Tale* (1992) helped to "disabuse me of the idea that the most direct representation is the best representation" and that providing quotations from one's fieldnotes was not necessarily "the best way to go. [Wolf] got me thinking about the transition from fieldnotes to the analysis."

Fieldnotes as Documents

As with my 1984–1985 interviews, the question about whether anthropologists "create" their own documents proved provocative in 2013. Some, who perhaps felt a bit defensive, said that fieldnotes "are very legitimate documents in their own right." To others, the answer was yes, anthropologists do create their own texts, because the "stories that people tell each other aren't documents until we document them." One interviewee responded that there was a "pretty big difference between looking at a document as opposed to looking at an event. Is one more true? No." Another termed fieldnotes "living documents"; still another said that they were not documents because they had been written "for other purposes. Fieldnotes are already a kind of interpretation."

Some of the interviewees commented on fieldnotes' complex relationship with memory and with the body, one advancing the idea that fieldwork, in contrast to studying documents in an archive, entails an "obvious" embodied dimension. Another interviewee suggested that it would be difficult to "operationalize" fieldnotes as data "without that kind of tacit embodied key" that accompanied them and was located in the fieldworker's mind.

Another definitional consideration of fieldnotes as documents concerned what fieldnotes "do." One interviewee stated that fieldnotes constitute the primary basis for the subsequent analysis, and another asserted that research that lacks "an accompanying inscription" cannot be scientifically meaningful. A third interviewee said that both "verbal and nonverbal prompts" can be considered fieldnotes if they are "part of the process of analysis, if it aids in that process."

Fieldnotes were often spoken about as a particular type of document—an aide-mémoire that helps the researcher "remember on a daily basis," helps to capture a moment "when it is still fresh in your memory and experience." Yet one interviewee admitted her discovery that after she had written down "everything," she "didn't go back and reread these fieldnotes. They're not so useful." For her, the act of writing certain fieldnotes so comprehensively was adequate for securing the information in the researcher's memory. Another interviewee described fieldnote-taking and writing up as a way "of keeping yourself honest so you don't color what happened in the past by what you want it to mean."

One of the interviewees brought up the role of fieldnote-taking during the ongoing interaction itself. "If you don't write anything down, they think you're not paying attention, or they think they haven't said anything important. So the writing down may be a sign to them that what they're saying is worthwhile." Another observed that in the field "fieldnotes are the link between the researcher and informant." A ritual specialist might tell her to "write this" or would take her notebook and draw something in it.

The Perversities of Fieldnotes

I now turn to what I call the "perversity" of fieldnotes. As many interviewees pointed out, fieldnote-taking, seemingly a straightforward and presumably "extremely teachable" methodology, turns out to be anything but. "It seems that taking fieldnotes should be a simple process. But it isn't, it's complex." "People think it's easier than it is. It takes a lot of discipline to do that . . . to convey that sense of being there and having been a part of something as it was happening." We can readily list reasons why fieldnote-taking presents a challenge. First, fieldworkers are unique human beings who have been trained at different times and in different universities. They have unique research proposals and work in different fieldsites. "It's unique, a unique kind of writing."

Fieldnotes represent risk. One might lose them. One's research community might not want fieldnotes to be taken. Or, as an interviewee explained, one's informant does not approve of the way one is taking them: "They'll tell me to 'write this down.' A shaman cut leaves and put them into my notebook to make sure I had it correctly." Fieldnotes also evoke anxiety. How do we respect confidentiality? What might occur here after I leave? "That's what I worry about more. If [in the future] there were some kind of class action suit in Guatemala, I may have some of the only existing records of that time."

Contradictions, complications, and odd juxtapositions were repeatedly remarked upon. "Some people say you have to maintain a . . . distance, but I think you can be close. But when there are exorcisms, suffering, when you're the ritual helper, you're performing, and it feels very odd to objectify people in that way. So I objectify and analyze myself in the process." "The writing [of your notes] can be accessing, drawing you close, or [it can be] creating a certain distance." Several interviewees pointed to the role of fieldnote-taking in developing the double consciousness needed in field-work, what one described as the anthropologist as "shape-shifter." Another discussed trying to teach students how fieldnotes were both an object in themselves and a regular, methodological exercise; how, moreover, "You're there, you do what you might be doing any day, and it's almost as if there was another you, and your fieldnotes are from that other person." Finally, one interviewee commented on using fieldnotes to analyze her reactions in the field: "The people's anxieties—you'd forget it very quickly. I resolved to also analyze myself in the process—why do I react that way?"

Fieldnotes and Affect

Although fieldnotes are material objects, to me they are most productively understood in terms of relationships: those between the fieldworker and the notes, between the fieldworker and his or her future self, between the fieldworker and "native" members of the group studied, between the field-worker and his or her advisor, and between the fieldworker and anthro-pology as a whole. As an illustration of the first three of these relationships, in my 1984–1985 project, one interviewee told me that a ceramic dish for roasting sausages could be a fieldnote because it communicated informa-tion not only about itself (composition, color) and its purpose or use but was a mnemonic of the social context within which sausage cooking occurred. Because of its power to evoke memories and provoke analysis, it served the same function as the scribbling in his field notebook. Even information lacking any material reality apart from impulses sent along neural pathways was spoken of as "fieldnotes" occasionally. (In *Fieldnotes*, Ottenberg called these "headnotes" [1990]).

Both in 1984–1985 and in 2013, interviewees had a wealth of points to make about memory as existing at times in a tense dialectical relationship with fieldnotes or as nearly coterminous with them. So not only can objects like that sausage dish play the role of fieldnote, so can one's self. As one of my 1980s interviewees put it when commenting about a situation she remembered vividly but whose importance she had not understood at the time and had not written down, "I am a fieldnote."

All these relationships to fieldnotes involve affect, and judging from the two sets of interviews, such relationships involving researcher and fieldnotes tend to be intense and complex. (Interviewees used "sacred," "taboo," "fetish," "exorcise," and "ritual" in discussing their fieldnotes.) The multiple roles fieldnotes play—as record, mnemonic, memento—can produce powerful feelings upon returning from the field. Nostalgia, even yearnings for the excitement of fieldwork, for one's research community, for one's youthful self, were frequently spoken about. Aversive feelings, like anxiety and anger, can also percolate up when thinking about or working with fieldnotes. As is always the case with something one creates, fieldnotes to some degree come to symbolize their creator—meticulous and comprehensive or, in contrast, inadequate. As one 1984–1985 interviewee put it, "Fieldnotes can reveal how worthless your work was, the lacunae, your linguistic incompetence, your not being made a blood brother, your childish temper." Clearly, the connection between fieldnotes and their creator that begins to elicit emotions in the field can continue for a long time afterward.

Fieldnotes Then and Now

Ethnography—the doing and the writing-up—is the hallmark of sociocultural anthropology. This volume explores how fieldnote practices are changing in a postmodern world characterized by new technologies and rapid transnational flows and articulations (Appadurai 1991), a world in which images and information that originate in European metropoles can instantaneously be accessed in extremely remote locales. The new technologies discussed in these pages play a role in contemporary field research that at times starkly contrasts with traditional notions about fieldwork and fieldnote practices of three decades ago.

Computers now regularly accompany the fieldworker, and Internet link-ups are available either at the fieldsite or can be regularly accessed in the nearest urban location. Today's technologies greatly expand the range of documents that qualify as fieldnotes. If the researcher's definition is broad and the study concentrating on an online community locked in controversy, for example, she or he will likely have exponentially more notes than the amount produced during fieldwork as conventionally understood. We also see that new ways of taking and storing fieldnotes can confound conventional assumptions about the relatively fixed position of a researcher's fieldnotes in time and space. (Such assumptions were already being upended by several anthropologists I interviewed in 1984–1985.)

Another question has to do with fieldnote authorship. What is the "fieldnote" status of writings produced by others? My recent interviewees spoke about utilizing both notes written by anthropologists who had previously worked at their site and notes produced by field assistants, literate informants, and a variety of local actors. Fieldnote-taking by assistants who are members of the study community has increased substantially. *Which* of these materials written by others may be referred to as "fieldnotes" varies from one researcher to another. For some, fieldnotes are by definition only written by the researcher. For others, fieldnotes may be defined to encompass everything that aids analysis or, by another definition, anything written whose meaning becomes understood via the researcher's mediation.

The traditional "ideal type" of field research envisioned a close connection, both physical and symbolic, between fieldnotes and fieldsite. Because the fieldsite was typically far away from home, fieldnotes represented the distance between these two locations. As material objects, sometimes smeared with smashed insects or chili paste, fieldnotes indexed the field in powerful ways. Insofar as fieldwork involved interaction with human beings in a far-off place, fieldnotes were seen to remain close to that interaction in all manner of ways. Interviewees also spoke of fieldnotes' ability to traverse temporal distance—they were a link to the younger anthropologist who was "there" in a way the present-day one could never be again, even if he or she were to return to the fieldsite.[2]

All ethnographic research today, without question, occurs in complex societies. Earlier research did too, but the traditional fieldworker was supposed to don blinders that would facilitate intensive, face-to-face research in a small community and would sideline the fact that that community was a part of a much larger society, usually with a complicated colonial and neocolonial history. Of course, contrary to this ideal type, traditional anthropologists in fact worked in all sorts of First World and urban settings (for example, Colson 1953; Powdermaker 1950). What has changed in the last thirty years is the relative *amount* of fieldwork in urban and First World settings and the requirement that one pay close attention to how a given community, no matter how remote, is entangled with myriad other venues and histories.³ The conventional ideal-type fieldwork was not supposed to concern itself with government agencies, labor unions, health-care delivery institutions, factories, NGOs, research and development wings of start-ups, or nuclear weapons laboratories.

The chapters in this volume reveal a variety of ways in which fieldnote practice has shifted in response to researchers' choosing to work in radically new kinds of fieldwork sites. Along with innovative theoretical underpinnings and new technologies and methodologies, the study of these sites has substantially increased the range of possible relationships involving fieldnotes. Numerous implications for fieldnote practice arise with these shifts in types of research site, and they involve ownership of fieldnotes, confidentiality issues, ethics, and the fieldworker's many other overall responsibilities with respect to his fieldnotes. All of these have been problematic issues since the beginning of ethnographic fieldwork, and they become extremely complex and thorny in these new contexts.

Although fieldnotes continue to be viewed as a close link to one's research, it seems to me that their propensity to acquire a "mystique" and to evoke particular feelings because they index a very different Otherness is lessening considerably. Given that most research projects now occur in much more accessible sites, the sharp temporal and spatial boundaries characterizing traditional ideal-type fieldwork have become blurred, and this has decreased the iconic "aura" of self-authored fieldnotes and their power to evoke firmly delineated memories and emotions. Traditional fieldwork constituted a distanced separation between fieldsite and home; in my earlier interviews, fieldnotes were often spoken of as mediating this distance: "The whole aspect of remoteness . . . not much written [about this place] . . . your fieldnotes become especially precious." Today, even when anthropologists work in another country, most report being engaged in constant, vigilant document gathering at home as well. Anthropologists now regularly download newspaper articles, NGO bulletins, and other media traces concerning their research community or institutions and events that impact it. Whether these electronic documents (or notes taken while perusing them) are fieldnotes depends only on the researcher's own definition. But whether classified as fieldnotes or not, the traditional image of fieldnotes as precious, exotic, irreplaceable, unique, and limited in quantity has for the most part gone the way of the dodo.

Conventional, ideal-type fieldwork requiring that research take place in one community and involve long-term, intense, face-to-face research no longer prevails. Investigators still "go to the field," but formal interviewing is much more the norm than was the case earlier. Many ethnographic projects today are multisited—for example, my interviewee studying an election. "The field" has become an increasingly abstract metaphor. There are also projects that involve a minimum of face-to-face interaction. Although fieldwork interactions might still be intense, they can be predominantly or totally electronic (see Tratner, Chapter 10, this volume). Fieldnotes from these modes of research project might not elicit the strong affect mentioned so often in my 1984–1985 interviews.

The nature of the fieldworker's relationship with "the natives" is also shifting. As anthropologists increasingly study topics such as social movements, humanitarian organizations, U.S. Army research labs, rural women's credit unions, or investment bankers, fieldnote practices are changing with the subjects. For example, the study population often will demand some mutually agreed-on return benefit before granting research permission, and such agreements often involve the fieldnotes (Erazo 2013), which may exist in electronic form. Researchers are also increasingly discovering how easily outsiders—often ones who do not have one's research community's interests uppermost in mind—might gain unauthorized access to their notes. Although concerns about writing down information that would endanger the community (about smuggling activities, for example) have surfaced in the literature for some time, the present-day ease of obtaining information in electronic form has considerably heightened this risk. (These concerns, of course, include not just fieldnotes but also published materials that can be put to uses never intended by the author—for instance, one interviewee expressed the concern that his Guatemala fieldnotes might be subpoenaed.)

Most assumed that traditional, ideal-type research was conducted, with some exceptions, by a single researcher, although often that researcher was accompanied by a spouse. Team-based research is nothing new (see Whiting and Whiting 1975), but it was once the exception. It is my impression that today, anthropologists increasingly participate in team research, which often includes community members, and the sharing of fieldnotes is increasingly made explicit in research contracts. Although common in sociology and social psychology, such built-in note sharing among members of a team lessens the Mystique of the Lone Fieldworker and, consequently, of the fieldnotes as well.

The moral and ethical status of the anthropologist is shifting, too. The role played by anthropology as a "handmaiden of imperialism" has been debated in the literature for decades (see Asad 1973), and many anthropologists interviewed in 1984–1985 voiced their concerns in this regard. The stereotype of "deep bush" fieldwork in communities of illiterate "natives," with its inevitable power imbalance and potential for misunderstanding and exploitation, bothered those interviewees, most of whom saw themselves as hardworking observer-participants and sensitive, moral persons who did not want to see themselves as manipulating their informants or benefitting from such power imbalances in an improper way. Today, "memsahib" images and consequent fieldworker anxieties are less likely to arise when "the natives" are literate, savvy, and understand contracts, indigenous intellectual property issues, and the like. This is especially the case in science studies (for instance, Helmreich 2009). However, except in work by anthropologists who "study up," power asymmetries during fieldwork continue to prevail. Fieldnotes probably continue to be a venue where researchers can vent their frustrations, but the nature of the venting is changing somewhat, given that fieldwork sites are increasingly populated by "natives" of near-equal or even superior social status to the anthropologist.

Ethnographic fieldwork remains the hallmark of anthropology, and fieldnote practice continues to play a very significant and multifaceted role in the endeavor. Given the multiple ways in which fieldnotes connect with anthropologists' identity, they will probably continue to be a space where fieldworkers grapple with challenges to their self-image as moral individuals carrying out ethical research. Fieldnote practice symbolizes what is unique about anthropological research and those engaged in it. The anthropologist creates fieldnotes that, in turn, play a part in creating the anthropologist. Both my earlier interviews and the most recent ones contain fascinating and unexpectedly revealing commentary about fieldwork and fieldnotes with respect to a broad range of issues—methodological, epistemological, ethical, political, and psychological.

Acknowledgments

Thanks to Roger Sanjek and Susan Tratner for organizing the AAA session and carrying this project forward. And very special thanks to the anthropologists I interviewed, who took the time to meet with me despite their very busy schedules.

Notes

1. Among the other responses were these:

Anthropology itself is about process, so insofar as fieldnotes are reminders of this process, linking our observations and thoughts and analysis of what's going on outside of us, and being in the process of doing fieldwork, the space of that process is fieldnotes.

Fieldnotes are all about process . . . you know, what we worked through. This is the method, the thing that makes this style of work distinctive from other styles of social science research.

A larger point for me was that the fieldnotes captured the play, the lived encounters and experiences.

They weren't formalized. . . . So that is our hallmark, making those informal encounters matter in bigger ways.

The ethnographer is using himself as a way of knowing, of learning.

We can only write that way when we have good fieldnotes.

2. The image of translation to a scale that would capture this notion of distance and different positions came up in the interviews as well. See Benjamin (1968) on the relationship between original and translated texts.

3. See Sylvain's (2014) discussion of the scholarly debates about research on the San Bushmen in southern Africa.

Bibliography

Appadurai, Arjun. 1991. Global Ethnoscapes: Notes and Queries for a Transnational Anthropology. In *Recapturing Anthropology: Working in the Present*, edited by Richard G. Fox, 191–210. Santa Fe, N.M.: School of American Research Press.
Asad, Talal, editor. 1973. *Anthropology & the Colonial Encounter*. London: Ithaca Press.
Benjamin, Walter, 1968. *Illuminations: Essays and Reflections*. New York: Schocken.

Colson, Elizabeth. 1953. *The Makah Indians: A Study of an American Indian Tribe in Modern American Society.* Manchester: Manchester University Press.

Erazo, Juliet S. 2013. *Governing Indigenous Territories: Enacting Sovereignty in the Ecuadorian Amazon.* Durham, N.C.: Duke University Press.

Gupta, Akhil, and James Ferguson. 1997. Beyond "Culture": Space, Identity, and the Politics of Difference. In *Culture, Power, Place: Explorations in Critical Anthropology,* edited by Akhil Gupta and James Ferguson, 33–51. Durham, N.C.: Duke University Press.

Helmreich, Stefan. 2009. *Alien Ocean: Anthropological Voyages in Microbial Seas.* Berkeley: University of California Press.

Jackson, Jean E. 1990a. "Déjà Entendu": The Liminal Qualities of Anthropological Fieldnotes. *Journal of Contemporary Ethnography* 13 (1): 8–43. Reprinted in 1995 in *Representation in Ethnography,* edited by John Van Maanen, 36–78. London: Sage; and in 2008 in *Representing Ethnography.* Vol. 3. Edited by Paul Atkinson and Sara Delamont, 22–51. Los Angeles: Sage.

———. 1990b. "I Am a Fieldnote": Fieldnotes as a Symbol of Professional Identity. In *Fieldnotes: The Makings of Anthropology,* edited by Roger Sanjek, 3–33. Ithaca, N.Y.: Cornell University Press.

Ottenberg, Simon. 1990. Thirty Years of Fieldnotes: Changing Relationships to the Text. In *Fieldnotes: The Makings of Anthropology,* edited by Roger Sanjek, 139–160. Ithaca, N.Y.: Cornell University Press.

Powdermaker, Hortense. 1950. *Hollywood, the Dream Factory: An Anthropologist Looks at the Movie-Makers.* New York: Little, Brown.

Sylvain, Renée. 2014. Essentialism and the Indigenous Politics of Recognition in Southern Africa. *American Ethnologist* 116 (2): 251–264.

Whiting, Beatrice B., and John W. M. Whiting, editors. 1975. *Children of Six Cultures: A Psycho-Cultural Analysis.* Cambridge, Mass.: Harvard University Press.

Wolf, Margery. 1992. *A Thrice-Told Tale: Feminism, Postmodernism, and Ethnographic Responsibility.* Stanford, Calif.: Stanford University Press.

PART II

FIELDWORK OFF- AND ONLINE

Chapter 4

The Digital Divide Revisited: Local and Global Manifestations

Mary H. Moran

In September 1982, I left the United States for Liberia, West Africa. I was twenty-five years old and a graduate student in anthropology at Brown University. I carried with me one suitcase, a backpack, a huge "boom box" combination tape player and shortwave radio (which ran on giant D batteries, the kind that did not last long in a moist tropical environment and leaked acid all over everything), a film camera, a Polaroid camera, and a 1940s-era Smith Corona manual typewriter that had belonged to my father. I had basically the same technological tool kit that was available to Margaret Mead and Gregory Bateson in the 1938 photograph that graced the cover of the paperback edition of *Fieldnotes: The Makings of Anthropology* (Sanjek 1990b).

The anthropology of my undergraduate and early graduate school days had not problematized fieldwork in the terms we now use. We were just beginning to consider how emplacement, location, and positionality shaped knowledge (the kinds of questions raised by Clifford and Marcus 1986 and Gupta and Ferguson 1997); existential states of being "in" and "out" of the field seemed easy to define, and the difference between "notes" and the people whose lives they were supposed to represent was blurry (see Sanjek 1990a).

I began my professional life when paper and pens were the primary tools of an ethnographer, and handwritten notes had to be laboriously typed up in detail and with carbon copies so you could send an extra set home to your advisor. Without electricity in my remote fieldsite on the country's southeastern Atlantic coast, it was quite a chore to get this typing done during the daylight hours, and I remember banging away at night on that old Smith Corona, with a candle on one side of the carriage (in perpetual danger of being knocked over and setting everything on fire) and a kerosene lantern on the other side, both of them throwing tremendous heat in the soggy Liberian night. Without the possibility of phone communication anywhere in the region, checking in with my family and friends in the United States involved a two-day trip to Monrovia, the capital, over terrible roads in any season. I do not remember feeling bothered by this somehow; there was no overwhelming sense of isolation or fear of being out of touch. To this day, most of my fieldnotes from that year and a half remain untyped, although the handwritten notebooks are covered with codes in different-colored markers, Post-it notes, and so forth, and I seem to have been able to make productive use out of them (Moran 1990), no matter how mystifying that may be to the students trained today in MAXQDA.

It is likely that I was technologically out of date even for 1982, but this was due to my personal and idiosyncratic avoidance of most mechanical devices. I have never been much intrigued with gadgets and still (in 2014) cling desperately to my old "un-smart" cell phone. It is therefore ironic that in the early 1990s I became something of an "early adopter" of technologies that enabled fieldwork at a distance, but this was owing to necessity rather than desire (see Moran 2006: 10–12). The Liberian civil war began in December 1989, when I was teaching at a small liberal arts college in rural central New York. I was desperately worried about my Liberian foster family and others I had come to know and care for, as well as for the country as a whole. It was hard to get any reliable, current news, and apart from a few phone contacts in Monrovia, which ended by the summer of 1990, I had no means of communication with anyone in the country for several years.

Then came the Internet. The World Wide Web became widely accessible to nonspecialist users in 1994 when Mosaic, the first graphical web browser, became available for popular software programs by Microsoft and Apple (Norris 2001: 27). By 1995, a group of former Peace Corps volunteers who had served in Liberia since the 1960s organized an email news service, collecting wire-service references to ongoing events and sending them out once or twice a week. Liberian expatriate communities in the United States and in Europe began websites and blogs.

At about the same time, members of my foster family who had relocated to the capital, Monrovia, began reaching out through a system of phone trees. Every few weeks, I would be jolted out of sleep in the middle of the night. The caller was usually someone in the United States, who would give me a number in Liberia and instruct me that "my family" was standing by. I would make the call, and at the end of a brief and rushed conversation with my foster brothers, they would give me a U.S. phone number and tell me to alert the next family to make their call. Given the level of background noise, I could imagine groups of Liberians gathered around shaky landlines, collaborating to reach multiple nodes of widespread global networks with one initial collect call to the United States. I can only imagine how important it must have felt for them, in those dangerous and deadly times, to feel that they could make a connection abroad, that the world had not completely forgotten them. Although I tried sending packages and letters, often with futilely concealed cash, these almost never reached my foster brothers. It was only when the war ended and digital money transfers became once again available that I was able to offer more than verbal and emotional support in the form of a brief phone exchange.

Alternatively, I got a lot of collect calls myself, again in the middle of the night. Because I usually took these calls sleepy and disoriented, behind a closed bathroom door, while trying not to wake my husband and children, I do not have accurate "fieldnotes" to document them, although I often tried to reconstruct them in writing the next morning. I was aware from fairly early on that these brief moments of contact did tell a story of how people survive through long periods of humanitarian crisis and make creative use of whatever technology is available—in this case, landline telephones—to reach out transnationally. In moments when the situation stabilized, these calls became the vehicle for transmitting authorization numbers for Western Union money transfers, as well as for the exchange of reassuring information. In other, more desperate times, I was able to use my access to news on the BBC and other websites to relay information to my foster brothers about the movements of armed factions across Monrovia's neighborhoods (see Moran 2006: 10–11).

Although it felt like there was constant slippage between notes, data, and family phone calls, the combination of new sources of information available on the web and telephone conversations made me feel like I was pioneering a new form of fieldwork at a distance. I would have preferred to do the more old-fashioned kind, but the alternative seemed to be moving my research agenda to a different country. My combining of web, phone, and face-to-face interviews with U.S.-based Liberians, however, allowed me to write a second book, *Liberia: The Violence of Democracy* (2006), without leaving the United States. Ironically, for all the emphasis that has been placed on how digital resources have "deterritorialized" fieldwork (see especially Bernal 2005), it was these technologies that allowed me to keep my scholarship firmly, if virtually, "in place."

The transition to cell phones, so celebrated in recent literature on the communications revolution in Africa, occurred during the second phase of the Liberian civil war, from 1999 to 2003. In the final, terrifying days of the last siege of Monrovia, during the summer of 2003, I discovered that my three foster brothers, living in three different parts of the country, could all call me, but could not reach each other. I became the conduit for their messages that each had survived the final stages of the war. Since that time, my engagement with this particular extended family has continued with phones, email, and Facebook, as well as with three trips back to Liberia since 2006. Just as when I lived physically in their household, I have been drawn into intrafamily feuds, accusations of witchcraft, revelations of previously unknown half-siblings, and of course requests for financial assistance with school fees, college tuition, weddings, funerals, and emergency medical treatment, not to mention new electronic devices.

While I have always taken seriously my fictive kin status and am grateful to be able to remain active in these networks, I have not really thought of these relationships in the context of the now-exploding literature on digital media in anthropology. Nor have I attempted, before now, to theorize on how these new channels of connection have reshaped my own conceptions of research. What is it that has been lost, and what has been gained, in the transition to more mediated forms of "fieldwork"? Am I closer to my Liberian foster family because I am more directly accessible to them (and because they are more accessible to me), and what are the implications for the kinds of information we share? Is this a form of privileged personal contact or grist for the anthropologists' mill, as my late-night phone conversations in the bathroom were?

In her 2010 article in *Annual Review of Anthropology*, Gabriella Coleman helpfully divides the literature on digital media into three overlapping categories: first, explorations of the relationship between digital media and the "cultural politics" of representations and imaginaries, such as ethnic identities, diasporas, and amorphous categories (such as "youth"); second, documentation of the vernacular cultures of the virtual world: SMS texting languages, gaming, digital genres, media workers such as bloggers, hackers, and programmers; and third, the "prosaics" of digital media, or the impact on practices applied to areas of social life such as economic exchange, maintenance of social hierarchies, religious identities, and so on (2010: 488). Coleman also notes the important critiques leveled by scholars such as Ginsburg (2008), van Binsbergen (2003), and Warschauer (2003), among others, against the notion of the "digital divide" between consumers and producers of electronic media and "others." This "powerful structuring emblem with material and cultural consequences" (Coleman 2010: 490) seems to have replaced older distinctions between the "modern" and "traditional" folk of anthropological fantasy. Warschauer notes that the "original sense of the *digital divide*, which attached overriding importance to the physical availability of computers and connectivity rather than to the issues of content, language, education, literacy or community and social resources, is difficult to overcome in people's minds" (2003: 6; see also Buys et al. 2008).

This "original sense" remains strong in the minds of my undergraduate students, who find it hard, at first, to believe that my Liberian informants all have cell phones and then, once they accept that notion, have difficulty believing that their lives and worldviews can still be very different from their own. In Ginsburg's words, the assumed presence or absence of communicative technologies in a particular place produces a "reinscribing onto the world a kind of 'allochronic chronopolitics' . . . in which the other exists in a time not contemporary with our own. This has the effect of re-stratifying the world along lines of a late modernity, despite the utopian promises by the digerati of the possibilities of a twenty-first century McLuhanesque global village" (2008: 130–131). The fact that many Liberians have cell phones does not mean that Liberia as a nation no longer struggles to recover from fourteen years of war, or that 85 percent of Liberians remain formally unemployed, or that the country is no longer on the list of the poorest places on earth.

As an alternative, Warschauer suggests that we consider the "institutional embeddedness" of technology in particular times and places, which includes the unequal power relationships inherent in those institutions (2003: 208–209). Once again, it is generally assumed that those on the "modern" side of the equation begin from a position of advantage, in terms of both access and knowledge. I have to say that my own experience has been the reverse; I often feel as if my Liberian foster family has left me behind technologically and are sometimes frustrated with my lack of expertise. I find myself limited in my ability to engage with them at the level and through the channels they prefer, both institutionally and in terms of competence. My failings in this area are also, admittedly, a means of controlling the stream of requests for assistance I receive from both old friends and a new generation of Liberians coping with the postwar context.

Lotte Pelckmans, in her 2009 article in the collection *Mobile Phones: The New Talking Drums of Everyday Africa*, notes that there has been considerable research on how cell phones have been adopted by users who were once assumed to be on the wrong side of the "digital divide." Early agonizing about how remote, rural communities the world over would be even further marginalized by technological change seems to have been complicated by the tendency of some localities to "jump over" stages of technology use that took years to become widespread in the industrialized countries. Proliferating studies have followed the rapid growth of cell phone use in Africa, the highest in the world since 2003 according to the UN Conference on Trade and Development. "Africa became the world's second most connected region after Asia in late 2011, with 616 million mobile subscribers" (Juma 2011: 6). Even war-devastated Liberia currently has four fiercely competitive providers of mobile service and a rate of cell phone penetration estimated to be 45 percent of the population (Lori et al. 2012: 295), even though the country is ranked as one of the most impoverished in the world. Numerous innovative projects use cell phones to record live births, collect health statistics, combat illiteracy, and promote postconflict reconciliation (see Bailey 2013; Best et al. 2007; Best et al. 2010; Lori et al. 2012; Thakur and Best 2008; and Virhia et al. 2010, among others). Furthermore, there is evidence that the published figures underrepresent actual phone use, as it is estimated that there may be as many as five users for each subscription, just as in the earlier days of landlines and collect calls, when many Liberians collaborated to share resources (Best et al. 2010: 92).

Less often noted, as Pelckmans points out, is how the relationships between these phone users and foreign researchers has been transformed by digital technologies. Attempting to document the "direct oral contact with people while on the move" or "the social life of phone mediated communication" (2009: 24), Pelckmans surveyed anthropologists on their use of phones in African fieldwork and in the transition back to the ethnographer's home country. She describes the practice in many African countries of "flashing," or allowing the phone to ring once while the user registers the number of the caller. The expectation is that the party who is "flashed" will return the call, thus using their prepaid minutes to pay for the time. This practice is generally understood as taking place between communication partners of distinct social and economic status; two friends who are equally strapped for cash would be less likely to try and foist the cost of talking onto each other.[1]

Pelckmans reports that the anthropologists she surveyed were continually flashed long after they had left their research sites. The flash functions as both a reminder ("I am thinking of you, are you thinking of me?") and an invitation to take up some of the financial obligations of transnational patrons and kin (2009: 28–29). Pelckmans notes that anthropologists, both in and out of the field, find that they have to develop strategies to manage the almost constant traffic of these calls. "Flashing practices definitely influence and (re)produce power relations among people; it is a continual process and impacts beyond the fieldwork period provided one does not consciously withdraw from keeping in touch" (29).[2] For foreign researchers, these flashes can literally "follow you home." I now understand the 1990's landline networks I was embedded in as a technologically earlier form of flashing, a process charged with decision making and negotiation about the duration, strength, and implications of these mediated relationships.

While relatively inexpensive phone credits and cheap texting rates are available in many African countries, Pelckmans's researcher respondents found themselves paying a high price for constant, continual contact with their African friends and informants when back in their home countries on differently configured phone plans (2009: 30). This is one way I have come to find myself on the "wrong" side of the digital divide in recent years, both in terms of my own lack of interest in and incompetence with new technologies and due to the differing economies of access in different locations. I am, as mentioned above, admittedly something of a technophobe, the kind who dreads institutional "upgrades" and tries to stick as long as possible with outdated versions of software, hardware, and everything else. Since returning physically to Liberia for the first time in 2006, I have been constantly asked to provide members of my foster family with phones, cameras, laptops, and other equipment. I do not mind paying for these items in most cases, but I often lack the technical expertise to purchase wisely. I now get digital photo invitations via email to birthday parties I cannot actually attend, with the note "your gift will be highly appreciated!" I have no idea how to construct such an invitation myself, but this more elaborate example of flashing must be answered and attended to.

Many of those emotions elicited by re-reading fieldnotes described by Jean Jackson (1990)—the complicated feelings of affection, ambivalence, guilt, and power—now come flooding back every time I open an email or get a phone call from Liberia. Jackson described fieldnotes as defined by location in place (notes taken down while "in" the field), but such displacements in time and space are dissolved by new technologies. As I do not have a research project going on new technologies or technological change, I do not classify these emails and invitations from Liberia as "data": they are simply human exchanges among people who share a long history of connection or, as Diane King notes (Chapter 15, this volume), "data that comes without prompting."

Yet, as Pelckmans argues, these technologies are now shaping our relationships in ways that are still unclear. She contends that the collapse of time and space achieved through continuous cell phone contact between anthropologists and "others" resolves Fabian's (1983) critique of the "discrepancy in the discipline of anthropology between the interactive fieldwork period and the objectifying process of writing about it afterwards (ethnography)" (Pelckmans 2009: 45). Contemporary fieldworkers use their phones not just to remain in contact with their informants but also as recording, writing, and data storage devices, challenging the "formerly separate processes of writing and conducting fieldwork. . . . Whether this results in an increased inclusion of the Other in our ethnography remains to be seen. Nevertheless, the reshaping of current anthropological epistemology and morality is definitely challenging. We seem to be witnessing an ICT-mediated epistemological 'turn' in 21st century anthropology" (47).

Pelckmans's use of the term "morality" is significant here because, as anthropologists have long acknowledged, moral economies have both a material and an emotional side. For me, the economics of keeping these lines of communication open exposes another digital divide between cost structures in the United States and those in Liberia. Back in the days of collect calls on landlines, I sometimes racked up two hundred dollars in charges in a single night of cut offs, bad connections, and repeat calls. Now, as a parent of two college-age young adults who depend on me for their phone plans as well as their health insurance, I am trapped in a Verizon "Friends and Family" plan that comes in at about the same amount per month (two hundred dollars for four phone lines, two of them with data plans, and not counting the charge for the remaining landline in the house). We pay for a shared allowance of 1,400 minutes of voice time per month, even though the four of us use only a fraction of that, in order to get unlimited texting. My husband and I hardly ever text to communicate, but our children send and receive more than three thousand texts a month, which would be exorbitantly expensive if paid for individually.

My Liberian friends and family, like most other African cell phone users, "charge" or "feed" their phones on a pay-as-you-go basis, with time purchased on widely available scratch cards. These minutes can be used for international calls as well as domestic calls, and my contacts call frequently (and not collect anymore, but still at inconvenient times in the middle of the night). I rarely call anyone in Liberia, because without an international plan it would cost about $2.50 a minute. For a $5.00 a month charge, I could add calls to Liberia to my plan and be charged only 60 cents a minute in addition to the monthly fee, but because I do not call very often, the service fee seems like an unnecessary added expense.

On the other hand, through my job as an academic, I have free and almost constant access to the Internet. I use it to communicate with those in Liberia who have email and Facebook, and I prefer this mode of communication, both for the ability to shift time in replying as well as its low cost (to me). However, unlike cell phones, this mode of communication is much more restricted in Liberia. A 2006 study estimated only 2 in every 1000 Liberians has regular access to the Internet (cited in Best et al. 2007: 36). Usually, this access comes through employment or must be paid for in Internet cafes. These different economic markets for communication create different circulations and patterns of use, as well as stimulating new forms of creativity in using them to maintain relationships. My "old ma," now in her seventies and with only shaky English literacy, can chat away on her cell phone but does not send me email; her sons, with their more sophisticated skills, can send me digital invitations constructed with cameras and sent on laptops I have provided. My location in space and in the developmental cycle of my household pushes me to make certain cost-effective choices in my phone plan, but they do not mesh easily with those of my Liberian family. The rapid changes in and spread of cell phone technologies have mitigated some aspects of the digital divide, but cost barriers remain in place, and the power structures underlying these, as Pelckmans noted, are manifest in those who are flashed and those who are flashing.

Old-fashioned fieldnotes, when they are read from a distance in time and space, evoke complex affective states of discomfort, loneliness, guilt, and nostalgia (Jackson 1990: 18). How much of my ambivalence about paying for international service is my own way of "managing" the constant flow of requests for assistance, of distancing myself from relationships now decades old and generational in nature? I tell myself that the less I am spending on monthly phone plans, the more disposable income I can afford to send in the form of Moneygram transfers or put into gifts of cameras and laptops when I travel to Liberia in person, but is this just my way of rationalizing the limits I impose on constant availability? Transnational Africans experience cell phones as the medium for the transmission of guilt, obligation, and affection, memory and identity; why would anthropologists be exempt from these same emotions?

Thinking back over my experience with cell phones as both research tools and a means of maintaining relationships, I realize that I initially thought of phone, and, later, Internet contact as primarily one-way channels for finding out "what was going on" during a chaotic and tragic period of Liberia's history. I never intended such contacts to substitute for what I considered "real fieldwork" that would produce "real fieldnotes," as Jackson says of those texts that are "en route from an internal and other-cultural state to a final destination" (1990: 14). Now I realize that my own history of connection, some of it documented in notes and much of it not, is also a source of data. It gives me, as an ethnographer, different points of access to things that might someday become useful to my research, even if I am not consciously setting out to "study it." I might even, as someone who lived through and experienced this transformation in both communications and fieldwork relationships end up as someone else's informant. More importantly, these technologies have been important in the maintenance of relationships that are now into their second and even third generation; the technologies allow the contact but cannot guide me in how to think or feel about the emotions they make possible. I see myself negotiating multiple cleavages rather than a single "digital divide," still with the hope that I can somehow contribute to the goal Ginsburg articulated: "Can we illuminate and support other possibilities emerging out of locally based concerns and speak for their significance in contemporary cultural and policy arenas?" (2008: 140).

Because that is how I think of the work I am doing now on the wartime experiences and choices of noncombatant men in Liberia (research based on the old-fashioned practice of face-to-face interviews), I do not know for sure how my ongoing digitally mediated relationships will figure into the mix. But because interviews with my three foster brothers, my most frequent phone and email correspondents, are among the ninety-some accounts I am working with, I am sure those communications will have a role. Technophobe that I am, I am dreading the day Liberia gets the equivalent of the Kenyan money transfer system, *mpesa*, because this will involve having to learn a whole new set of ways to meet my financial obligations (a radio report from June 2013 announced the launch of just such a mobile money platform on a pilot basis). Try as I might to avoid opening all aspects of my "home" life to the global reach of new communication technologies, I know I cannot prevent this infiltration from "the field," nor, in the larger scheme of things, would I want to. All I can do is situate myself in the ongoing flow, as the changing technoscape transforms me and my Liberian friends.

Acknowledgments

Bibliographic research for this essay was ably provided by my Colgate student research assistant, Stefan Oliva. Dr. Peter Rogers of the Colgate University Libraries was also a valuable source of assistance.

Notes

1. Anthropologist and novelist Francis Nyamnjoh has incorporated the strategic use of flashing and its gendered dimension as a form of exchange between men and women into his fiction, set in Cameroon. Explaining the practice to a foreign researcher, the character Bobinga Iroko says, "Normally beepers and flashers are low income people and generally women consider themselves to be low income so they beep even when they have much more than the men. . . . And with my private number, if I receive a beep, it doesn't matter who is there, if I do not know you I will never respond. You know how many people out there are just seeking for notice?" (Nyamnjoh 2009: 9–10). The story also includes commentary on the increasingly transnational pattern of relationships, as more Africans seek to improve their economic chances by "bush falling" or hunting for opportunities abroad:

> The new means of communication makes relating over distances easier, which is not perceived by all as positive, as ease of communications comes with heightened demands and expectations of remittances on the part of relations back home. In the face of the challenges of coping in the margins abroad,

many bush-fallers feel the weight of the pressure of constant communication with folks back home who often do not understand the difficulties confronting them as economic migrants. (de Bruijn, Nyamnjoh, and Brinkman 2009: 16)

2. Their practices replicate those described by Nyamnjoh's high-status fictional characters, including having multiple phones and numbers that are selectively distributed and even giving out false numbers while trying to maintain just enough contact to avoid destroying the relationships. Anthropologists often learn these options from local elites trying to manage similar cascading requests; these are another index of relative power, as only those with resources can afford multiple lines and phones.

Bibliography

Bailey, Jennifer G. 2013. The Role of ICTs in Illiteracy Eradication and Workforce Development in Liberia and Under-Resourced Countries. Paper presented at the annual meeting of the Liberian Studies Association, Rutgers University, New Brunswick, N.J., April 4–6, 2013.

Bernal, Victoria. 2005. Eritrea On-Line: Disapora, Cyberspace, and the Public Sphere. *American Ethnologist* 32 (4): 660–675.

Best, Michael L., Kipp Jones, Illenin Kondo, Dhanaraj Thakur, Edem Wornyo, and Calvin Yu. 2007. Post-Conflict Communications: The Case of Liberia. *Communications of the ACM* 50 (10): 33–39.

Best, Michael, Thomas N. Smyth, John Etherton, and Edem Wornyo. 2010. Uses of Mobile Phones in Post-Conflict Liberia. *Information Technologies and International Development* 6: 91–108.

Buys, Piet, Susmita Dasgupta, Tim Thomas, and David Wheeler. 2008. Determinants of a Digital Divide in Sub-Saharan Africa: A Spatial Econometric Analysis of Cell Phone Coverage. Policy Research Working Paper no. 4516. Washington, D.C.: The World Bank Development Research Group Sustainable Rural and Urban Development Team.

Clifford, James, and George Marcus, editors. 1986. *Writing Culture: The Poetics and Politics of Ethnography.* Berkeley: University of California Press.

Coleman, E. Gabriella. 2010. Ethnographic Approaches to Digital Media. *Annual Review of Anthropology* 39: 487–505.

de Brujin, Mirjam, Francis Nyamnjoh, and Inge Brinkman, editors. 2009. *Mobile Phones: The New Talking Drums of Everyday Africa.* Leiden: African Studies Centre.

Fabian, Johannes. 1983. *Time and the Other: How Anthropology Makes Its Object.* New York: Columbia University Press.

Ginsberg, Faye. 2008. Rethinking the Digital Age. In *Media and Social Theory*, edited by David Hesmondhalgh and Jason Toynbee, 127–144. New York: Routledge.

Gupta, Akhil, and James Ferguson, editors. 1997. *Culture, Power, Place: Explorations in Critical Anthropology.* Durham, N.C.: Duke University Press.

Jackson, Jean. 1990. "I Am a Fieldnote": Fieldnotes as a Symbol of Professional Identity. In *Fieldnotes: The Makings of Anthropology*, edited by Roger Sanjek, 3–33. Ithaca, N.Y.: Cornell University Press.

Juma, Calestous. 2011. Africa's New Engine. *Finance & Development* 48 (4): 6–11. "International Monetary Fund." Accessed February 9, 2015. http://www.imf.org/external/pubs/ft/fandd/2011/12/juma.htm.

Lori, Jody R., Michelle L. Munro, Carol J. Boyd, and Pamela Andreatta. 2012. Cell Phones to Collect Pregnancy Data from Remote Areas in Liberia. *Journal of Nursing Scholarship* 44: 294–301.

Moran, Mary H. 1990. *Civilized Women: Gender and Prestige in Southeastern Liberia*. Ithaca, N.Y.: Cornell University Press.

———. 2006. *Liberia: The Violence of Democracy*. Philadelphia: University of Pennsylvania Press.

Norris, Pippa. 2001. *The Digital Divide: Civic Engagement, Information Poverty, and the Internet Worldwide*. New York: Cambridge University Press.

Nyamnjoh, Francis B. 2009. *Married but Available*. Excerpt. In *Mobile Phones: The New Talking Drums of Everyday Africa*, edited by Mirjam de Brujin, Francis Nyamnjoh, and Inge Brinkman, 1–10. Leiden: African Studies Centre.

Pelckmans, Lotte. 2009. Phoning Anthropologists: The Mobile Phone's (Re-)Shaping of Anthropological Research. In *Mobile Phones: The New Talking Drums of Everyday Africa*, edited by Mirjam de Brujin, Francis Nyamnjoh, and Inge Brinkman, 23–49. Leiden: African Studies Centre.

Sanjek, Roger. 1990a. Fieldnotes and Others. In *Fieldnotes: The Makings of Anthropology*, edited by Roger Sanjek, 324–340. Ithaca, N.Y.: Cornell University Press.

———, editor. 1990b. *Fieldnotes: The Makings of Anthropology*. Ithaca, N.Y.: Cornell University Press.

Thakur, Dhanaraj, and Michael L. Best. 2008. The Telecommunications Policy Process in *Post-Conflict Developing Countries: The Case of Liberia*. Paper presented at the 36th Research Conference on Communications, Information, and Internet Policy, George Mason University School of Law, Arlington, Virginia, September 26–28.

Van Binsbergen, Wim. 2003. Can ICT Belong in Africa or Is ICT Owned by the North Atlantic Region? In *Situating Globality: African Agency in the Appropriation of Global Culture*, edited by W. M. J. van Binsbergen and R. van Dijk, 107–146. Leiden: Brill.

Virhia, Tuulia, Timo Itala, Gama Roberts, and Tornorlah Varpilah. 2010. Mobile Solution for Birth Registration in Liberia: A Case Study of Using ITCs in Statebuilding. Paper presented at the Ninth International Conference on Mobile Business/2010 Global Mobility Roundtable, Athens, Greece, June 13–15.

Warschauer, Mark. 2003. *Technology and Social Inclusion: Rethinking the Digital Divide*. Cambridge, Mass.: MIT Press.

Chapter 5

Writing eFieldnotes: Some Ethical Considerations

Mieke Schrooten

Many ethnographers have emphasized the central place of writing, not only in their own research but in ethnographic fieldwork in general (Clifford and Marcus 1986; Geertz 1973; Sanjek 1990). Ethnographic research is at the core of what Stocking has called anthropology's fundamental "methodological values"—"the taken-for-granted, pretheoretical notions of what it is to do anthropology (and to be an anthropologist)" (1992: 282). Exemplary anthropological research is widely understood to be based on experience "in the field" (Gupta and Ferguson 1997: 1), and fieldnotes play an important role, therefore, in "doing anthropology." As Jean Jackson, one of the contributors to *Fieldnotes: The Makings of Anthropology*, stated: "If 'the field' is anthropology's version of both the promised land and an ordeal by fire, then fieldnotes symbolize what journeying to and returning from the field mean to us: the attachment, the identification, the uncertainty, the mystique, and, perhaps above all, the ambivalence" (1990: 33).

Since the publication of *Fieldnotes* in 1990, much has changed within anthropology. Globalization, defined by Castles as a "proliferation of cross-border flows and transnational networks" (2002: 1143), has profoundly changed the anthropological research context, urging this field science to expand its boundaries. Owing to significantly increased human mobility and a revolution in communication, the everyday lives of many individuals often transcend the geographical locations in which classical fieldwork took place, challenging ethnographers to include these social spaces in the demarcation of their fieldwork sites. Not only the choice of fieldwork sites but also the issues that are being researched, the methods used, and the way fieldnotes are taken have all been impacted by these changes.

One of the most compelling new fieldwork sites ethnographers encounter today is the Internet. The continuing growth of global Internet access lies at the root of new and diverse kinds of imagination that link together people living in various geographic locations (Schrooten and De Brouwer 2012; Schrooten and Lamote 2013). It has become a commonplace that twenty-first century migrants maintain transnational lifestyles, keeping in close touch with their regions of origin and with other regions around the world in which significant others have settled (Schrooten, Geldof, and Withaeckx 2015). Transnational contacts are gaining in importance, and many transnational spaces and communities are developing (Faist, Fauser, and Reisenauer 2013; Vertovec 2007). Most migrants can therefore no longer be characterized as cut from their existing social ties or "uprooted." On the contrary, various means of long-distance communication, such as mobile telephones, the Internet, and digital broadcasts, have strongly facilitated interaction across geographical and political borders (Kissau and Hunger 2010; Schrooten 2011b).

These new media are being used for several purposes on macro, micro, and meso levels. The Internet has, for example, played an important role in several recent protests, such as the 2011 protests in Egypt and Tunisia, the 2013 protests in Turkey, and the worldwide mobilization of Brazilians in the spring of 2013. But social media are also of great importance for many globally dispersed families, as they allow them to have contact on a daily basis and to share news in real time. The research of Madianou and Miller (2012) demonstrates, for example, how parents and children who are separated because of migration use new media to maintain long-distance relationships (between the Philippines and the United Kingdom, in this case) and care for each other. In my own research with Brazilians living in Belgium, I found that many migrants frequently make use of social media, not only to remain connected with their durable networks all over the world but also to forge new connections in their new place of residence (Schrooten 2012a).

Following the connections of the people they study, migration researchers are challenged to expand the scope of their fieldwork to include online research sites as well, extending ethnographic traditions of fieldwork into the virtual world. The willingness to incorporate the Internet both as part of "the field" and as a method of data collection is tinged, however, with anxiety about how far existing research methods are appropriate for technologically mediated interactions (Hine 2006).

When online phenomena are studied, there are adjustments in data collection and analysis that must be made. Ethnographers who decide to conduct research in an online environment are faced with several challenges: To what extent are the procedures and assumptions that are currently taken for granted in ethnography suitable for online research? How does one take ethnographic fieldnotes on a social network site (SNS), a multiuser dungeon (MUD), or a community blog? How do we deal with the large amount of data available online?

Another obvious difference from conventional ethnography is the way in which researchers have to find an entrée into the community they want to study. Although the problem of how to present oneself also exists within traditional ethnography, the challenges involved in obtaining access differ, as ethnographers cannot rely solely upon their physical presence and personal interactional skills (Garcia et al. 2009; Mann and Stewart 2003).

Online ethnographic research, moreover, has raised a number of ethical questions. The fact that participation on social network sites leaves online traces offers unprecedented opportunities for researchers. Even so, the specificities of this research setting also necessitate a re-examination of the institutionalized understandings of research ethics. Ethnographers must learn how to apply standard principles of human subject protection to a research environment that differs in fundamental ways from the face-to-face research contexts for which they were conceived and designed. The easy access to online data, the ability of a researcher to record these data without the knowledge of participants, the complexities of obtaining informed consent, and the question of guaranteeing the respondents' anonymity fuel the need for directive guidelines for ethical online ethnographic research. In this chapter, I discuss some of the ethical issues I encountered in my own research on the use of social network sites by Brazilian migrants in Belgium in order to provide an understanding of the challenges that are related to online research and, consequently, to the ethical responsibilities of online researchers.

Discovering the Online Field

In 2004, after obtaining my bachelor's degree in social work, I enrolled in a postgraduate intercultural social work course. The one-year program included an internship of six months in a "developing country." On September 24, 2004, I arrived in Palmas, the capital of the Brazilian state Tocantins, where I was going to work in a *Centro de Direitos Humanos* (human rights center) and a *Conselho Tutelar* (guardianship council). I promised my family and friends to keep in touch through email and letters and, I hoped, an occasional Skype conversation. At that moment, I did not yet have an account on a social network site, nor did most of my friends and relatives. It was only earlier that year that Mark Zuckerberg had created Facebook (then still called "The Facebook"). This social network site already provided access to several college and university networks, as well as some high school networks, but it was not open to everyone.

During the first weeks of my stay in Palmas, one of my roommates asked if she could add me as a friend on Orkut. My question about what she meant by "Orkut" was met with considerable astonishment, and she immediately introduced me to this social network site. I soon learned that Orkut was enormously popular in Brazil. Although the site was only launched in January 2004, and originally had only an English-language interface, Portuguese-speaking Brazilians quickly "invaded" and became the dominant user group (boyd and Ellison 2007: 214).

Later, when I spoke about the widespread popularity of Orkut in her home country with Sônia, a Brazilian woman I met in Belgium upon my return from Brazil in April 2005, she told me:

> I know! I entered in the very beginning. I went to Brazil and someone told me "Look, there is this new website in Brazil and everyone is becoming a member." But I didn't know it, so I asked them what it was. "It is Orkut." So I entered, in the very beginning. So everyone was becoming a member and today everyone in Brazil is on Orkut, really everyone. If you get to know someone on the street, you always ask: "Are you on Orkut? Give me your Orkut. I'm going to add you on Orkut." . . . Everyone has it, because nobody wants to be left out. Everybody wants to participate. And it is a lot easier to keep in touch.

After my return from Palmas, I continued to use Orkut to keep in touch with my friends from Brazil. Of the many features of interpersonal communication that Orkut offered, I mainly used the scrapbook that was linked to everyone's personal profiles, which I regularly read, and on which I left public comments or "scraps." I also chatted with friends who were online and looked at the information they shared on their personal profile, such as pictures and messages they posted on their own scrapbooks.

In 2007, I returned to Brazil for my master's thesis fieldwork, which focused on the (re)creation of ethnic boundaries (Schrooten 2008, 2011a). The aim of the research was to study internal migration and the reproduction of Brazilian race relations in the city of Palmas. Palmas is a very young city, constructed in 1989 to become the capital of the newest Brazilian state, Tocantins. My Palmas research explored the possibility that, during an era in which the national government began to implement measures to combat racial discrimination, the creation of a "planned city" could avoid reproducing the pattern of race relations that characterized the rest of the country.

Although nearly everyone I met during this fieldwork used the social network site Orkut on a daily basis, at the time I never considered utilizing this online environment as a research location. I did not yet realize how much impact these new technologies had on the everyday lives of people, nor how useful this "fieldwork location" was for the study of the construction of ethnic boundaries. To me, as to many Brazilians, Orkut was just an easy (and cheap) way to keep in touch with the people I met.

When I wrote my Ph.D. research proposal in 2009, I decided to shift my focus to international Brazilian migration. After my return from fieldwork in Brazil, I had met several Brazilian migrants in Belgium. Because I was surprised by the growing number of Brazilians I encountered, I decided to look for quantitative data on their presence in the country. I soon found out that Brazilians represented a significant portion of the total current migration flow into Belgium (Schrooten 2012b). Although Brazilian migration constituted a relatively recent phenomenon for Belgium, it had been acknowledged as an important trend by Brazilian policy makers (Pedroso 2011), the Ministry of the Brussels Capital Region (Ministerie van het Brussels Hoofdstedelijk Gewest 2008), and the International Organization for Migration, located in Brussels (Góis et al. 2009).

Again, when I wrote my 2009 research proposal, I did not refer to Orkut, or even to the Internet in general, as a possible research site. However, soon after my fieldwork in Belgium started, I decided to make it one of my central fieldwork locations. Within the variety of Brazilian websites, magazines, and satellite channels I encountered in the course of the research, Orkut and, more recently, Facebook and WhatsApp, were often mentioned as the most important media for keeping in touch with other Brazilians, both inside and outside Brazil.

Social Media Use by Brazilian Migrants in Belgium

For most Brazilians I met during my research, computer-mediated communication via social network sites (SNSs) was already embedded in their daily life practices before they migrated to Belgium. In Brazil, they mainly used these sites to connect with friends and relatives. After migrating to Belgium, many also found social media to be a valuable tool for maintaining continuous personal and transnational contacts. When I started looking at how people enact transnationality on a daily basis, it became apparent that migrants' use of new media affects the nature of migration and the conditions of life as a migrant (Schrooten 2012a).

SNSs allow migrants to remain connected with their durable networks all over the world (Faist 2004; Horst 2006; Madianou and Miller 2012). But there is more. Computer-mediated communication in general helps migrants not only in maintaining relationships with their networks back home but also in tracing and contacting other migrants from the same place of origin in their new place of residence (Hiller and Franz 2004). Thus, as Diminescu argues, "The paradigmatic figure of the uprooted migrant is yielding to another figure—one that is as yet ill-defined but which corresponds to that of a migrant on the move who relies on alliances outside his own group of belonging without cutting his ties with the social network at home" (2008: 567).

Most of my informants told me that they had frequent contact with their relatives living beyond Belgium. Dije, for example, who left her four daughters in Brazil when she migrated to Belgium in the beginning of 2010, spoke with them nearly every day: "We talk to each other every day on MSN. I also call about three times a week. I have that VoIP, do you know it? Two cents a minute to call there. So I call almost every day, to talk to them. And if I don't call, we talk on MSN. So we talk to each other every day. It hardly ever happens that we don't talk." When I was invited to my informants' homes, I was often introduced to family members or friends in Brazil through Skype. In many homes, the webcam was left on for nearly the whole day, creating a sense of copresence.

Mobile phones, social network sites, and emails all provided opportunities for maintaining these long-distance relationships. In the course of my research, there was a shift in the social media that were most often referred to. Whereas in 2010, Orkut and MSN were by far the most popular, by 2014, Facebook and WhatsApp had become the most used social media, not only to keep in touch with those left behind but also to organize one's migration journey and to find an entrée into the Brazilian community in Belgium. Since 2008, the Brazilian Internet population has strongly increased, but the popularity of Orkut sharply declined in favor of Facebook. In September 2014, Orkut even officially shut down.

On SNSs such as Orkut or Facebook, members can create groups and invite others to become members. In cities all over the world with a significant number of Brazilian migrants, these newcomers have formed online migrant groups related to their presence in the city, as well as to the country in which their city of residence is located. Many of my informants told me that the first place where they "met" other Brazilians was on one of these social network sites.

The story of Amélia, who migrated to Belgium in 2006, is illustrative of that of many other Brazilians I talked to:

> So, when I came here in 2006, it was already starting. Orkut already existed. Orkut started working. And it was through Orkut that small [online] groups were formed. These small groups transformed into larger groups. And there, people started to meet and started to get to know each other. Friendships and relationships were made. The group that I mainly visit today on Facebook was originally created on Orkut. The first activity of this group was a party that was organized in the city of Ghent. . . . When I arrived in Belgium, I didn't know any Brazilian here. It was through Orkut that I started to build a network.

The following words of Sônia, the moderator of one of the groups I studied, illustrate how the existing online networks make it possible for migrants to forge new connections with people they do not know, building new individual "weak tie" networks (Haythornthwaite 2005):

> The people who are in Brazil already think, "Ah, I'm going to participate in the community of Antwerp or Brussels or Leuven or

Ghent . . . because I'm going to that city." So they enter the community, they already start looking for information among those who are already living in that city. So when they arrive here, they already know everyone, they already make arrangements to meet and have a drink, they already know where there will be a party. This is a very good thing, when I came here there was nothing like this. But nowadays, it is very easy, someone who didn't even leave Brazil already knows everyone over here. So it helps a lot.

Besides offering a possibility to trace and contact other migrants from the same place of origin in their new locale, the online groups on social network sites also have several other important functions. In an earlier article (Schrooten 2012a), I described how these functions are different in each stage of the migration process, ranging from finding information that assists in the decision to migrate to sharing stories of the difficulties faced, giving each other material advice, or even reaffirming themselves as Brazilian. Also, the degree of users' involvement varies, ranging from consumption or practical advice to "lurking" (observing online without making themselves known) to pursuing a strong social life online.

Ethics in Online Ethnography

Because people's lives increasingly are shifting into the digital domain, which is becoming more and more public, emergent technologies offer many interesting research opportunities. In contrast to the field of consumer and marketing research, for example, anthropologists seem to have been rather slow and reluctant to follow social groups online (Hine 2000; Kozinets 2010). Although the Internet is an efficient means for gaining access into subcultures, social movements, and many other groups, it is only recently that social researchers in significant numbers have begun examining the Internet as a meaningful research space and conducting ethnographic work on social network sites, blogs, and other online media (Murthy 2013).

I have used and continue to actively use digital technologies in my qualitative research on Brazilian migrants in Belgium. However, my fieldwork is not conducted wholly online; it also involves face-to-face ethnography. Whereas many researchers use digital methods to provide an access point to respondents who would have been inaccessible or much harder to reach through "conventional" ethnographic approaches (Miller and Sønderlund 2010; Murthy 2013), I initially gained access to the online groups I studied through my traditionally conceived offline fieldwork. It was my respondents who then invited me to become a member of the online groups for Brazilians in Belgium. Because the Internet was intimately interwoven with my respondents' offline lives, the integration of both offline and online qualitative data-gathering methodologies turned out to be an important research strategy.

From the moment I decided to include the social network site Orkut in my research, I found that research ethics were one of the most important differences between traditional ethnography and online ethnography. As I posed it then:

> Does the posting of things on the Internet make these public property, available for researchers to use without asking permission? Some researchers would answer affirmatively to this question, arguing that all cyberspace postings are in the public domain and thus imply an implicit permission for their use by others (e.g. Denzin 1999; Finn & Lavitt 1994; Magnet 2007; Schaap 2002; Sharp & Earle 2003; Slater 1998). Many of these researchers have explicitly chosen to conduct physically "invisible" research, maintaining a covert position in their research site. One of the major advantages of this approach is its entirely unobtrusive character and the chance this provides to research naturally occurring behaviours. . . . [On the other hand], other researchers (e.g. Döring 2002; Kozinets 2010; Roberts, Smith & Pollock 2004; Schrum 1995; Walther 2002; Waskul & Douglas 1996) . . . argue that some Internet locations are inherently private. They urge online researchers to communicate who they are and to ask for permission to use the online data for their research.
>
> While there may be advantages to immediately announcing one's presence as an online researcher, in some cases disclosing one's presence to ask for consent may disturb the normal activity of the site (Garcia et al. 2009: 58–60). An inappropriate entrée into a community can also cause a hostile reaction towards the researcher (Kozinets 2010: 74–94). For this reason, some ethnographers have

chosen to begin a participant observation study of online phenomena by lurking in order to familiarize themselves with the setting before asking questions. Still, while this silent lurking can give the researcher important information about the norms of the online setting, participating immediately in the online setting can give researchers a more authentic experience. Moreover, this allows online researchers to gain the informed consent of research participants, another cornerstone of ethical research (Sveningsson 2004: 50–51). Given my stance that respect for the expectation of privacy overrides the distinction between public and private spaces, I found it important to obtain informed consent from people to be interviewed in the environment of Orkut. (Schrooten 2010)

Although in the emerging literature some concrete examples can now be found of how to conduct ethical research using SNSs (Bull et al. 2011; Hesse-Biber and Leavy 2010; Wilkinson and Thelwall 2011), an internationally accepted framework for online ethnographic research ethics does not as yet exist. Without these guidelines, I found that the onus was on the individual researcher to make ethical decisions in the course of her or his research.

As my fieldwork began, I had specific questions related to many aspects of my fieldwork ethics: Could I use all the data I found on the Orkut and Facebook groups I studied for analysis? How should I write fieldnotes in an environment where all the data were automatically stored and always available? Did I have to ask for informed consent before using quotations? Should I announce my presence as a researcher, and if I did, would this disturb the naturalness of the activities of the online group?

One of the first concrete dilemmas I encountered was precisely how to obtain informed consent. How could I give the online group members the opportunity to decide whether they wanted to take part in my research? In my offline fieldwork, I informed my respondents about the purpose of the study, confidentiality and privacy protocols, their rights as research subjects, the possibility of withdrawing, and how the information during the face-to-face interview would be used. The lack of face-to-face contact with Brazilian online group members, however, impeded me from using the same study consent procedures. What is more, in the online research environment I also studied the interactions among members of these lively online groups. This is a totally different research context than the individual face-to-face interviews during which I had obtained informed consent.

There were two more aspects of online environments that made it difficult to secure such consent. First, the data I use in my research are gathered from Orkut and Facebook groups that require membership. For that reason, I cannot consider such data as being gathered in a public space where the individuals who have posted messages have no expectation of privacy. Second, the online groups can have a large number of members, ranging from two hundred to almost four thousand, and new participants join on a frequent basis. Therefore, during my analysis of the discussion threads of the groups I study, I know I will encounter postings of some group members who know that I am doing research but also of other group members who do not. As all posted messages are parts of ongoing conversations, it would become quite difficult and problematic to include some messages within the same thread in my analyses but to exclude others (Flicker, Haans, and Skinner 2004).

The first thing I did to obtain informed consent was try to meet each group moderator in person. After explaining the aims of my study, I requested their permission to conduct participant observation and to contact members for research purposes. This was of great importance for my work, as these moderators turned out to be influential "gatekeepers" who strongly eased my access to their group, to its individual members, and to offline gatherings. Not only did all the moderators approve my presence in their online groups, they encouraged people to participate in the research.

Next, I introduced myself as a researcher on the discussion threads of each group I participated in, and I always announced my presence when going online. I described the study aims, provided information about what data would be collected and how they would be used, and invited people to participate in online and in face-to-face interviews. I also posted my university email address as a way to authenticate my identity as a researcher.

Still, these efforts were insufficient to obtain consent from all participants in the changing, fluid online groups. My strategy, therefore, has been to use the postings on each forum only to make general observations about the uses of social network sites by current and prospective migrants. If I want to quote anyone verbatim, I approach that person to ask for consent. Also, I try to meet as many group members as possible in person. Not only does this give me the chance to verify information gathered online and to extend my focus to my other fields of interest, it is also an opportunity to seek informed consent in a more explicit way.

Besides the question of obtaining informed consent, another ethical dilemma I faced was how to fully utilize online data in my publications. The profiles on social network sites often explicitly connect online and offline identity information. This presented radically different challenges than those online environments that de-link users from any personal or distinctive offline identifiers. Furthermore, as Keenan (2008) states, "on the internet, things never go away completely." Data placed by individuals on the Internet, including discussion thread posts on social network sites, continue to persist in cyberspace. This poses specific challenges to not revealing the identities of research participants (Bull et al. 2011; Zimmer 2010), and, consequently, it is not always possible to guarantee complete and total anonymity through pseudonyms and the removal of identifying information (Murthy 2013).

To maximize protection of the identities of online group members in the dissemination of my research results, I quote only those postings of members who have consented to be part of my study. I also replace all names with pseudonyms so that people's real names are never tied to any quotations. The fact that online membership in the groups I study is required to view the message board also makes it more difficult for outsiders to find the actual quotation that I use in my writing.

To further assure as much anonymity as possible within these online groups, I translate the Portuguese-language postings into English so that both Google and Facebook searches cannot connect the quotation to the identity of the individual who posted the message. The anthropologist Tom Boellstorff, who conducted virtual fieldwork on the Second Life site (2008), similarly used pseudonyms for Second Life residents, paraphrased their quotations to make them difficult to identify by using a search engine, and in some cases also combined quotations from more than one person.

Conclusion

The fact that there has been a lack of clarity in terms of ethics forces online researchers to carefully think through the implications of their research, not only for the dynamics of the sites they study but also for their respondents. As Murthy cautions, "researchers should take care to specify storage of ethnographic material, anonymization, and risks regarding identification of respondents through web searches in informed consent agreements" (2013: 31).

Online activities are part of how people live today, and they affect offline aspects of social life. Fieldworkers must include technologically mediated communication in their research agendas, either through online ethnographic study or by placing such communication within the wider spectrum of communicative modes people employ in living together. Because Internet media are "continuous with and embedded in other social spaces" (Miller and Slater 2000: 5), we should adopt a dialectical research praxis, trying to understand how our different research sites are interrelated. A balance between offline and online ethnography, including data gathered in both face-to-face and online interaction, can provide a fuller, more comprehensive account of the increasingly transnational and mediated phenomena we seek to understand.

Bibliography

Boellstorff, Tom. 2008. *Coming of Age in Second Life: An Anthropologist Explores the Virtually Human.* Princeton, N.J.: Princeton University Press.

boyd, danah m., and Nicole B. Ellison. 2007. Social Network Sites: Definition, History, and Scholarship. *Journal of Computer-Mediated Communication* 13 (1): 210–230.

Bull, Sheana, Linsey Breslin, Erin Wright, Sandra Black, Deborah Levine, and John Santelli. 2011. Case Study: An Ethics Case Study of HIV Prevention Research on Facebook: The Just/Us Study. *Journal of Pediatric Psychology* 36 (10): 1082–1092.

Castles, Stephen. 2002. Migration and Community Formation Under Conditions of Globalization. *International Migration Review* 36 (4): 1143–1168.

Clifford, James, and George E. Marcus, editors. 1986. *Writing Culture: The Poetics and Politics of Ethnography.* Berkeley: University of California Press.

Denzin, Norman K. 1999. Cybertalk and the Method of Instances. In *Doing Internet Research: Critical Issues and Methods for Examining the Net*, edited by Steven G. Jones, 107–126. Thousand Oaks, Calif.: Sage.

Diminescu, Dana. 2008. The Connected Migrant: An Epistemological Manifesto. *Social Science Information* 47 (4): 565–579.

Döring, Nicola. 2002. Studying Online Love and Cyber Romance. In *Online Social Sciences*, edited by Bernard Batinic, Ulf-Dietrich Reips, and Michael Bosnjak, 333–356. Seattle: Hogrefe & Huber Publishers.

Faist, Thomas. 2004. *The Volume and Dynamics of International Migration and Transnational Social Spaces.* Oxford: Clarendon.

———, Margit Fauser, and Eveline Reisenauer. 2013. *Transnational Migration.* Cambridge, Mass.: Polity Press.

Finn, Jerry, and Melissa Lavitt. 1994. Computer Based Self-Help Groups for Sexual Abuse Survivors. *Social Work with Groups* 17 (1–2): 21–46.

Flicker, Sarah, Dave Haans, and Harvey Skinner. 2004. Ethical Dilemmas in Research on Internet Communities. *Qualitative Health Research* 14 (1): 124–134.

Garcia, Angela Cora, Alecea I. Standlee, Jennifer Bechkoff, and Yan Cui. 2009. Ethnographic Approaches to the Internet and Computer-Mediated Communication. *Journal of Contemporary Ethnography* 38 (1): 52–84.

Geertz, Clifford. 1973. *The Interpretation of Cultures*. New York: Basic Books.

Góis, Pedro, Pascal Reyntjens, Annika Lenz, Christiane Coelho, and Diana Gouveia. 2009. *Assessment of Brazilian Migration Patterns and Assisted Voluntary Return Programme from Selected European Member States to Brazil*. Brussels: International Organization for Migration.

Gupta, Akhil, and James Ferguson, editors. 1997. *Anthropological Locations: Boundaries and Grounds of a Field Science*. Berkeley: University of California Press.

Haythornthwaite, Caroline. 2005. Social Networks and Internet Connectivity Effects. *Information, Communication & Society* 8 (2): 125–147.

Hesse-Biber, Sharlene Nagy, and Patricia Leavy, editors. 2010. *The Practice of Qualitative Research*. Thousand Oaks, Calif.: Sage.

Hiller, Harry H., and Tara M. Franz. 2004. New Ties, Old Ties and Lost Ties: The Use of Internet in Diaspora. *New Media & Society* 6 (6): 731–752.

Hine, Christine. 2000. *Virtual Ethnography*. London: Sage.

———. 2006. *Virtual Methods: Issues in Social Research on the Internet*. Oxford: Berg.

Horst, Heather A. 2006. The Blessings and Burdens of Communication: Cell Phones in Jamaican Transnational Social Fields. *Global Networks* 6 (2): 143–159.

Jackson, Jean E. 1990. "I Am a Fieldnote": Fieldnotes as a Symbol of Professional Identity. In *Fieldnotes: The Makings of Anthropology*, edited by Roger Sanjek, 3–33. Ithaca, N.Y.: Cornell University Press.

Keenan, Thomas P. 2008. On the Internet, Things Never Go Away Completely. In *The Future of Identity in the Information Society*, edited by Simone Fischer-Hübner, Penny Duquenoy, Albin Zuccato, and Leonardo Martucci, 37–50. New York: Springer.

Kissau, Kathrin, and Uwe Hunger. 2010. The Internet as a Means of Studying Transnationalism and Diaspora. In *Diaspora and Transnationalism: Concepts, Theories and Methods*, edited by Rainer Bauböck and Thomas Faist, 245–266. Amsterdam: Amsterdam University Press.

Kozinets, Robert V. 2010. *Netnography: Doing Ethnographic Research Online*. Los Angeles: Sage.

Madianou, Mirca, and Daniel Miller. 2012. *Migration and New Media: Transnational Families and Polymedia*. London: Routledge.

Magnet, Shoshana. 2007. Feminist Sexualities, Race and the Internet: An Investigation of suicidegirls.com. *New Media & Society* 9 (4): 577–602.

Mann, Chris, and Fiona Stewart. 2003. Internet Interviewing. In *Postmodern Interviewing*, edited by Jaber Gubrium and James Holstein, 81–105. Thousand Oaks, Calif.: Sage.

Miller, Daniel, and Don Slater. 2000. *The Internet: An Ethnographic Approach.* Oxford: Berg.

Miller, Peter G., and Anders L. Sønderlund. 2010. Using the Internet to Research Hidden Populations of Illicit Drug Users: A Review. *Addiction* 105 (9): 1557–1567.

Ministerie van het Brussels Hoofdstedelijk Gewest. 2008. *Jaarverslag 2007.* Brussels: N. De Cooman.

Murthy, Dhiraj. 2013. Ethnographic Research 2.0: The Potentialities of Emergent Digital Technologies for Qualitative Organizational Research. *Journal of Organizational Ethnography* 2 (1): 23–36.

Pedroso, Luiz Eduardo Villarinho. 2011. *O Recente Fenômeno Imigratório de Nacionais Brasileiros na Bélgica.* Brasília: Fundação Alexandre de Gusmão.

Roberts, Lynne, Leigh Smith, and Clare Pollock. 2004. Conducting Ethical Research Online: Respect for Individuals, Identities and the Ownership of Words. In *Readings in Virtual Research Ethics: Issues and Controversies*, edited by Elizabeth Buchanan, 156–173. Hershey, Pa.: Information Science Publishing.

Sanjek, Roger, editor. 1990. *Fieldnotes: The Makings of Anthropology.* Ithaca, N.Y.: Cornell University Press.

Schaap, Frank. 2002. *The Words That Took Us There: Ethnography in a Virtual Reality.* Amsterdam: Aksant Academic Publishers.

Schrooten, Mieke. 2008. The Influence of the Racial Democracy Myth in Contemporary Brazil. *Kolor: Journal on Moving Communities* 8 (2): 63–77.

———. 2010. Virtual Migrant Communities: "Orkut" and the Brazilian Case. COMCAD Working Papers no. 80. Bielefeld, Germany: Centre on Migration, Citizenship and Development. Accessed February 11, 2015. http://www.uni-bielefeld.de/tdrc/ag_comcad/downloads/workingpaper_80_Schrooten.pdf.

———. 2011a. Internal Migration and Ethnic Division: The Case of Palmas, Brazil. *The Australian Journal of Anthropology* 22 (2): 203–219.

———. 2011b. Online Gemeenschappen. In *Een verhaal van één taal, één stad en drie continenten: De Angolese, Braziliaanse en Portugese Bevolking van Brussel*, 86–88. Brussels: Regionaal Integratiecentrum Foyer Brussel vzw.

———. 2012a. Moving Ethnography Online: Researching Brazilian Migrants' Online Togetherness. *Ethnic and Racial Studies* 35 (10): 1794–1809.

———. 2012b. (Trans)Forming Boundaries in a Contact Zone: The Experience of Brazilian Migrants in Brussels. *Revista de Ciencias Sociales* 29: 89–104.

———, and Stefanie De Brouwer. 2012. Werken aan Netwerken in de Hulpverlening aan Migranten. Met het Ecogram als Werkmodel. *Tijdschrift voor Welzijnswerk* 36 (323): 13–18.

———, and Frederik Lamote. 2013. Translokaliteit als Nieuwe Context voor Sociaal Werk. *TerZake*, December, 30–33.

———, Dirk Geldof, and Sophie Withaeckx. 2015. Transmigration and Urban Social Work: Towards a Research Agenda. *European Journal of Social Work*, January 23. Accessed February 10, 2015. http://www.tandfonline.com/doi/abs/10.1080/1369 1457.2014.1001725?journalCode = cesw20#.VNpTVPldUfY.

Schrum, Lynne. 1995. Framing the Debate: Ethical Research in the Information Age. *Qualitative Inquiry* 1 (3): 311–326.

Sharp, Keith, and Sarah Earle. 2003. Cyberpunters and Cyberwhores: Prostitution on the Internet. In *Dot.cons: Crime, Deviance and Identity on the Internet*, edited by Yvonne Jewkes, 36–52. Cullompton, Devon: Willan Publishing.

Slater, Don. 1998. Trading Sexpics on IRC: Embodiment and Authenticity on the Internet. *Body & Society* 4 (4): 91–117.

Stocking, George W., Jr. 1992. *The Ethnographer's Magic and Other Essays in the History of Anthropology*. Madison: University of Wisconsin Press.

Sveningsson, Malin. 2004. Ethics in Internet Ethnography. In *Readings in Virtual Research Ethics: Issues and Controversies*, edited by Elizabeth A. Buchanan, 45–61. Hershey, Pa.: Information Science Publishing.

Vertovec, Steven. 2007. Super-Diversity and Its Implications. *Ethnic and Racial Studies* 30 (6): 1024–1054.

Walther, Joseph B. 2002. Research Ethics in Internet-Enabled Research: Human Subjects Issues and Methodological Myopia. *Ethics and Information Technology* 4 (3): 205–216.

Waskul, Dennis, and Mark Douglass. 1996. Considering the Electronic Participant: Some Polemical Observations on the Ethics of On-Line Research. *The Information Society* 12: 129–139.

Wilkinson, David, and Mike Thelwall. 2011. Researching Personal Information on the Public Web: Methods and Ethics. *Social Science Computer Review* 29 (4): 387–401.

Zimmer, Michael. 2010. "But the Data Is Already Public": On the Ethics of Research in Facebook. *Ethics and Information Technology* 12 (4): 313–325.

Chapter 6

File Sharing and (Im)Mortality: From Genealogical Records to Facebook

Martin Slama

The sharing of digital (or digitized) data represents a ubiquitous phenomenon in today's social media age. In the natural sciences, it forms the basis of networked knowledge production, giving rise to new forms of sociality in the scientific community (Beaulieu 2005); and fundamental to so-called hacker ethics, it is a constitutive part of the universe of free software developers (Karanović 2012; Kelty 2008). In the social sciences and humanities, it supports experimentation with ethnographic representation, as when, for example, visitors in a virtual ethnographer's office can read fieldnotes (Underberg and Zorn 2013: 39). Even more than in these uses and examples, file sharing attests to new ways of expressing friendship, kinship, and a range of further relationships and socialities in the everyday lives of many people across the globe. This includes the cultural and emotional repertoires that unfold within these societal realms.

Asserting that it is a ubiquitous phenomenon, however, does not mean that file sharing is devoid of problematic aspects. One has only to think of legal battles over copyright issues or the appetite of IT corporations for "big data," not to mention instances in which users unintentionally "share" their data with national security agencies. Yet, concerns such as these over sharing clearly preceded the digital age, and this seems to be particularly true for anthropology, which brings us to ethnographic fieldwork and fieldnotes in particular.

Although there were instances of sharing fieldnotes with students and colleagues (Sanjek 1990a: 327–334), especially in larger projects of collaborative research, the contributions to *Fieldnotes: The Makings of Anthropology* (Sanjek 1990b) amply attest that sharing fieldnotes remained a sensitive issue among anthropologists, not least since the "scandal" of Malinowski's posthumously published field diary (Malinowski 1989). As the Malinowski case indicated, the anxieties over sharing and archiving fieldnotes were often associated with the problem that anthropologists, like all human beings, will ultimately pass away. In *Fieldnotes*, one thus encountered reflection on the questions: What will happen with my fieldnotes after my death? Can other people interpret them correctly? Can they make sense to anyone else at all? Can they harm informants due to their political implications? (See, for example, Jackson 1990: 10.)

Such questions in the original *Fieldnotes* volume were interlinked with concerns about durable ways to archive fieldnotes. Back then in the 1980s, the advent of the digital era added this "new" dimension to these worries: "Today's new fear, in addition to fire, loss, and death, is computer wipeout" (Sanjek 1990c: 38). Such worries can become particularly significant when, in his or her "desire for personal immortality," the anthropologist senses "the possibility that no one will ever be interested in looking at them [the fieldnotes] at all—the ultimate death!" (Ottenberg 1990: 143, 155). Fieldnotes thus might evoke death as well as lasting remembrance.

In today's digital era, however, when ethnographic data are digitized or are often digital from the start, concerns about loss of field data are not restricted to the scholarly community, as our data now can easily be shared between anthropologists and their interlocutors by a click of one's mouse or by a touch on the screen of one's smartphone. This chapter focuses on these changing circumstances of generating and sharing data and, as we will see, the mortality of fieldwork data and those involved in producing them.

I approach this topic by resorting to my fieldwork experience in Indonesia, beginning in the early 2000s and spanning more than a decade. This provides the opportunity to reflect upon how the digital began to inform my research and how the problem of (im)mortality, which we know from the first version of *Fieldnotes*, continues to be relevant in the digital era as well.

A Short (Hi)Story of the Digitization of Fieldwork

Digital communication and digital files early on played a role in my anthropological work. My field research in Indonesia as a doctoral candidate during 2000–2001 concerned young Internet users, especially their activities in chatrooms online and in Internet cafés offline (Slama 2010; see also Burrell 2012). At that time, no mobile Internet access existed in Indonesia, and Internet connections had only recently started to enter private homes. Internet cafés were the places to go online. Middle and upper class Indonesians owned mobile phones, which were also used for texting. The first digital cameras were in use, and a rare few mobile phones were equipped with cameras that allowed taking pictures at very low resolution. In addition to participant observation in Internet cafés and recording interviews with a conventional tape recorder, my online conversations in the chatrooms became a major source of "fieldnotes" that, as Bonnie Nardi puts it (Chapter 11, this volume), "seem[ed] to write themselves."

More than a year after I had completed the fieldwork for my dissertation, I was given the opportunity to return to Indonesia as a researcher for a new project that, this time, was not so pointedly focused on digital realms.[1] Still, it became clear quite early that this did not mean I would resort to a predigital mode of conducting fieldwork.

In March 2003, I began fieldwork among Indonesians of Arab descent whose ancestors, mainly between the middle of the nineteenth and middle of the twentieth centuries, had migrated to what is today Indonesia from the Hadhramaut in eastern Yemen. In addition to longer stays of about a year in 2003–2004 and in 2007–2008, I visited certain of my new fieldwork sites on an annual basis for periods of several weeks and was thus able to observe the technological changes that informed the everyday lives of my interlocutors. Of course, my own uses of new technologies for communication and documentation were also adapting and changing during this period.

When, in March 2003, I began fieldwork in the Arab neighborhood of the central Javanese city of Solo, the only digital device I employed was a digital camera—from today's perspective, a clumsy, "stone age" model. I had planned to do digital recordings of interviews but quickly came to realize that most of my interlocutors did not feel comfortable with this, a situation that had much to do with the geopolitical context and timing of my fieldwork. That same month, March 2003, the United States and its so-called "coalition of the willing" invaded Iraq, an action of which many Indonesian Muslims, and Indonesians of Hadhrami descent in particular, were highly critical. Their stance also found its expression in general anti-Western sentiments and suspicion. Moreover, in the years before 2003,

Indonesia was haunted by terrorist attacks that were linked to perpetrators of Hadhrami descent. This gave rise to stereotyped media reports, and to a revival of older, colonial discourses that targeted so-called "extremist Arabs" in an imagined "land of moderates" (moderate local Muslims; Mandal 2011). As a result, I cancelled my plan to record interviews and instead took notes by hand during and after conversations, producing "scratchnotes" that were expanded later (Ottenberg 1990: 148; Sanjek 2014: 69), thus replicating the makings of predigital anthropology (Sanjek 1990d: 95–99).

In 2003, most of my interlocutors, like other middle class Indonesians, owned mobile phones, which were widely used not only for making calls but for sending text messages. Some of them also had a home computer connected to the Internet, which Indonesians cynically liked to call the World Wide Wait (Hill and Sen 1997: 70). Despite less than ideal serivce, Hadhramis, like others, used email and participated in listservs for various purposes. Yet the most popular form of non–face-to-face communication was texting, and my research would have been impossible had I not engaged in this practice as well. Texting at that time permitted brief, pointed, and promptly returned conversation, as many messages were deleted within a few days, or even hours, in order not to exceed the limited memory capacity of the mobile devices then in use (compare Horst and Miller 2006).

When I began my second long period of fieldwork in 2007, I concentrated on peripheral eastern Indonesia rather than on Java. At that time, violence-prone Islamism had peaked in Indonesia, and time had passed since the events of 9/11 and the invasion of Iraq. In addition to participant observation, I tried again to record interviews and this time did not confront major obstacles. On the contrary, many of my interview partners felt honored to participate in a somewhat official-seeming interview session, which I recorded using my digital voice recorder. They apparently enjoyed the idea that a European anthropologist was interested in their community and their personal lives, something they could not recall ever happening before. This was also the time when mobile phones with improved built-in cameras became widespread in Indonesia. My interlocutors freely used them to take pictures of me occasionally, whereas I always asked for permission to photograph them with my brand new digital camera, which was much simpler to use than the old one. So, in this phase of my research, the digital became manifest in the form of images, taken from various perspectives, as well as of voice recordings.

The succeeding years were marked by the rise of the smartphone and the mobile Internet (see also Barendregt 2012: 208). Sending pictures electronically, chatting with BlackBerry Messenger or WhatsApp, participating in social networking sites such as Facebook and others, became and remains extremely popular in Indonesia. In 2013, with more than 48 million users, Indonesia was home to the world's fourth largest Facebook community (Kunad 2013).

As less expensive devices have more recently entered the market, these digital practices have trickled down to the popular classes. Today, one can find Indonesians living at minimum wage levels who are on Facebook, which they access from their low-priced, Chinese-branded smartphones. Given the manifold spread of mobile uses of the Internet, my digital data sources also multiplied (see also Kelty 2009: 187; Boellstorff et al. 2012: 113–119). They now comprise interview recordings and images that I produced, pictures and texts created by my interlocutors, and a range of online interaction traces. They are all much easier to store due to the extended memory capacities of today's devices and to the ease of transferring data from one device to another.

Now, before I discuss digital file sharing as an example of how changing technological affordances became significant in my fieldwork, I turn to the modes of written documentation widespread among Hadhramis and how they indicate some intriguing parallels between the digital and predigital eras. This may also prevent us from imagining the introduction of digital technologies as a total or radical break with the past or from succumbing to the utopian or dystopian discourses that often accompany the rise of new technologies, especially digital ones (for fuller discussion, see Slama 2010).

Genealogies as (Digital) Files to Be Shared

Hadhramis have a particularly rich tradition of producing and sharing documents, one that long predates the digital age. Thus, for Hadhramis, the possibilities of digital production and reproduction did not represent instances of absolute novelty. They clearly did not enter a cultural vacuum but rather appeared as contemporary varieties of already existing forms and techniques. This led, as we shall see, to a relatively smooth appropriation of the digital for uniquely Hadhrami purposes.

Perhaps the most significant text genre produced by Hadhramis is the genealogy. In the sixteenth century, when Hadhramis started to spread across the Indian Ocean, they already carried written genealogies with them. Beyond the facts of patrilineal descent, their genealogies often contained additional information, such as the locations where their Hadhrami ancestors passed away and were buried, and in this manner, Hadhramis constructed a geography of their diaspora through their genealogies. As Engseng Ho points out in his seminal book, these genealogies constituted an "older technology for traversing distance and duration" (2006: 182). This type of text was complemented by other genres, such as hagiographies of Hadhrami Sufi saints, travelogues called *rihla* (Alatas 2005), manuals for visiting graves, and litanies (Ho 2006). And importantly, all these texts were copied and shared.

The most recent innovation in Hadhrami document production is a form of "genealogical passport" issued by Rabitah Alawiyyah, a Hadhrami organization in Jakarta (Ho 2006: 325). This organization was founded by Hadhramis who claim descent from the Prophet Mohammed and are thus particularly concerned with matters of ancestry; their elevated descent is formally indicated by the titles *sayyid* (pl. *sada*) or *habib* (pl. *habaib*). At the Rabitah office, genealogies of Hadhrami *sada* are registered and digitized with the intention that the ancestry of every Hadhrami *sayyid* in Indonesia and elsewhere can be readily authenticated and false claims be exposed (Heiss and Slama 2010: 41). Like every passport, these genealogical documents constitute evidence that must be presented in particular situations. Although they are not of relevance when crossing the borders of nation states, they will be consulted, for instance, when parents want to check the suitability of their children's potential marriage partners.

The sharing of documents among Hadhramis has now entered the twenty-first century through digitization of their genealogies, and their genealogical "passports" have become digital documents to be shared. In addition, images of Hadhrami ancestors, especially those who have gained saint-like status (Slama 2014a), have also been digitized and are now shared on social media interfaces.

It is important to note that my recorded interviews contain some of the same thematic elements as the Hadhrami text genres. Because conducting fieldwork among Hadhramis is impossible without including such topics as genealogy, geographic mobility, and Islamic practice and piety, most of my interviews contain significant passages dealing with the ancestry and migration history of my interlocutors and their families. This information is similar to what was written down in the genealogies. In my interviews, one finds accounts of pilgrimages and visits to graves of family members that are reminiscent of travelogues (*rihla*) and manuals, and interview topics such as Islamic practice, exemplary piety, and involvement in Islamic organizations evoke the hagiographies of Sufi saints.

Given these parallels, it was not surprising that some Hadhramis developed an interest in my recorded interviews and viewed them as being of potential benefit to them. The following two examples from my fieldwork demonstrate how my interviews came to be appreciated by Hadhramis and how this led to their being shared as digital files. The discussion also touches on the link between file sharing and the question of (im)mortality.

Interviews and Pictures as Digital Files to Be Shared

The first interview was recorded in May 25, 2008, in Ternate, North Moluccas. My interview partner was Ilham Alatas,[2] a Hadhrami man who was sixty-seven years old and suffered from what may have been an ophthalmic tumor. During the interview, his wife, his youngest son Alwi, and one other family member were present. We began our conversation with the migration history of his family, and proceeded to where he was born, how he came to Ternate, and where his brothers and sisters lived in Indonesia. We continued with his secular and Islamic education and his career as a civil servant in Ternate after he had graduated from college. We then discussed his nine children, where they lived, and whom they married, and then his eleven grandchildren. Before Ilham Alatas had retired, he held a high position in the local government as the head of the accounting office. He was a respected figure not only in society at large but also within the Hadhrami community. After retirement, he led the Ternate branch of the Al-Khairaat Foundation, an organization established by Hadhramis that is concerned with Islamic education and welfare and operates several kindergartens and schools in Ternate.

In view of the Hadhrami preoccupation with genealogies, diasporic family histories, and Islam, the value of my interview was apparent not only to the ethnographer but to many Hadhramis, including my interview partner's family members. When Ilham Alatas passed away one month after I interviewed him, his youngest son Alwi contacted me and asked me to send him the digital interview file, which, as he later emphasized, represented "the most important thing for us . . . not only because of the content, but also because we can hear our father's voice."[3]

At that time, I was in central Java. I copied the file onto a CD, which I sent him by mail. I did not attempt to use email because of the poor Internet connection in Ternate. After Alwi had received the CD, the family assembled in the dining room to listen together to the recording: their family history as it was narrated by Ilham Alatas (interrupted only by my questions and some brief comments of the other family members present). As Alwi later emphasized to me, the voice of Ilham Alatas recreated his presence in a way that other forms of remembering and recalling him and their family history could not match.

The second interview I will discuss was recorded in April 2008 in Manado, North Sulawesi. My interview partner was Aisyah Alatas; she was sixty-one years old at that time, and our meeting to record the interview became the starting point of a longer relationship, as *Ibu* (or Mother) Aisyah, as she was respectfully called, developed a deeper interest in my research. In the following weeks, she introduced me to many Hadhrami men and women in North Sulawesi, and we met again later in Ternate and in Jakarta. (It was she who had accompanied me to Ilham Alatas's house and was the fourth person present when I interviewed him.)

Ibu Aishya's support was crucial in obtaining particularly valuable data for exploring the gendered dimensions of my Hadhrami research (Slama 2012). I also took several pictures of her and her only son Rahmat, who sometimes joined us. Sadly, however, when we met for the first time in Manado, Ibu Aisyah was already suffering from breast cancer. Apart from the topics also discussed with Ilham Alatas, such as the migration history of the Alatas family and their sponsorship of Islamic education, she also talked to me during the interview about the state of her health:

> I suffer from cancer, which I concealed from my family for about two years, so that they don't prevent me from travelling. I didn't tell them because I know that when the time has come, when Allah is calling us, then this is it; that's how far we have come. Why should we complicate things? And the medicine that is available for cancer treatment today is not yet working maximally anyway. Family members who suffered from cancer were not cured, although they had surgery. So I concealed it and went to religious gatherings [*haul*].[4]

There, at the graves of our pious ancestors I asked Allah for good health. If I can continue doing good deeds for my family, hopefully I will be cured. But if he wants to call me, that's it. I like travelling to see new things. Travelling from one world to another [meaning from this world to the hereafter] is also something new. (Interview with Aisyah Alatas, Manado, December 4, 2008)

Ibu Aisyah Alatas passed away in April 2011. Once I heard, I prepared a CD onto which I copied the interview as well as the pictures I had taken of Ibu Aisyah and Rahmat. I sent it to Rahmat, with whom I remained in contact. He was deeply moved when he received the CD. In February 2013, I contacted him via email again and we also had a Skype conversation. In the meantime, he had married and become the father of a son. He told me in one of his emails (today's variant of "letters from informants" [Sanjek 1990a: 107]):

I store the files of my mother on several personal computers so that they are safe from viruses and the breakdown of hard disks. . . . The pictures and the recordings that you have sent are very special gifts to me and my family. Something very beautiful can be stored and shared with close family members or friends for remembering beautiful moments. . . . Sometimes, at certain moments, I open these memories; and digital [images and words] are perfect media for all this. Sadness and happiness converge; these memories are a special medicine that can bring peace to my heart. (Email from Rahmat Alatas, October 2, 2013)

Rahmat told me that his family had listened to the interview with his mother multiple times at his uncle's house. His wife, whom Rahmat met after Ibu Aisyah passed away, has only heard her mother-in-law's voice from the recording. The pictures I took of his mother are now posted on Rahmat's Facebook account, a "medium for expressing the private and intimate" (Miller 2011: 174), stored in a folder named "My Mom."

Exhibiting pictures of deceased family members or legendary Hadhrami figures on social media constitutes a "digital genre" (Coleman 2010: 497) or "cultural genre of content" (Miller 2011: 212) among Indonesian Hadhramis and has become a common online practice. By sharing the pictures of his mother with Rahmat, I now participate in this already established genre. In the case of my interview recordings of both Ilham Alatas and Aisyah Alatas, however, something new was added to the acceptable ways of remembering family members—the digitized interviews now complement images (analog or digital) and religious practices such as grave-site visits. The digital files can evoke emotions ranging from sadness and joy to deep grief and mourning for the dead to finding peace with the irreversible condition of losing one's father or mother.

Given the significance that digital records can have for close family members, it is no surprise that it is not only anthropologists who worry about data loss but the interlocutors with whom they now share files as well. To avoid this, Rahmat saved the interview recording and the pictures on multiple computers. So now, for both anthropologists and interlocutors, the mortality of human beings is linked to the potential mortality of data. Thus, anthropologists are not alone in their concerns about how to store and save "their" files.

At the same time, in the age of digital data and file sharing, certain other concerns of anthropologists we know from *Fieldnotes* seem to have become less relevant. It would be absurd today if I worried about whether my interlocutors were able to interpret the shared interview recordings "correctly," as anthropologists in the 1980s worried about whether anyone could make sense of their handwritten or typed fieldnotes. We understand and expect that shared digital files may generate different interpretations among those who produce, read, look at, or listen to them. They live on through these new interpretations. Yet this is an immortality that anthropologists of earlier generations might not have imagined.

Conclusion

My short personal (hi)story of the digitization of fieldwork and the two examples of file sharing suggest that today, at least in the Indonesian context, field research without producing and managing digital data has become impossible. An anthropologist comes into contact with people via email, texting, BlackBerry Messenger, WhatsApp, Facebook, and other media while in the field, as well as before and afterward. Moreover, researchers and their interlocutors become producers of digital data such as texts, images, videos, and voice recordings that can be shared and exchanged.

I have argued that in the case of the Hadhrami diaspora, one can detect parallels and continuities between older forms of Hadhrami text production and documentation, the digitization of these older genres, and the sharing of digital data generated today. Against this backdrop, my interview recordings and images can be seen as complementing these older genres, as well as the newer digital documentation practices of Hadhramis themselves. Still, one has to consider, at the same time, the specifics of each form of data, in my case particularly the differences between interviews and images. Pictures of family members and Sufi saints that often decorate the walls of Hadhrami homes have belonged to the repertoire of Hadhrami visual documentation for quite a long time, whereas my voice recordings added a new dimension and resulted in new ways in which people utilize such data, including in offline family gatherings. With regard to images, a novel aspect is the ease and alacrity with which pictures can be exchanged and shared in digital form today.

As my examples show, Hadhramis highly value both the genres of voice recordings and of visual files on Facebook and other social media. Digital data thus become not only the makings of anthropology but materials for making personal memories and family histories of people with whom anthropologists work. Through file sharing, an interview that is part of our ethnographic project can be part of our interlocutors' projects as well. "We" thus can assist "them" through our ethnographic fieldwork, where hitherto the role of "assistant" was undertaken by selected informants and revealed the social hierarchies of anthropology's "hidden colonialism" (Sanjek 2014: 72–81).

This brings us to one further aspect of how file sharing might undermine the hierarchies between academia and the social realms where fieldwork takes place: interviews, images, and a range of other digital files—as "raw" data still to analyze—can become relevant in the immediate here and now and be shared soon or not long after they were generated. In contrast, the "cooked" end products of ethnographic research—the monograph or journal article—take other trajectories and are often difficult to access from outside academia, frequently posing language barriers and displaying inaccessible and coded academic jargon. The immediacy of unedited fieldwork data is far different from academic writings that may become relevant perhaps only to future generations of the people with whom anthropologists work.

My discussion of file sharing indicates that two supposedly different audiences for batches of documentary production—the academic ethnographic and the intimate familial—can intersect in accessing digital fieldwork materials. Certain academic genres, like the ethnographic interview, can convey very different meanings to various publics in the digital age when they are disembedded from the solely academic context. Consequently, such digital data represent more than the raw materials of anthropological interpretation; they are charged with particular emotions and can become part of personal memories and family histories.

This also has ramifications for how anthropologists continue to reengage their data, both in the short term and over their careers. As João Biehl reminds us, "There are of course many different ways, both figurative and literal, of returning to our ethnographic sites and subjects or of reengaging notes, memories, and visual archives" (2013: 578). In the digital age, one of these ways is to reengage dialogically with informants and interlocutors with whom recent, and even long-archived, files can be shared. For example, one can "return" to a site by contacting people on social media to discuss shared files that are now located on their accounts, such as the pictures of Rahmat's mother. And one can trace the online and offline trajectories of shared files, such as the interview with Alwi's father.

In such highly emotional cases as the digital traces of deceased persons, the anthropologist may become part of the family history of interlocutors by virtue of being the one who is present in interview recordings and in images. The sharing of such data also has consequences, of course, for the continuing relationships established during fieldwork. The level of intimacy and privacy that may be reached raises the ethical questions of what should be shared with whom.

Such ethical concerns were less pressing in the two cases I presented here, as sharing interview recordings and pictures of deceased persons with their sons was hardly problematic. One might even argue that they have the moral right to receive these files, and it would be unethical not to share them. Certainly, in other cases, this is less clear, and anthropologists need to think carefully about the digital realms in which their files should live on and thus contribute to their "immortality."

This durability of digital fieldwork records may be the vexing side of today's digital age. Not so long ago, anthropologists worried about the mortality of their data (and of themselves), but today's maxim is that "the Internet never forgets." Before our data today become subject to misuse, we thus need to think not about their mortality but about their immortality.

Acknowledgments

This chapter discusses fieldwork over a time span of more than a decade. Dissertation research in Indonesia was rendered possible by grants from the Office of International Relations at the University of Vienna and from the ASEA-UNINET (ASEAN-European University Network). Research on the Hadhrami diaspora was funded by two projects based at the Institute for Social Anthropology (ISA) of the Austrian Academy of Sciences, namely "Hadhramis in Indonesia: Ethnic Identity of Yemeni Diaspora Groups Today" (duration: March 2003 to August 2006; project director: Helmut Lukas) and "Networks of a Diaspora Society: Indonesian Hadhramis in the Homeland and in Peripheral Regions" (duration: February 2007 to July 2010; project director: Andre Gingrich). Both projects were funded by the Austrian Science Fund (FWF). In the years 2003 and 2004, research was partly carried out together with my ISA colleague Johann Heiss. I would like to thank the Indonesian Institute of Sciences (LIPI) for issuing research visas for the projects. I also wish to express my gratitude to our Indonesian partner institutions for their excellent cooperation, namely the Centre for the Study of Culture at Gadjah Mada University, led by Faruk HT, and the Centre for the Study of Religion and Culture at the State Islamic University Syarif Hidayatullah, directed by Chaider Bamualim. A postdoctoral grant from the Austrian Programme for Advanced Research and Technology (APART) of the Austrian Academy of Sciences allowed me to add to my research data more recently (project title: "Among National Elites and Local Muslims: The Hadhrami Diaspora in Contemporary Indonesia"; duration: January 2010 to April 2013). Since June 2014, I have been given the opportunity to conduct research on issues of social media usage and Islamic practice in Indonesia thanks to the Austrian Science Fund, which approved the project "Islamic (Inter)Faces of the Internet: Emerging Socialities and Forms of Piety in Indonesia" (duration: June 2014 to May 2017).

Notes

1. For an overview of the research projects that rendered fieldwork in Indonesia possible, see the acknowledgments at the end of the text in this chapter.

2. The names of my interlocutors are here anonymized, using typical Hadhrami names.

3. Text message from Alwi Alatas, December 2, 2013. All translations of Indonesian sources are by the author.

4. A *haul* takes place at the anniversary of a prominent Islamic scholar's death. In addition to *haul*, *maulid* (the celebration of the Prophet Mohammed's birthday), and *ziarah* (grave visits) are important aspects of Hadhrami *sada* religious practice. This article draws on material gathered among Hadhrami *sada* only. For Hadhramis who do not consider themselves descendants of the Prophet Mohammed and their religious practices and beliefs, see Slama (2014b).

Bibliography

Alatas, Ismail Fajrie. 2005. Land of the Sacred, Land of the Damned: Conceptualizing Homeland Among the Upholders of the *Tariqah ʿAlawiyyah* in Indonesia. *Antropologi Indonesia* 29 (2): 142–158.

Barendregt, Bart. 2012. Diverse Digital Worlds. In *Digital Anthropology*, edited by Heather A. Horst and Daniel Miller, 203–224. London: Berg.

Beaulieu, Anne. 2005. Sociable Hyperlinks: An Ethnographic Approach to Connectivity. In *Virtual Methods: Issues in Social Research on the Internet*, edited by Christine Hine, 183–197. Oxford: Berg.

Biehl, João. 2013. Ethnography in the Way of Theory. *Current Anthropology* 28 (4): 573–597.

Boellstorff, Tom, Bonnie Nardi, Celia Pearce, and T. L. Taylor. 2012. *Ethnography and Virtual Worlds: A Handbook of Method*. Princeton, N.J.: Princeton University Press.

Burrell, Jenna. 2012. *Invisible Users: Youth in the Internet Cafés of Urban Ghana*. Cambridge, Mass.: MIT Press.

Coleman, Gabriella E. 2010. Ethnographic Approaches to Digital Media. *Annual Review of Anthropology* 39:487–505.

Heiss, Johann, and Martin Slama. 2010. Genealogical Avenues, Long-Distance Flows and Social Hierarchy: Hadhrami Migrants in the Indonesian Diaspora. *Anthropology of the Middle East* 5 (1): 34–52.

Hill, David, and Krishna Sen. 1997. Wiring the Warung to Global Gateways: The Internet in Indonesia. *Indonesia* 63: 67–90.

Ho, Engseng. 2006. *The Graves of Tarim. Genealogy and Mobility Across the Indian Ocean*. Berkeley: University of California Press.

Horst, Heather, and Daniel Miller. 2006. *The Cell Phone: An Anthropology of Communication*. Oxford: Berg.

Jackson, Jean E. 1990. "I Am a Fieldnote": Fieldnotes as a Symbol of Professional Identity. In *Fieldnotes: The Makings of Anthropology*, edited by Roger Sanjek, 3–33. Ithaca, N.Y.: Cornell University Press.

Karanović, Jelena. 2012. Free Software and the Politics of Sharing. In *Digital Anthropology*, edited by Heather A. Horst and Daniel Miller, 185–202. London: Berg.

Kelty, Christopher. 2008. *Two Bits: The Cultural Significance of Free Software*. Durham, N.C.: Duke University Press.

———. 2009. Collaboration, Coordination, and Composition: Fieldwork After the Internet. In *Fieldwork Is Not What It Used to Be: Learning Anthropology's Method in a Time of Transition*, edited by James Faubion and George E. Marcus, 184–206. Ithaca, N.Y.: Cornell University Press.

Kunad, Kirk. 2013. Top 10 Countries with Most Facebook Users in 2013. "ClickTop10: Internet," April 18. Accessed February 11, 2015. http://www.clicktop10.com/2013/04/top-10-countries-with-most-facebook-users-in-2013/.

Malinowski, Bronislaw. 1989. *A Diary in the Strict Sense of the Term*. Stanford, Calif.: Stanford University Press. First published in 1967.

Mandal, Sumit. 2011. The Significance of the Rediscovery of Arabs in the Malay World. *Comparative Studies of South Asia, Africa and the Middle East* 31 (2): 296–311.

Miller, Daniel. 2011. *Tales from Facebook*. Cambridge, U.K.: Polity Press.

Ottenberg, Simon. 1990. Thirty Years of Fieldnotes: Changing Relationships to the Text. In *Fieldnotes: The Makings of Anthropology*, edited by Roger Sanjek, 139–160. Ithaca, N.Y.: Cornell University Press.

Sanjek, Roger. 1990a. Fieldnotes and Others. In *Fieldnotes: The Makings of Anthropology*, edited by Roger Sanjek, 324–340. Ithaca, N.Y.: Cornell University Press.

———, editor. 1990b. *Fieldnotes: The Makings of Anthropology*. Ithaca, N.Y.: Cornell University Press.

———. 1990c. Fire, Loss, and the Sorcerer's Apprentice. In *Fieldnotes: The Makings of Anthropology*, edited by Roger Sanjek, 34–44. Ithaca, N.Y.: Cornell University Press.

———. 1990d. A Vocabulary for Fieldnotes. In *Fieldnotes: The Makings of Anthropology*, edited by Roger Sanjek, 92–121. Ithaca, N.Y.: Cornell University Press.

———. 2014. *Ethnography in Today's World: Color Full Before Color Blind*. Philadelphia: University of Pennsylvania Press.

Slama, Martin. 2010. The Agency of the Heart: Internet Chatting as Youth Culture in Indonesia. *Social Anthropology/Anthropologie Sociale* 18 (3): 316–330.

———. 2012. "Coming Down to the Shop": Trajectories of Hadhrami Women into Indonesian Public Realms. *The Asia Pacific Journal of Anthropology* 13 (4): 313–333.

———. 2014a. From Wali Songo to Wali Pitu: The Travelling of Islamic Saint Veneration to Bali. In *Between Harmony and Discrimination: Negotiating Religious Identities Within Majority/Minority Relationships in Bali and Lombok*, edited by Brigitta Hauser-Schäublin and David Harnish, 112–143. Leiden: Brill.

————. 2014b. Hadhrami Moderns: Recurrent Dynamics as Historical Rhymes of Indonesia's Reformist Islamic Organization Al-Irsyad. In *Dynamics of Religion in Southeast Asia: Magic and Modernity*, edited by Volker Gottowik, 113–132. Amsterdam: Amsterdam University Press.

Underberg, Natalie M., and Elayne Zorn. 2013. *Digital Ethnography: Anthropology, Narrative, and New Media*. Austin: University of Texas Press.

PART III

DIGITALLY MEDIATED FIELDWORK AND COLLEGIALITY

Chapter 7

Doing Fieldwork, BRB: Locating the Field on and with Emerging Media

Jordan Kraemer

Are you online right now? How do you know? Maybe you are reading this in print, but your phone is buzzing, or you are taking breaks to check your email, and will BRB (be right back). Maybe you downloaded the digital edition of this text but are not connected to the Internet at the moment. Or maybe, by the time you read this, Internet access has become truly ubiquitous, and you are successfully tuning out distractions.

I frequently faced this question of when one is "online" while studying social and mobile media practices among several friendship clusters in Berlin in the late 2000s (Kraemer 2012, 2014). But it also echoes questions anthropologists raised in the 1980s and 1990s about the role of communication technologies in changing the nature of the "field" itself (Appadurai 1996; Burrell 2009; Gupta and Ferguson 1992, 1997; Marcus 1995). Globalizing processes, entwined with emerging communication technologies, provoked anthropologists to rethink what constitutes "the field" as a place ontologically distinct from "home." These questions pushed scholars to look more closely at what makes anthropological fieldwork distinctive, particularly that key (and often underexamined) component of fieldwork, fieldnotes. The first *Fieldnotes* volume (Sanjek 1990a) demystified much about the practice of writing fieldnotes and helped reimagine the field—and anthropology itself.

The current volume revisits these questions by asking how emerging technologies are again transforming fieldwork and the everyday practices of anthropologists. In this chapter, I examine how social and mobile media—that is, social network sites (Facebook, MySpace, LinkedIn), blogs, "microblogging" services (Twitter, Tumblr), and media sharing platforms (YouTube, Flickr, Instagram) and mobile networking, especially on Internet-enabled mobile phones—are remaking anthropological understandings of the field, fieldwork, and fieldnotes. Social media often overlap with mobile platforms, and by "mobile" I mean technologies that depend on wireless networking—cell phones, especially Internet-enabled smartphones; laptops; cellular and WiFi networks; and other portable devices.[1] I address these questions by comparing the binary of online versus offline to home versus field, drawing on work in anthropology, science and technology studies (STS), and information studies to rethink these binaries in relation to place-making practices.

I use one particular day from my fieldwork to illustrate some conceptual and practical challenges for conducting ethnographic fieldwork on and with social and mobile media, but these considerations affect anthropologists and ethnographers studying a broad range of topics. Our research methods must now contend with the reality that digital, networked technologies are integral to daily life both for scholars and the worlds, peoples, and places we study.

The day was March 31, 2010. It was the day before abstracts were due for the annual meeting of the American Anthropological Association (AAA). I was more than halfway into a ten-month research stay, based in Berlin, and was deeply steeped in my fieldwork. Early fieldwork anxieties about gathering data were giving way to struggles writing all of my observations down. I was collaborating with a close friend and co-conspirator, Jenny Carlson, to plan our first AAA panel. Over the course of thirty-six hours, I cowrote the panel abstract, maneuvered the AAA's online system (no mean feat!), wrangled other panelists, and conducted fieldwork on Facebook, with a group of Berliners in their apartment, and with another circle of friends at a music event. I moved between online and offline sites, circles of friends, and "home" or "not-the-field" (which may not always be the same) and "the field," movements facilitated by email, instant messaging, mobile telephony, and social network sites (see Figure 7.1). So what constituted distinctions between different spaces or settings, and what are some consequences for anthropological fieldwork?

Of course, media and communication technologies are not new to anthropology or ethnographic fieldwork—from letters and photography to

Jordan Kraemer
April 1, 2010 • Twitter • [Public]

i just lost 16+ hours working on a panel & abstract submissions for big fall anthro
conference in the US (#AAA2010). back to fieldwork pls.

Like • Comment • Share

Figure 7.1. "Back to fieldwork pls."

film and audio recordings, anthropologists have been recording their subjects and observations since Boas and Malinowski (see also Bateson and
Mead 1962; Brady 2002; Mead 1956), not to mention writing letters to
family, colleagues, and mentors back "home" (Sanjek 1990c). Fieldnotes
represent a key medium through which anthropologists inscribe ourselves
and our work, as intermediate texts between interacting with research participants and their worlds and more final forms of "writing up." But fieldnotes also serve to make the field a certain kind of place. Social and mobile
media are remaking these practices in multiple ways, providing new platforms and formats for creating field materials and bringing relationships
and interactions from different parts of life into closer proximity. In this
chapter, I consider specific capacities and entailments of emerging media[2]
that reshape fieldnotes and the field, including challenges in recording
activities on social media, managing disparate audiences and social worlds,
and conducting fieldwork when one can never fully disconnect from
"home." Thinking through these issues and their consequences offers new
insights into long-standing issues in anthropology and ethnography on the
nature of the field, fieldwork, and the texts we produce.

Making Online and Offline Worlds

Anthropologists and other scholars have been grappling for some time with
questions of how to conceptualize the Internet, virtual worlds, and digital
media. How should we even denote interactions or communications that
involve networked computing technologies: digital? virtual? online?
Rethinking binaries such as "online" and "offline" offers a means to recon-
sider the relationship between "the field" and "not-the-field" (which may
not always not be "home") as places in the making.[3]

Social and mobile media can be considered a subset of digital, net-worked communication technologies, where "digital" differentiates binary encodings (literally, a discrete code made up of ones and zeros) from analog formats (see Lévy 2001: 33–43). I use "social media" to refer to networked communication platforms that are organized around interlinked user profiles or pages, depend on users to create content or share media, and articulate participants' "social networks" (boyd and Ellison 2008; Ellison, Steinfeld, and Lampe 2007), that is, linkages between users.[4]

In describing these approaches, I consider specific and material qualities of mobile and social media, such as their capacity to be enmeshed in everyday practice.[5] Mobile devices, for example, integrate practices such as checking email or Facebook into other daily activities. Users often fit online activities into little gaps throughout the day, stretching and contracting experiences of time in a way Rattenbury, Nafus, and Anderson (2008) describe as "plastic." Other scholarship attends to the multiplicity of connections that social media facilitate, such as Madianou and Miller's (2013) conceptualization of polymedia, to theorize how users move between platforms, applications, devices, and other communicative modes (see Figure 7.2).[6]

Social and mobile media, then, affect everyday social worlds by allowing users to switch rapidly between conversations and contexts. This rapid movement can risk "context collapse," a situation in which one social world impinges on another (boyd 2014: 31–32). But users also manage audiences and publics through practices such as linguistic code switching (Kraemer 2012: 149–157). Worlds can collide without blurring or merging. In fieldwork, too, emerging media bring into close proximity people, places, and activities considered "in the field" with those we associate with "home." As with online worlds, the "field" must be constructed as a kind of place. These boundaries are not necessarily dissolving—on the contrary, we as fieldworkers continue to reinstantiate them. I was "in the field," for example, when I was chatting online with those whose practices I was observing, recording, and analyzing; other times, I conversed with colleagues, friends, and family from "home." Yet when I began discussing my fieldwork experiences with my panel co-organizer, our chatlogs became part of my field record in ways that complicate these distinctions. Fieldwork takes place across (and constitutes) diverse sites and spaces, and I therefore propose attending to this plurality of encounters, technologies, activities,

---

Jordan Kraemer
[date redacted] • Twitter • [Public]

are young people rethinking attitudes towards privacy, or rather reacting to its
increasing erosion? http://tumblr.com/xkb9p64fn

Like • Comment • Share

Facebook Friend > Jordan Kraemer
[date redacted], 2010 • [Friends]

jordan, ich komm so gegen halb neun vorbei. ist das ok???

Like • Comment • Share

> **Jordan Kraemer** naja, kein problem. aber willst du dass ich vorbei komme?
> [date redacted], 2010 • [Friends]
>
> **Facebook Friend** ich komm rüber zu euch. is doch noch spargel über ☺
> [date redacted], 2010 at 6:41pm • Like

Figure 7.2. Connection strategies and polymedia: switching between
audiences and platforms such as Facebook and Twitter.

and actors. Just as possibilities are proliferating of communicating, interacting, and engaging through emerging media, so are new means to lurk, disconnect, or withdraw, which are equally important in constructing
experiences of place.[7] To explore these, I next recount examples of how I
navigated the field and not-the-field, as well as the field materials that constituted these spaces.

Thirty-Six Hours in the Life of a Fieldworker

These issues came to the fore that day in March 2010 when I was struggling
to balance fieldwork with the demands of submitting a conference panel.
My account of the following thirty-six hours illustrates the kinds of fieldnotes I generated as I moved between media, sites, and encounters and the
places constituted through them.

The final AAA deadline was April 1, and I had spent most of the day
working in my apartment. The apartment itself had become part of my

fieldwork as my roommates maintained ties to a circle of friends from the same region of eastern Germany. In my research, the regional emerged as a key geographic scale that was often enacted through social and mobile media.

I was working at my laptop in the afternoon when I received an instant message from Jenny, my panel co-organizer. She was working on her dissertation prospectus from her home in Austin, Texas, where it was still morning. Our conversation in some sense took place out of the field (though not necessarily at my "home"); for example, when we referenced professional activities:

> *jenny*: Hey!!
> *jenny*: How goes
> *jordan*: GOOD MORNING
> *jordan*: good!
> *jenny*: I am looking at all the emails
> *jordan*: i have my abstract drafted, just need to edit, which i will do tomorrow.
> *jenny*: I have to do this today too
> *jordan*: i'm just now trying to tackle the session abstract
> *jenny*: I know!
> *jenny*: Wanna workshop it?

Our chat also became a record of fieldwork, akin to fieldnotes, as we turned from discussing the abstract to reflecting on my ongoing fieldwork. As our conversation progressed, I moved my laptop into the kitchen so I could begin cooking dinner. I was preparing foods for Passover, the Jewish holiday, which led to discussing my experiences in Germany as an American Jew:

> *jordan*: what was REALLY interesting was going to a German-Jewish seder on monday
> *jenny*: ??
> *jordan*: in Schöneberg
> *jordan*: and they were like, Friedrichshain, where's that? we're Wessies
> *jenny*: I know
> *jordan*: no one here says Wessies.

jordan: or Ossies.

jenny: I know. . . . I find that Ossi and Wessi is only invoked ironically in regard to cultural artifacts

jordan: another interesting thing was watching *Inglorious Basterds* a few months ago, with my German friends

This led to discussing fieldnotes themselves:

jenny: I hope you took fieldnotes on that

jordan: i take fieldnotes on EVERYTHING

jenny: are you a scratch note/jot note person?

jordan: it's so time consuming

jordan: i have a notebook for handwriting but i type almost everything up longform for better future use

jenny: OKAY. But point being. . . . *Inglorious Basterds*

As this conversation was taking place, I was moving between other media and interactions, launching Skype with my partner in San Francisco and coordinating plans with other contacts in Berlin. Instant messaging provided a space for me and Jenny to reflect on our work as we were conducting it, while producing a record that became part of my field materials. Even within a single format, our conversation moved quickly between topics and language registers, just as online chat made it possible to jump between the field and not-the-field, bringing online conversations into the space of the kitchen.

The following day, we ran into technical difficulties submitting the abstracts, exacerbated by the fact that one panelist, also conducting fieldwork, did not have Internet access during the day. She asked her boyfriend to use her computer as her intermediary while she talked him through the process over the phone:

doris[8]: are you online? This is kinda urgent!

jordan: yeah, i'm here

jordan: the system looks like it's back up for me

doris: Hey Jordan. This is not Doris; but her boyfriend. Doris is out in the boonies with no net access. She wanted me to get in touch with you about the AAAS [sic] stuff

jordan: Hi!

doris: she is in fact on the phone with me.
jordan: great

Like me, Doris was straddling the field and not-the-field (but again, not "home") to upload her abstract while contending with infrastructural limits to Internet access. Her boyfriend was similarly positioned both in and out of the field while accessing her IM account and wrestling with the submission system. Our chat linked us across fieldsites and brought us momentarily "out" of the field—even as the field exerted its presence by hampering our ability to communicate.

Along with these conversations, I was engaged simultaneously—or perhaps, in rapid succession—in chats "in" the field. A friend of my roommate's, Claudia, messaged me on Facebook to coordinate cooking a meal. She had moved to Berlin in the past few years, around the same time as many of her friends from rural Saxony-Anhalt. She reached out to me over Facebook chat because Daniele would not be home when she wanted to cook:

Claudia: jordan—when will you be home tomorrow evening?
Claudia: [I] want to cook at your place, but dani doesn't come home
        til half past nine
Jordan: all day long, at the most
Claudia: will you be home at 7pm?

Here, indexical words pointed to the space of my apartment ("your place") and upcoming times ("tomorrow evening"). I misunderstood which day she wanted to cook on, however, which led to miscommun ication:

Claudia: ja! see you tomorrow
Jordan: oh wait
Jordan: you mean today or tomorrow?
Claudia: tomorrow
Jordan: ACHSO [OH OKAY]
Claudia: from 7
Jordan: nevermind! :)
Jordan: no problem.

Jordan: i'm cooking THIS evening. i didn't understand.
Claudia: ok.

In this sense, our chat took place "in" the field, both because Claudia was one of my research participants and because we referred to spaces and times where I conducted fieldwork. While I was chatting with Claudia, a potential interviewee in the Netherlands, linked to networks of electronic music fans I was also studying, messaged me to schedule a meeting over Skype. My fieldsite in this sense did not constitute a single geographic place; it could span multiple locales over the same media platforms.

I reproduce these chatlogs here to illustrate how "the field" was made online. But they also offer multiple possibilities for "creat[ing] our own documents" (Sanjek 1990b: xii), as a record of fieldwork and a space in which to reflect while "in" the field. The field here emerged out of the attention I brought to particular people and activities; that is, when I was observing and recording (see Jackson 1990: 16–17; Lederman 1990: 88–89). As one interviewee told Jackson in her study of anthropologists' relationships to their fieldnotes, he took breaks from fieldwork by not taking notes: "'Sometimes I don't take notes on purpose. Around here I use it as a protective device. My way of turning off'" (Jackson 1990: 17). But even attention breaks down as a rubric to delineate the field, because I often made observations without taking notes or created fieldnotes unintentionally when I thought I was just chatting with a friend from "home."

When Claudia arrived to begin cooking, I returned to my chat with Jenny to let her know I would have to go shortly:

jordan: people are arriiving here in an hour so i can't keep doing
   this
jordan: sorry

At this point, I shifted from working at the computer to spending time in the kitchen with Claudia, Daniele, and their friends before leaving to meet with another fieldwork circle of friends later that evening. This did not necessarily mean going "offline," however, as I remained connected via mobile phone to the Internet (and to text messaging). Alongside the friends from Magdeburg, I was conducting fieldwork with a circle of DJs, music producers, and their friends, most of whom lived in Berlin. They participated in broader networks of electronic music fans that I considered translocal; that is, taking place across locales. "Translocal" here indicates not just linkages between places but dynamic connections that create new experiences of place (Zhan 2009: 8), and, like the regional, emerged as a key form of scale-making. A DJ and music promoter named Alex had messaged me earlier that day via Skype, his preferred messaging platform for close friends, to coordinate meeting later at a music show. I want to describe next two key moments from the evening that illustrate moving between modes of communication, media, and places.

That evening, a Friday, a well-known music project was heading the bill at Berghain, a nightclub that has come to symbolize Berlin's postunification nightlife and licentious club culture[9] (Rapp 2009; see also Borneman and Senders 2000). Saturdays were notorious for kicking off multiday dance parties fueled by repetitive techno and less licit intoxicants. But Friday nights were calmer affairs, with live performances that attracted a specialist crowd of self-described "music geeks." When I arrived, the crowd was milling about before the set began. Another friend proposed that we "get into position" or "into place"—that is, find a good spot to hear the music before the floor became tightly packed. We made our way forward shortly before the lights dimmed. A wall of deep, droning sound washed over us and the crowd surged forward, hemming us in on all sides. Eventually, the relentlessly vibrating bass and tight quarters overwhelmed my commitment to fieldwork, and I snuck away to the bar. Reflexively, I checked email on my smartphone for updates regarding our conference panel. Just as I had moved between chat conversations in and out of the field in my apartment, I switched from participant observation to email with fellow panelists.

Yet this switching was never seamless. I felt conspicuous in the dim, smoky bar, staring at a brightly lit screen. Although this has become a norm in many places, it was still unusual there. I walked down to the ground floor, where I found a quiet spot on a couch to take handwritten notes. A few moments later, I was interrupted by a man in his thirties, with short hair and a trim beard. "Hallo? Hallo? Are you doing homework?" he asked. I debated how to reply. "No, I'm taking notes," I said finally, and explained that I was an anthropologist, which led to a longer conversation until he excused himself. The moment illustrates, on one hand, how note-taking can disrupt fieldwork, as others have commented (Sanjek 1990c: 96; Clifford 1990: 51). Both checking my mobile phone and taking notes could provoke curiosity, even suspicion, because such actions stood outside the bounds of context-appropriate behavior. On the other hand, moments of

disruption and disconnection could spark unexpected, and potentially productive, encounters, as I discuss next. Afterward, I eventually returned to
my apartment—where I still had to finalize my conference presentation
title, briefly switching "out" of the field once more.

Colliding Worlds and Strategies for (Dis)Connection

Digital communication technologies do not dissolve boundaries between
field and home, but they can bring disparate worlds into close proximity.
This entails numerous challenges for conducting fieldwork on and with
emerging media, three of which I want to relate regarding fieldnotes and
place making. First, I found it difficult to write notes while "observing" on
Facebook and similar platforms, so I developed alternative means for creating field records of social media activities. Second, it was often awkward to
conduct fieldwork on the same social network sites I used with friends and
contacts from "home"; I had to negotiate these usages. Third, although it
is technologically possible to study social media practices from a distance,
it is surprisingly hard to conduct this research without "being there" (Lederman 1990: 88–89) to observe the everyday contexts of social and mobile
media. I want to discuss the first two of these in more detail, to suggest
reframing the issues of connection and disconnection as forms of attention
that constitute the field. I hope this will shed light on the third challenge.

Initially, I envisioned taking fieldnotes while observing activities on
Facebook, Twitter, and other platforms—literally sitting at my laptop and
switching between Facebook and a word processor—yet was quickly sty-
mied. Alongside my detailed daily fieldnotes, I have a lone document titled
"Facebook/Social media notes," which remains blank. I was able to describe
visual content on user profile pages and popular media (such as news and
streaming television sites), and I often wrote about events or exchanges that
happened on Skype or Facebook or over mobile phones. But I found it
difficult, for example, to report on the stream of posts and actions that
constitutes the Facebook News Feed, until I discovered screenshots.

At first, I saved pages on Facebook as images, preserving how they
looked but sacrificing the ability to copy, paste, or search for text. I found
it more effective to save entire webpages—all HTML, links, and image
files—to my computer, which allows me to retrieve pages later in a web
browser (although elements sometimes break or expire when sites change

their architecture). I could then save pages periodically and analyze them later as documents or stills. My difficulty recording social media practices in real time may reflect ways people use Facebook, checking it periodically throughout the day rather than spending sustained periods of time there. But screenshots provided a snapshot that became part of my ethnographic record, like a photograph—an ethnographic still life I could return to and analyze in the context of daily fieldnotes, interview transcripts, and other data (compare Edwards 1997 for a discussion of the material entailments of photographic stills in anthropology).

This leads to the challenge of maintaining disparate social worlds with people back "home" and those in "the field." Facebook, like other social media, can make visible relationships from different parts of people's lives, especially through the News Feed, which aggregates the activities of one's Friends according to proprietary algorithms. I had to decide whether to create a new Facebook account for my research, which, with few contacts, might appear suspicious or artificial—outside the bounds of usual sociality. There are ethical advantages, however, to identifying as a researcher, and anthropologists have historically found that participants adjust to their presence. A separate research profile, moreover, might signal that I did not consider those I met in the field to be "real" or "actual" friends (cf. Ellison, Steinfield, and Lampe 2011: 878) and required deciding in advance who were potential research subjects. I addressed these issues by creating instead a separate "Group" on Facebook for interlocutors in Berlin and other sites. This group allowed me to browse status updates and activities in one place without making the group's boundaries visible to other users—or disconnecting from my existing network.

I continued posting updates to all of my Facebook Friends, but this led to awkward moments. A German-speaking friend complained that she had trouble understanding my posts in English, but I risked alienating, or at least discomfiting, friends from "home" when I wrote in German. One, for example (see Figure 7.3), quipped "bless you" in response to the name of a central plaza, Gendarmenmarkt—a humorous response that may have belied discomfort.

Sometimes, I switched between German and English to target different audiences, a strategy many of my interlocutors used. At other times, I posted the same update twice—with notable variations. For example, one Sunday I posted in German about relaxing and enjoying soup my roommate had cooked:

Facebook Friend in Germany Gendarmenmarkt!
[date redacted], 2009 at 5:53pm • [Friends]

Facebook Friend in U.S. bless you!
[date redacted], 2009 at 5:54pm • Like

Figure 7.3. "Gendarmenmarkt!" "bless you!"

broccoli soup from my roommate, now on the couch. Totally nice
Sunday. (*broccoli suppe meiner Mitbewohnerin, jetzt auf den
Couch. Ganz schöne Sonntag*)

I then followed with a second post:

which is to say, delicious broccoli soup thanks to my roommate,
now couch time. also got in my first real bike ride, to and from
a Jewish café in Mitte to buy matzah.

This latter addition seems aimed at a different audience, friends back
"home," perhaps because I associated the Jewish holiday more with my
personal life.

The encounters in Figure 7.4 illustrate the awkwardness, disconnections, and disjunctures that often characterize moving between places and
worlds on social media. Facebook could create online spaces at multiple
geographic levels simultaneously—translocal linkages, local rhythms of living, regional ties—but this switching was never seamless. Just as checking
email or taking notes at a club marked my behavior as inappropriate, moving between social worlds on Facebook generated moments of discomfort
and sparked encounters between friends from "home" and those in "the
field." In this sense, the field became a spatial scale of its own, as I will
discuss next. I therefore suggest reframing connection strategies for moving
between media in the field as strategies for (dis)connection, to encapsulate
ways in which we manage attention by pulling away, sneaking off, or putting down the notepad—to write, reflect, or just catch a break. To shift
attention away from one place is always to take it somewhere else, and
therefore it plays a key role in constituting the field as a place.

Jordan Kraemer
[date redacted] • Twitter • [Public]

haven't really done any academic writing in 6+ months. having serious writer's block trying to work on an abstract due asap.

Like • Comment • Share

> **Facebook Friend 1** We all experience writer's block sometimes. You can fight it!
> [date redacted] at 1:04pm • Like
>
> **Jordan Kraemer** it's just gotten so pleasantly foreign ☺. i had to just engage in some stream-of-consciousness rambling to get myself going again. thank goodness i have more fieldwork left before i have to write for real!
> [date redacted] at 1:08pm • [Friends]
>
> **Facebook Friend 2** omg! i knooooooooooooow! i hate it, simply hate it! can you imagine having to write a dissertation. Agh!
> [date redacted]] at 10:58pm • Like

Figure 7.4. Difficulties moving between "the field" and "not-the-field."

Final Words: Digitalia as Marginalia That Produce the Field

What it means to do fieldwork is changing as emerging technologies bring us into closer contact with "home" while we must navigate a shifting "field." It is no longer practical to conduct fieldwork in isolation, if ever it was. Still, because these shifts also affect the people and worlds we study, to be immersed in our fieldsites now includes these movements between spaces and places, across media and encounters. Fieldnotes occupy a central position in constituting the field as a place (or multiple places), even as emerging media provide new platforms and possibilities for creating field materials. In this chapter, I have considered how social and mobile media are transforming fieldwork by turning to accounts of digital materialities, connection strategies, and polymedia to emphasize plural and diverse practices that include media technologies. These approaches seek to account for ways that people move between media and other modes of engagement without dividing them into online or offline. Yet binary distinctions can create online and offline worlds as spaces in their own right, comparable to the ways in which anthropological fieldwork can create the "field" in opposition to "home" or "not-the-field."

In this vein, I have recounted myriad materials I generated over thirty-six hours of fieldwork, which included handwritten notes; chatlogs with friends, colleagues, and research participants; a Twitter post about my conference panel; screenshots of Facebook; and, of course, "headnotes" (Ottenberg 1990: 144–146), recollections that helped flesh out my notes when I typed them up later and continue to inform my ethnographic writing. Some I created intentionally (my daily field log and Facebook screenshots), but others emerged as digital marginalia—"digitalia"—that became invaluable sources of data.

Rather than divide these materials into "online" and "offline," I want to call attention to how they created "the field" and "not-the-field" as places. The field could be on Facebook, when I observed participants' activities and took screenshots. It was also constituted through attention to my informants' daily activities, whether cooking or attending a music show. Online and offline worlds did not merge, but Facebook brought together diverse scales and spheres of social life, for me and for those I was studying. The field, in consequence, came into more immediate, even dialectical, relation with "home" or "not-the-field," as I moved between conversations with colleagues, family, research participants, and friends (categories that were rarely static), on Skype, mobile phone, Facebook, in my apartment kitchen, or at a concert. The space of my apartment in Berlin, in effect, became multiply constituted as both "in" and "out" of the field, as did the space of instant message conversations.

As I have argued elsewhere (Kraemer 2014), emerging media reshape experiences of place partly by bringing different levels or scales of social life into new configurations (compare Tsing 2005: 57–58). In this sense, the field represents a spatial scale that was made through the field materials I generated, and their particular medium—digital, analog, verbal, or otherwise—shaped particular experiences of place. Emerging media, as I have said, make it possible to alternate rapidly between settings and contexts. These possibilities are never determinative, as technologies are taken up in culturally specific ways that cannot be predicted from their affordances alone.

New modes of connectedness, I have argued, also generate new possibilities for disconnection. I do not suggest that mobile phones or social media are simply sites of distraction and isolation, as I found that this was rarely the case. But switching between media could disrupt or interrupt a field-work encounter, thus shifting attention from instant messaging to my apartment or from a music show to email. I have therefore suggested that we reframe connection strategies as strategies for (dis)connection, to encap-sulate how we manage attention—and our field-making practice—by turn-ing elsewhere. Movements between sites, media, and contexts constructed everyday encounters as much around moments of disconnection as around moments of connection—moments that could equally elicit new encoun-ters, new experiences of place, and new entanglements between the field and not-the-field as places in the making.

Acknowledgments

I thank Roger Sanjek and Susan Tratner for their insights and for organiz-ing this excellent collection and Jenny Carlson for allowing me to quote our conversations and for her comments.

Notes

1. DeNicola (2012) has noted that these technologies are increasingly character-ized by their locatability as much as by their mobility.

2. I use "emerging" to account for how such technologies are still developing and being adopted in contingent ways, without emphasizing a binary between "new" and "old" because today's "new media" may quickly become tomorrow's old hat.

3. My approach is informed by literature on the materiality of information (Blanchette 2011; Dourish and Mazmanian 2013; Hayles 2004; Rosner et al. 2012) that considers material qualities of digital technologies to be inseparable from their mean-ing, use, and consequences for social life. These approaches call attention to specific practices that constitute "online" and "offline" without implying that these spheres are blurring or collapsing, as Tom Boellstorff (2012) has shown. Similarly, "the field" and "not-the-field" are not collapsing or merging but must each be created as places. Fieldnotes remain key to this field-making practice, even as social and mobile media are transforming their practice.

4. But I would caution against conflating social networks, social network sites, and broader social worlds. Miller and Horst note that one feature of anthropological approaches to digital culture are our units of analysis: "where some disciplines priori-tize collectives, minds, individuals and other fragments of life, anthropologist focus upon life as lived and all the mess of relevant factors that comes with that" (2012: 4).

5. Material qualities are not necessarily fixed, though—instead, as Hayles has argued, they are a component of media that derive from "the interplay between a

text's physical characteristics and its signifying strategies" (2004: 67). Although digital texts can appear as stable (albeit dematerialized) objects, our experiences of them depend on qualities specific to their physical encodings (and decodings).

6. Ellison, Steinfield, and Lampe, for example, describe diverse ways through which college students manage social relations both on and off Facebook in terms of "connection strategies," to emphasize the "overlapping nature of online and offline interactions" (2011: 876). Madianou and Miller (2013) coined the word "polymedia" to account for media environments in which people navigate (and generate) social relationships by switching between media modes and platforms, whether these be voice calls, videochat, Facebook updates, or direct messaging.

7. It is interesting to note how many of the latest popular platforms (such as Snapchat and Post Secret) revolve around secrecy, anonymity, and temporariness.

8. Not her real name. Names of research participants are also pseudonyms.

9. Berghain has received a good deal of sensationalist coverage in the U.S. media as well (see, for example, Rogers 2014).

Bibliography

Appadurai, Arjun. 1996. *Modernity at Large: Cultural Dimensions of Globalization.* Minneapolis: University of Minnesota Press.

Bateson, Gregory, and Margaret Mead. 1962. *Balinese Character: A Photographic Analysis.* Special Publications 2, 17–92. New York: New York Academy of Sciences. First published in 1942.

Blanchette, Jean-François. 2011. A Material History of Bits. *Journal of the American Society for Information Science and Technology* 62 (6): 1042–1057.

Boellstorff, Tom. 2012. Rethinking Digital Anthropology. In *Digital Anthropology*. Edited by Heather A. Horst and Daniel Miller, 39–60. London: Berg.

Borneman, John, and Stefan Senders. 2000. Politics Without a Head: Is the "Love Parade" a New Form of Political Identification? *Cultural Anthropology* 15 (2): 294–317.

boyd, danah. 2014. *It's Complicated.* New Haven, Conn.: Yale University Press.

———, and Nicole B. Ellison. 2008. Social Network Sites: Definition, History, and Scholarship. *Journal of Computer-Mediated Communication* 13 (1): 210–230.

Brady, Erika. 2002. Save, Save the Lore! In *The Anthropology of Media: a Reader*, edited by Kelly Askew and Richard R. Wilk, 56–72. Malden, Mass.: Blackwell.

Burrell, Jenna. 2009. The Field Site as a Network: A Strategy for Locating Ethnographic Research. *Field Methods* 21 (2): 181–199.

Clifford, James. 1990. Notes on (Field) Notes. In *Fieldnotes: The Makings of Anthropology*, edited by Roger Sanjek, 47–70. Ithaca, N.Y.: Cornell University Press.

DeNicola, Lane. 2012. Geomedia: The Reassertion of Space Within Digital Culture. In *Digital Anthropology*, edited by Heather A. Horst and Daniel Miller, 80–98. London: Berg.

Dourish, Paul, and Melissa Mazmanian. 2013. Media as Material: Information Representations as Material Foundations for Organizational Practice. In *How Matter Matters: Objects, Artifacts, and Materiality in Organization Studies*, edited by Paul R. Carlile, Davide Nicolini, Ann Langley, and Haridimos Tsoukas, 92–118. Oxford: Oxford University Press.

Edwards, Elizabeth. 1997. Beyond the Boundary: A Consideration of the Expressive in Photography and Anthropology. In *Rethinking Visual Anthropology*, edited by Howard Morphy and Marcus Banks, 1–26. New Haven, Conn.: Yale University Press.

Ellison, Nicole B., Charles Steinfield, and Cliff Lampe. 2007. The Benefits of Facebook "Friends": Social Capital and College Students' Use of Online Social Network Sites. *Journal of Computer-Mediated Communication* 12 (4): 1143–1168.

———. 2011. Connection Strategies: Social Capital Implications of Facebook-Enabled Communication Practices. *New Media and Society* 13 (6): 873–892.

Gupta, Akhil, and James Ferguson. 1992. Beyond "Culture": Space, Identity, and the Politics of Difference. *Cultural Anthropology* 7 (1): 6–23.

———. 1997. Ethnography at the End of an Era. In *Culture, Power, Place: Explorations in Critical Anthropology*, edited by Akhil Gupta and James Ferguson, 1–15. Durham, N.C.: Duke University Press.

Hayles, N. Katherine. 2004. Print Is Flat, Code Is Deep: The Importance of Media-Specific Analysis. *Poetics Today* 25 (1): 67–90.

Jackson, Jean E. 1990. "I Am a Fieldnote": Fieldnotes as a Symbol of Professional Identity. In *Fieldnotes: The Makings of Anthropology*, edited by Roger Sanjek, 3–33. Ithaca, N.Y.: Cornell University Press.

Kraemer, Jordan. 2012. Mobile Berlin: Social Media and the New Europe. Ph.D. diss., University of California, Irvine.

———. 2014. Friend or Freund: Social Media and Transnational Connections in Berlin. *Human-Computer Interaction* 29 (1): 53–77.

Lederman, Rena. 1990. Pretexts for Ethnography: On Reading Fieldnotes. In *Fieldnotes: The Makings of Anthropology*, edited by Roger Sanjek, 71–91. Ithaca, N.Y.: Cornell University Press.

Lévy, Pierre. 2001. *Cyberculture*. Translated by Robert Bononno. Minneapolis, Minn.: University of Minnesota Press.

Madianou, Mirca, and Daniel Miller. 2013. Polymedia: Towards a New Theory of Digital Media in Interpersonal Communication. *International Journal of Cultural Studies* 16 (2): 169–187.

Marcus, George E. 1995. Ethnography in/of the World System: The Emergence of Multi-Sited Ethnography. *Annual Review of Anthropology* 24 (1): 95–117.

Mead, Margaret. 1956. Some Uses of Still Photography in Culture and Personality Studies. In *Personal Character and Cultural Milieu*, edited by Douglas Gilbert Haring, 79–105. Syracuse, N.Y.: Syracuse University Press.

Miller, Daniel, and Heather Horst. 2012. The Digital and the Human: A Prospectus for Digital Anthropology. In *Digital Anthropology*, edited by Heather A. Horst and Daniel Miller, 3–35. New York: Berg.

Miller, Daniel, and Don Slater. 2000. *The Internet: An Ethnographic Approach*. Oxford: Berg.

Ottenberg, Simon. 1990. Thirty Years of Fieldnotes: Changing Relationships to the Text. In *Fieldnotes: The Makings of Anthropology*, edited by Roger Sanjek, 139–160. Ithaca, N.Y.: Cornell University Press.

Rapp, Tobias. 2009. *Lost and Sound*. Frankfurt am Main: Suhrkamp.

Rattenbury, Tye, Dawn Nafus, and Ken Anderson. 2008. Plastic: A Metaphor for Integrated Technologies. *Ubicomp'08*, 232–241. Seoul, Korea, September 21–24. http://dl.acm.org/citation.cfm?id = 1409635.

Rogers, Thomas. 2014. Berghain: The Secretive, Sex-Fueled World of Techno's Coolest Club. *Rolling Stone*, February 6. Accessed February 13, 2015. http://www.rollingstone.com/music/news/berghain-the-secretive-sex-fueled-world-of-technos-coolest-club-20140206.

Rosner, Daniela, Jean-François Blanchette, Leah Buechley, Paul Dourish, and Melissa Mazmanian. 2012. From Materials to Materiality: Connecting Practice and Theory in HCI. *CHI 2012*, 2787–2790. Austin, Texas, May 5–10. http://dl.acm.org/citation.cfm?id = 2207676.

Sanjek, Roger, editor. 1990a. *Fieldnotes: The Makings of Anthropology*. Ithaca, N.Y.: Cornell University Press.

———. 1990b. Preface to *Fieldnotes: The Makings of Anthropology*, edited by Roger Sanjek, xi–xviii. Ithaca, N.Y.: Cornell University Press.

———. 1990c. A Vocabulary for Fieldnotes. In *Fieldnotes: The Makings of Anthropology*, edited by Roger Sanjek, 92–121. Ithaca, N.Y.: Cornell University Press.

Tsing, Anna. 2005. *Friction: An Ethnography of Global Connection*. Princeton, N.J.: Princeton University Press.

Zhan, Mei. 2009. *Other-Worldly: Making Chinese Medicine Through Transnational Frames*. Durham, N.C.: Duke University Press.

Chapter 8

"Through a Screen Darkly": On Remote, Collaborative Fieldwork in the Digital Age

Jenna Burrell

In July 2012, I embarked on a methodological experiment, a six-month study of fisheries and mobile phone use in a series of towns and villages in north and south Kerala, India. To use the word "embarked" in this case is to employ the term purely as metaphor. My intention was to never board a plane or set foot on the sand of the Kerala coast. It was an experiment in remote ethnography and the new possibilities following from these two trends: (1) evolving ideas in ethnographic practice about the relationship between a social phenomenon and the space of its unfolding, and consequently where the ethnographer might legitimately locate him- or herself and (2) the global spread of networked technologies and the improving bandwidth quality and declining cost of connection, which have made ever more remote locales possible to access.

At the same time, my collaborator and co–principal investigator, Janaki Srinivasan, a 2011 Ph.D. from the University of California, Berkeley, School of Information, where I teach, embarked more literally to spend several months in the field. The experiment then, more modestly, was to gauge how closely I, as the remote collaborator, could come to the comprehensive understanding she would develop through her onsite immersion. I was to follow along with the fieldnotes and other documentation that she produced, practically in real time. This would also include multimedia fieldwork data—photos, short videos—all made available through a shared Dropbox folder.

A Long History of Sharing Fieldnotes

Reading and relying upon someone else's fieldnotes is not at all a new practice. As I have read about how others have approached the matter, such efforts seem often to be inspired by the need to grapple with and make the most of the limited resources (time, money) available to us. Such limits are determined by the institutions that support and govern our work. The transition from graduate student, poor in funds but rich in time, to faculty member, usually dealing with the reverse distribution, often leads to thoughts about whether it is possible to delegate fieldwork to others. At the same time, in light of what we learn as graduate students about the methods of ethnography and what defines its distinctive epistemological contributions, such a temptation is also likely to generate feelings of professional inauthenticity. Yet, as Sanjek notes, "The lone ethnographer designing, conducting, and writing up his or her own fieldwork adventure is mainly Malinowskian myth and post-1960s individual grant practice"; prior to this era, "fieldnotes were shared" (1990a: 329). Thus returning attention to collaboration and the sharing of fieldnotes is really rediscovering a practice with a long history. With this awareness, we can avoid reinventing the wheel.

New possibilities for remote participation in fieldwork seem to follow also from advances in communication technology—not merely the invention of the Internet, mobile phones, and other media and devices but the present-day reality of their global diffusion. In recent years, digital connectivity and improving data bandwidth capacities are almost ubiquitously available and relatively inexpensive (or at least to funded foreign researchers) in practically every corner of the world. Yet, having spent the bulk of my career studying such technologies and their appropriation within diverse cultural contexts, it is clear to me that a long view is necessary to guard against the common temptation to attribute unwarranted transformative, even revolutionary, change to new technologies (Burrell 2012b). Such technologies do not make participation in fieldwork from afar a brand-new possibility, but they do alter the research terrain in some way. Furthermore, the practice of attempting to engage with these new possibilities also makes clear the continuing complications and barriers to effective collaboration across distances and to relying upon another's fieldnotes and field materials, no matter how readily available and communicative that researcher is.

In *Fieldnotes: The Makings of Anthropology* (Sanjek 1990b), several contributors discussed using the fieldnotes of others and sharing their own
fieldnotes. In her informal survey of attitudes toward fieldnote writing, Jean
Jackson (1990) found that many anthropologists were reluctant to share.
Some were self-conscious about the inadequacy of their notes or about
being measured and judged by others based upon them. Christine Obbo
(1990) discussed the politics of sharing in light of cutthroat competition in
academia. I am willing to accept the charge of naiveté. I maintain faith in
my collaborator's positive intentions and focus here instead on the epistemological questions that arise when interpreting the notes of others, notes
that are inevitably interpretations themselves.

Reviewing what limited documentation there is of such efforts in *Fieldnotes* and other sources uncovers similar reflections about the challenges to
comprehension in third-party fieldnote reading. The circumstances of
doing so, in some cases, follow from the death of the original ethnographer
while in the field (sometimes from accident or disease), reflecting the often
extreme dedication and demands of this practice of physical immersion.
Generally, exercises in analysis and writing from third-party fieldnotes have
been cast along the lines of archival research, of reconstructing observations
from the past. The original author of the fieldnotes may no longer be living
and thus cannot be consulted (as in Nancy Lutkehaus's use of Camilla
Wedgwood's notes from a village on Manam, Papua New Guinea), and the
information about people and practices inscribed in the notes are frozen in
time within a recent or more distant past that cannot be returned to (Lutkehaus 1990).

One example that helps shed light on my attempt at collaboration from
afar is Robert J. Smith's (1990) account of working with Ella Lury Wiswell
to write *The Women of Suya Mura*, an account that relied upon Wiswell's
extensive fieldnotes produced in a Japanese village in 1935–1936. This was
a case in which the writer of the original fieldnotes was still living, and the
reader, Smith, never actually visited the site but relied entirely on Wiswell's
notes and on conversations with her to ultimately produce a published
ethnographic monograph. Still, the handling of the fieldnotes in this project
gave it the flavor of archival work, using the fieldnotes as a completed
corpus. This finiteness is underlined by Smith's description of the retrieval
of Wiswell's notes. They had been "stored in the attic of a friend's house in
New Haven" (Smith 1990: 359). Sitting there for some time, they awaited

an effort to analyze the raw fieldwork material and offer it to a wider audience.

A Novel Proposition

By characterizing these examples as a form of archival work, I have alluded to a new direction that such collaboration and sharing of fieldnotes might take in the present-day era of near ubiquitous connectivity and the capacity for immediate, inexpensive, and media-rich communication across great distances. The principle distinction between this prior work and my own was in Janaki's and my effort to realize a nearly simultaneous writing of fieldnotes by Janaki and their remote reading by me. As with other such collaborations, the fieldnotes themselves were only one component of the process. We also attempted a weekly Skype phone call while Janaki was in the field. In this way, I did not access the fieldnotes as a completed text but as something living and evolving that, through our synchronous communication, although I was located remotely, I had the unique opportunity to shape. Anyway, that was the idea. . . .

The reality of the situation was that a number of barriers beyond what I had initially envisioned interfered with my ability to establish the deep familiarity and mental index of people and place that I had hoped to realize. Yet there was also an unexpected value in this struggle. It helped me to understand something more about the nature of ethnographic practice and the fieldnotes that result. In particular, it provided an unanticipated education about the workings of embodiment and immersion on memory and cognition in fieldwork. My somewhat more conventional fieldwork experiences in the past (Burrell 2012a, 2012b) served as a point of comparison and aided in this emerging understanding. My attempt at reading and interpreting the fieldnotes of another pointed also to their inevitable incompleteness. In attempting to comprehend the notes of another, I found this easier to see and specify than when reading my own fieldnotes.

The Notions of the Fieldsite and of Immersion

I want briefly to step aside from considering the role of bodily immersion and sensory experience on memory and how the writing of fieldnotes relates to this. For a moment, it is worth considering also the matter of professional identity and fieldwork as a rite of passage. Formation of the professional self is not a frivolous concern. A cultural analyst who dismisses such "rites" among his or her own tribe is one who studies culture as external and exotic and fails to recognize its more immediate and personal relevance.

Ethnographers immerse themselves in the field through a process called "participant observation." This immersion is so "deep" that it involves not observation alone but also an attempt to experience a social world as members experience it (or as closely as possible to that) while the researcher still retains his or her outsider viewpoint and motivation to write fieldnotes and eventually bring the findings to a professional research community. This defines the uniqueness and the appeal for many of us of doing ethnographic work. So to delegate that immersion to someone else seems, on some level, to succumb to a compromised version of ethnographic practice.

Yet, these procedures of earning one's professional identity, as imparted to aspiring and novice ethnographers, have at times been confused, I will suggest, with a particular ontological notion of the social or cultural. This particular notion is that social phenomena unfold coherently in continuous Cartesian space: space that is unproblematic for us as participant observers to inhabit (beyond the usual access and acceptance issues faced by any outsider). To the extent that a proposed fieldwork site does not fit this criterion (does not unfold coherently and continuously, or does not offer a recognizable way for the participant observer to locate him- or herself), it may be deemed unsuitable for the practice of ethnography or, going even further, cast as not properly the site of the social or cultural.

To the extent that a professional rite—eighteen months solo in a geographically remote and culturally "strange" fieldsite—becomes confused with an ontological claim, it poses a limitation on more far-ranging and, I would argue, by now necessary developments toward advancing anthropological knowledge. I emphasize *by now* to refer to a set of disciplinary developments in anthropology and the expansion of ethnographic approaches into other disciplines, which have accomplished considerable groundwork to bring us to this point. I refer also to this transition to near ubiquitous connectivity (among other changes in the "global order") as producing new cultural formations that are as deserving of study and may richly reward those willing to take on the unconventional.

Pushing against and sometimes past the imposed limitations in what constitutes an appropriate fieldsite has been a major theme in work that defines or attempts virtual ethnography. This started with some early efforts—generally exploratory, chapter-length, or primarily methodological elaborations—that stopped short of the full-scale production of an ethnographic monograph (Hine 2000; Markham 1998; Paccagnella 1997; Taylor 1999). It has been built upon as a central concern in the latest wave of ground-breaking monographs in "unconventional" fieldsites, sometimes produced with an intentional mindfulness of placement within an anthropological genealogy, for example Tom Boellstorff's *Coming of Age in Second Life* (2008).

In another unconventionally sited ethnography, Gabriella Coleman's (2013) study of hacker culture in the United States, she points out that "participant observation" as a practice is undertheorized to begin with. The muddling of professional identity and career strategy with the choice of an epistemologically sound research venue is reflected in her account of arriving at a dissertation topic and seeking buy-in from advisors. As she recounts, she was warned by her, ultimately, very supportive advisors about employability and encouraged to consider a study of hacker culture as a *second* project. There were concerns about whether the subject matter was social or cultural enough, that "the very activity of computing (usually seen as an instrumental and solitary activity of pure rationality) could be subject only to thin, anemic cultural meanings" (5). There was a sense, then, that this population lacked the necessary "social milieu" for Coleman to locate herself within.

Efforts to establish the "virtual" spaces of the Internet and the domain of computing as legitimate subject matter raised questions about what being "in situ" really meant. The assumption that a person seated before a computer was necessarily doing something "solitary" was cast into doubt. Convincing efforts along these lines showed how participants in networked games such as World of Warcraft (Nardi 2010) and online worlds such as Second Life developed their own cultural codes and practices arising from the materially novel circumstances of digital existence. In such special cases, an ethnographer seated at the screen was as much a participant as anyone else, as all members of such worlds were similarly situated.

Granted, there is not quite a direct analogy from the ethnographer seated at home having a digitally mediated experience to a conventional physical social world such as the fishing villages of Kerala in India. However, such work functions as a bridge to broader thinking about the question of what it means to be "immersed" under circumstances where a conventional understanding of physical copresence is not applicable, where all members communicate and interact in some sense from afar. Likewise, efforts to carry out cultural analysis on many other topics, such as the urban, transnationalism, and global institutions that do not present fieldsites in neatly packaged, self-contained bounded spaces have generated further expansion of thinking (see especially Hannerz 1992; Marcus 1998; Trouillot 2003).

Still, this expansion of thinking should not mean that we start to treat immersion and being physically present in the fieldsite (as understood in more conventional terms) as merely an obsolete and unnecessary symbolic gesture. There is another aspect of "being there" that defines and underpins the epistemological logic of ethnographic practice, namely as a logic of discovery in the field. This entails the first of a two-phase science, the phase we as ethnographers favor—the "imaginative logic of discovery"—rather than its successor—the "harsh discipline of proof" (Taussig 2011: xi). This requires improvisation in situ, not a protocol entirely thought out in advance. It is critical to the principles of inductive analysis and of iteration upon an emerging understanding.

Without the ethnographer being in situ, physically there to hear and observe firsthand and respond flexibly, how can he or she pursue this necessary improvisation? For many years, this is what made me reluctant to forgo immersive fieldwork and leave it to research collaborators. The element of recurrent and real-time communication with Janaki while she was in the field was an attempt to explore the possibility of contributing to this improvisation and thus maintain the legitimacy of my role as a researcher on the project.

Where the New Networked Technologies Might Take Our Fieldwork Practices

Given recent efforts to stretch the definition of fieldsites beyond bounded spaces and the increasingly high-quality connections that link one corner of the globe to another, has the time arrived when we might in some sense *do* fieldwork without immersion? Is it possible to approximate this immersion experience with the right real-time updates, multimedia data captures, and network technologies? In discussing, from here on, my own mixed experience attempting such a feat, I offer a roughly chronological recollection of the Kerala fieldwork as it unfolded, as reflected from my remote position.

The work began very promisingly. Less than two weeks after Janaki's arrival in Kerala, we had our first Skype phone conversation from the field. Her notes had also started appearing in a shared Dropbox folder. At our first check-in call, there were only three files (one for each day of fieldwork), as Janaki was becoming situated in the field. Images also soon appeared, sorted into folders by date and labeled by location or event. But these folders were kept separate in the file structure from the unfolding flow of chronological fieldnotes, and as simple as it may seem, this separation of textual fieldnotes and images was a practice that made my efforts to conceptualize the field more difficult.

At first, the notes were limited enough that I could keep up with them. Janaki spent the first few days talking to "experts" who were able to narrate at a general level the history of the fishing community and its major events and issues. As the notes began to pile up more quickly, and as Janaki moved on to the actual beach landing sites, the diversity of fieldwork locales and types of people spoken with increased, and so did my confusion. The volume of details grew, along with a dawning awareness of the complexity of roles and practices in the fishing industry. Inevitably, as is generally the case in ethnographic fieldwork, interviewees started to say things that seemed to contradict what others said. I began to create comment boxes (a feature provided in Microsoft Word) in the margins of Janaki's fieldnotes (see Figure 8.1). Looking back, my comments referred mostly to baseline information and thoughts from two sources: background reading on our research topic, and my own fieldwork in fishing communities in Uganda.

Our decision to conduct fieldwork at this site in India stemmed from a study by an economist about information flows in the fishing sector using mobile phones and their effect on market efficiency (Jensen 2007). That study took place in some beach landing sites in northern Kerala that Janaki later visited. At first, cross-referencing the economist's precise model with the actual, messy fieldsite as Janaki experienced it turned up contradictions and more confusion, especially as we tried to compare her ethnographic work in south Kerala with a model using data collected in north Kerala.

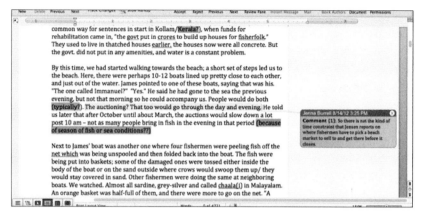

Figure 8.1. Janaki Srinivasan's fieldnotes with Jenna Burrell's comment. Used with permission of Janaki Srinivasan. Screenshot by Jenna Burrell.

This cross-referencing, however, turned out to be a useful way of preliminarily organizing her observations. In retrospect, I can see how critical were these three initial anchor points—the economist's study, my vivid recall of fishing in Uganda based on immersive fieldwork, my efforts at synthesis and at making sense afterward—to us being able to engage with and find a path into the fieldnotes.

Fieldwork and the Value of Sequestering Time

It was only three weeks into the fieldwork that my fall semester started and I was called back to the frenzied pace of prepping for the class I was teaching (on fieldwork methods), advising students, and reconnecting with the department after the summer break. By that time, Janaki and I had had a second Skype phone call to confer. Unsurprisingly, perhaps, I then started to fall behind on reading the fieldnotes as they arrived, and the notes themselves were written up more sporadically through the rest of August and during September.

We managed to continue our Skype check-in calls, one on September 9 and another on September 25. In these calls, Janaki attempted to offer a compressed summary of her comings and goings and a bird's-eye view of the fishing industry, of how mobile phones (and other technologies) were a factor in fishing itself as well as the trade in fish, and of how things overall related to our expectations. Besides cross-checking the conclusions of the economist's study (which focused on fish prices and marketing practices), our attention was drawn more broadly to the history of religious conflict in the south, the role of the Catholic church as tax collector, changes in fishing equipment over the years, ocean topography, weather and seasonal factors, and the widespread use of GPS devices, along with other wide-ranging topics introduced by the fishers and others in the fish supply chain and given importance in their conversations. We spent our periodic Skype conversations untangling these complexities.

Reading the fieldnotes (if only rapidly and incompletely) raised many questions, but only a few seemed relevant to Janaki's further lines of inquiry in the field. Both I and our third collaborator, Richa Kumar of the India Institute of Technology in Delhi, who also joined the Skype calls, only modestly shaped the fieldwork from afar. As our emerging and now more focused attention to fishing industry roles, investment structures, money flows, and auctioning practices threatened to overwhelm the study with greater complexity, I reminded the rest of the team that it was our interest in the mobile phone that distinguished our efforts from those of other scholars who had done considerable work to map fish supply chains and document fisher union organizing and local protests against foreign trawlers.

In the process of falling behind, I began to grasp how critical my being physically away was to the practice of doing fieldwork and, specifically, how important being away from my office and my department at the university was. I realized I needed to sequester my time and retreat from other demands in order to process complex field observations and experiences. In the past, emphasizing my unavailability while doing fieldwork had always helped to block off competing demands. My "out of office" email message informed others that I was somewhere far flung, with "unreliable access to email," often belying the truth of my generally continual connectivity in this day and age. However, when intimately involved in remote fieldwork in Kerala, India, but spatially located in Berkeley, California, the ongoing obligations to the place where I am physically present cannot be so easily avoided.

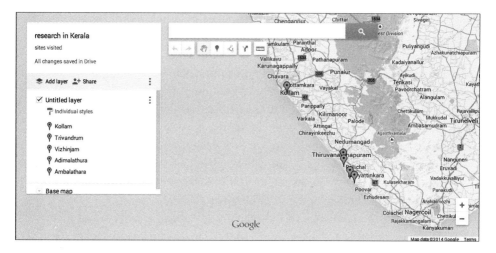

Figure 8.2. Google Map of the Kerala coast. Screenshot by Jenna Burrell.

Sense of Place and Sense of Time

Five weeks into the fieldwork period, I sat down to study the accumulated fieldnotes with more dedicated focus and greater concentration. This effort was motivated by an upcoming Skype call with Janaki—in other words, a deadline to prepare for. Reading the notes, I found that what I was struggling with were the proper nouns: visualizing and remembering the specific people spoken with and the places visited. I turned to the archive of photos in our Dropbox folder and also to Google Maps to do some cross-referencing. I used a Google Map feature to place markers on locations visited (see Figure 8.2), and then I set a search for travel directions between Kollam and Vizhinjam, calculating the distance between these two fishing villages at eighty kilometers. In the process, I tried to imagine the state of the roads and the kind of travel it would involve. The maps, of course, were not a stand-in for first-person immersion and observation. They offered something entirely different from a visual awareness obtained through "being there"—a virtual view possible only from high above the ground, one perhaps even created by satellite.

Turning to the photos that Janaki, with her first-person view, had captured and shared, I found they integrated within their frames great quantities of detail that were not reflected in the fieldnotes. They offered a

Figure 8.3. Vizhinjam shoreline: photo taken from Catholic church.
Photograph by Janaki Srinivasan and used with her permission.

memorable sense of the dense shoreline in the village of Vizhinjam (see
Figure 8.3), thick with boats, fishermen, auctioneers, and fish. Looking at
the photos, I could get glimpses of scenes illustrating the types of objects,
persons, and activities coexisting in space: for example, the size and quantity of fish and how they are handled, the gender composition of the
crowds, clothing styles, implements, and boat sizes. I was intrigued by the
sarong styles of men, worn mostly short above the knee but sometimes long
and nearly touching the ground. From Janaki's photos, I also grasped better
the significance and singular influence of the Catholic church in some
southern Kerala villages, seeing the pristine white church of Vizhinjam and
a photographic view taken from its tower (Figure 8.3). From this very highest point in the area, there was a panoptic, 360-degree view of the entire
village below.

This inspired another effort at cross-referencing. I wanted a view of the
church from a distance, not looking out from it (as in Figure 8.3), to see

where it was located relative to the beach. I went onto Flickr, the photo-sharing site, and searched for the village name "Vizhinjam" and "church." I was stunned to find what I was looking for immediately, a photo by a user named Trailblazing Tomtom, taken in February 2012 (available here: https://www.flickr.com/photos/trailblazingtomtom/8293943082/), that gave me exactly the perspective that was not available in our own fieldwork photos.

Just as over the years I have found that transcribing audio interview files myself helps to structure and focus my engagement with my fieldwork, this work of tracing locations on the map and studying photos was intended to help me do the same. Reflecting a similar dilemma, Robert J. Smith noted, "The more deeply I got into the journal [of ethnographer Ella Wiswell], the more completely at sea, I felt" (1990: 363). Seeking to bring into prominence the people named in the accounts in her journal, and overwhelmed by Wiswell's well-assimilated familiarity with background information and inconsistent use of names and nicknames, as well as her own distinct authorial voice, he set himself the task of retyping passages verbatim.

Despite the multimedia and multiperspective visuals from our Kerala fieldsite and despite my cross-referencing tasks, I still could not quite envision fully the layout of a fishing village, could not piece the sequence of photos together to map out the space in the same way as I do automatically when I look at my own photos from stints of more traditional immersive fieldwork. What neither the photos nor Google Maps could offer, moreover, was a more navigational and three-dimensional sense of place. With the photos and fieldnotes I had produced through my own physically immersive fieldwork in Uganda, I can effortlessly recall what was to the left or the right or what was behind me, even without deliberately thinking about it. In trying to absorb the moorings of someone else's (here Janaki's) fieldwork, still images can seem quite limited, cropping out all but what fits in a rectangular frame.

Hand-in-hand with this incompleteness of the visual record and, consequently, the patchiness of my visual comprehension of the sites Janaki visited in Kerala, there was also the problem of how fieldnotes compress and abbreviate the temporal span of fieldwork. As much as there might be an efficiency to reading in a short period fieldnotes that took weeks of lived experience to generate, it comes at a cost. The temporal rhythm of fieldwork is difficult to replicate in fieldnotes: the periods of sitting around or of

Figure 8.4. Fish auction, northern Kerala. From video by Janaki Srinivasan and used with her permission.

traveling in different kinds of vehicles versus the periods of intense activity. Fieldnotes do not provide a metronomic gauge of the hours of the day. Rather, their quantity seems to correlate with or provide a measure of the intensity of research activities. A key event, one with a great deal of observed interaction or a breakthrough experience of cultural illumination, might last only an hour or so yet still generate pages and pages of fieldnotes.

On documenting (and, for me, reconstructing) this temporal dimension, one technological advance that I have found surprisingly useful in my own fieldwork is a now readily available, and rather inexpensive, small and unobtrusive digital camera with large data storage capacity, one that can easily switch between still photo and video modes. It is now an essential in my fieldwork kit and was part of Janaki's as well.

Along with the still photos she captured, Janaki placed, without specific commentary, a few short videos in our shared Dropbox folder. One video featured the repetitive monotone of an auctioneer trying to sell several lots of fish ordered by size and carefully laid out in rows and columns (see Figure 8.4). A few men walking by carefully stepped around the fish, which were laid out on the sand in the confined area of the busy landing site. Potential buyers leisurely stood around nearby. To my novice's eyes and ears, the fish did not appear to be sold or even bargained for during the one minute and twenty second clip.

Later, when we began to write up the project results, this video became significant. It illustrated the tempo of fish auctioning in northern Kerala and differed from a similar video Janaki captured in southern Kerala, where the auctioning, as I came to understand, was much more frenetic. The first video ultimately became intelligible and memorable as an example of the much larger scale of trade in the north, where huge quantities were purchased by fewer buyers and with larger price increments between each auctioning step. This was the opposite of the tempo and scale in southern Kerala fish auctions. In this example, temporal rhythms could be captured very effectively. The particular camera equipment we employed, however, was limited by memory and battery constraints that afforded only short, one-minute video clips.

Reflecting on How Physical Immersion Solidifies Memory

The bodily experience of immersive fieldwork is captured through multiple senses. Although individual senses, especially sight and hearing, may alternately dominate, they always operate in parallel. Experiencing the fieldsite virtually through the mediation of various screens and through the disaggregating effect of different formats, I felt powerfully the loss of this sensory simultaneity. As I assembled it from fragments, Janaki's fieldwork presented me with a struggle. Besides the more obvious modes of sight and hearing, there was the loss of the kinesthetic sense of one's body moving through space, of one's eyes gazing back and forth across a broad scene and in this way internalizing a three-dimensional memory of a space. An interview involves observing the animated movement of the speaker at the same time one is listening to and decoding his or her words. These aspects of the speaker may not be possible (or, at least, not easy) to consciously observe so that they become inscribed in one's fieldnotes but nonetheless still reside in one's memory. From this, a recall of the person, of their experienced essence, helps to secure that mental index that is so necessary to call upon in *analyzing* fieldnotes. The absence of this is what I identified as the source, in part, of my problem with retaining the proper nouns in Janaki's notes and particularly in identifying recurring characters.

Immersion plays numerous roles in ethnographic practice. Perhaps least widely appreciated are the roles immersion and an actively embodied and kinesthetic sensibility play in securing memory. It is this struggle with memory that was the most significant part of my difficulty in participating in fieldwork remotely. The archive of fieldnotes and other field materials is critically important in memory work, and fieldnote writing is carried out for this very purpose. Geertz describes how the ethnographer "'inscribes' social discourse; he writes it down. In so doing, he turns it from a passing event, which exists only in its own moment of occurrence, into an account, which exists in its inscriptions and can be reconsulted" (1973: 19).

On first glance, the purpose of writing fieldnotes is to make up for the weakness of our own memories, not only of the ephemerality of events unfolding in the world but of our inability to recall them without external prompting. However, it is clear that these materials inscribed or collected in the field do not accomplish this by being totally and utterly complete. They do not, at the end of the day, encompass all of the data used in analysis. Instead, they continually serve their author as memory jogs. Inscribed fieldnotes are an index to "headnotes," as Simon Ottenberg terms them in *Fieldnotes* (Ottenberg 1990). The written notes help to recreate and re-enliven the original fieldnote writer's recall of things not written—the headnotes—things that become relevant and are recovered and remembered long after the event is impossible to comprehend without them. Consequently, reading the fieldnotes of someone else is to do so with the major handicap of being without access to headnotes.

To realize this, in part through this difficult experience of reading someone else's fieldnotes, was an immense relief. For a long time, in my own conventional practice of writing my fieldnotes during immersive fieldwork stints and analyzing them later, I felt guilty whenever I drew from something that was not specifically documented in the notes. I thought this was evidence of my failure to be complete, of my laziness in fieldnote writing. Now, in reading these notes of another, I saw rather the impossibility of completeness; I understood the many kinds of things that are so difficult to inscribe, perhaps to some extent because our memories are poor, but also because, as powerful as it is, language has limits. The value of the fieldnotes is partly in their explicit contents but also in what they unlock in the fieldworker's memory.

Relying on the fieldnotes of another placed me a layer removed from the experience of immersion, so the component of dialogue proved essential for reaching a minimal point of intelligibility and an ordering of the fieldwork results that I could remember and grapple with. While Janaki was in the field, our ongoing conversations on Skype proved most useful in my efforts to capture the fieldsite in my mind. Such conversations had at least two purposes: for Janaki to help me assemble an understanding of the fieldsite and its complicated social worlds and for me to offer another mind, another interpretive perspective that might shape future fieldwork in Kerala. In practice, our dialogue seemed weighted toward the former purpose, as the Skype calls were perhaps too infrequent, and I was generally too confused to be able to offer much toward the future course of the fieldwork, such as the selection of new sites and people to talk to or questions arising from on-site observations. This would have required a better semblance of understanding and a tighter cycle of absorbing and responding than our too-brief, twice-weekly calls probably allowed.

In reflecting on the historical cases of shared fieldnotes recounted in *Fieldnotes*, although these at first seem to be studies conducted from "completed" archival sources, the ethnographer/archivist in fact always brought an indispensable component of dialogue into the mix. For Nancy Lutkehaus, who used Camilla Wedgwood's posthumous notes from 1933 to 1934, her visit in 1978 to the Papua New Guinea village where the notes were written allowed Lutkehaus to restart a dialogue with some of the very same people depicted in Wedgwood's notes. For Robert J. Smith, writing *The Women of Suya Mura* involved lengthy conversations with the original author of the fieldnotes, Ella Lury Wiswell, and, ultimately, her coauthorship of the resulting ethnographic monograph.

Dialogue is also identified explicitly as a critical feature of ethnographic practice in an account by Solon Kimball and William Partridge of the latter's fifteen-month period of studying "the social place and cultural meaning of marijuana in a community in Colombia" (Kimball and Partridge 1979: 11). Partridge was Kimball's student, and they maintained unusually frequent written communication throughout Partridge's fieldwork sojourn. They noted several forms of dialogue, including that between fieldworker and informants but also that between fieldworker and advisor and other colleagues, all of them important to the "intellectual ferment which adds knowledge and shapes theory" (ix).

In our case, my role was not one in which I was strictly an advisor, a voice of experience to a novice fieldworker, but rather that of a colleague. I dedicated considerable time to our shared fieldwork library of readings, referencing relevant passages and details from the articles that we had collected for the project. My collegial role was to continue to mull over the ways that Janaki's fieldwork tied back to the external audience and the existing body of scholarship to which we might hopefully contribute. Although I can identify the value of dialogue from *my* perspective—of gaining a firmer grip on the fieldsite and a basic understanding of how things unfolded there—perhaps the question might be raised of whether Janaki gained as much from the time spent overcoming my confusion from afar on points that had become quite clear to her.

Conclusion: A Failed Experiment?

A multitude of tools may be used by the fieldworkers of today to document and share snippets of their immersive experiences, and these can be channeled immediately to research collaborators participating anywhere. Yet the processes of data collection according to multiple technological *formats* effect a *dis*-integration of visual, audio, tactile, artifactual, and textual dimensions. Photos, videos, and inscribed notes separate into different modalities what was, for the fieldworker, an experience that seamlessly integrated the various senses. The remote colleague must attempt from these formats and modalities to reassemble these dimensions, but with the disadvantage of even more missing pieces. As I have discussed, there is a kinesthetic sense of orientation and direction, a sense of the temporal and a sense of scale and distance not easily categorized into one of the familiar five senses, which seems to somehow still evade capture by any of the newer technologies of enhanced documentation. It is not, on reflection, that this kinesthetic sense perhaps generates some unique data that remains missing from the record but that it is in some way what holds the whole fieldwork experience together.

Today, participating remotely in fieldwork is usually to experience the fieldsite as mediated by different software interfaces and through a series of screens. Increasing global connectivity adds the possibility of a dialogue between those immersed in fieldwork and those participating from afar, a dialogue that can be more tightly interwoven with the fieldwork process. This was something approximated in the past through a slower, more sparse exchange of letters via the postal system. Yet despite the new immediacy of connectivity today, there is still somewhat of a lagging element in these cycles of conversation. Generally, they require fieldworkers to exit the immersive experience and direct their attention, time, and energy toward explanation to another person. This can be a distraction; it is not like having a collaborator standing at your side in the field, sharing the experience.

The promise of enhanced video presence, new wearable technologies, and more massive storage capabilities has been touted for decades within the high-tech sector as the ultimate realization of the total capture of life experience, in real time, from a first-person perspective . . . an instantly accessible archive of "being there." In some small ways, this has already happened. I regularly see bicycle commuters, for example, with video cameras mounted on their helmets, presumably to capture bad driving behavior that threatens their safety.

So, in place of an admittedly incomplete text, what if we had a complete video record of all observations from a period of fieldwork? This is a real question raised predictably once a year by a student in my fieldwork methods class. Isn't this the ultimate solution—something that will inevitably be realized, and probably soon?

I argue in response that as much as we strive to be complete in our fieldnote writing, to inscribe observations or experiences that we may not as yet anticipate will be important to our later analysis, in their incompleteness, fieldnotes helpfully condense and organize the ambiguous and disorderly firsthand experiences of the stranger in a new social milieu. The vision of total experiential capture is also problematic, because it is fundamentally unidirectional; it does not allow for the participation or disruption of questioning and dialogue that helps us to relate observation to meaning. Such "total" capture, moreover, is not really total (at least in its most recent proposed versions). It must conform to existing formats; it does not integrate all of the senses, particularly those quasi-senses of movement and bodily positioning in space.

Still, the massive and expanding archives (such as Google Maps and Flickr) now publicly available on the Internet do seem to already serve as a kind of panoptic eye on the world. I continue to find it astounding that, in a few seconds, using just a two-word search, I could pull up an image from a particular angle of a specific church in a small Kerala village. Yet the vast gulf between observation and meaning remains. The technological tools help us work around and grapple with a research role that does not entail fieldwork immersion, but they are still not, nor are they likely to be, sufficient to supplant the need for and value of that immersion both for securing memory and for arriving at meaning.

Bibliography

Boellstorff, Tom. 2008. *Coming of Age in Second Life: An Anthropologist Explores the Virtually Human*. Princeton, N.J.: Princeton University Press.

Burrell, Jenna. 2012a. *Invisible Users: Youth in the Internet Cafés of Urban Ghana*. Cambridge, Mass.: MIT Press.

———. 2012b. Technology Hype Versus Enduring Uses: A Longitudinal Study of Internet Use Among Early Adopters in an African City. *First Monday* 17 (6). Accessed February 15, 2015. http://firstmonday.org/ojs/index.php/fm/article/view/3964/3263.

Coleman, E. Gabriella. 2013. *Coding Freedom: The Ethics and Aesthetics of Hacking*. Princeton, N.J.: Princeton University Press.

Geertz, Clifford. 1973. *The Interpretation of Cultures: Selected Essays*. New York: Basic Books.

Hannerz, Ulf. 1992. *Cultural Complexity: Studies in the Social Organization of Meaning*. New York: Columbia University Press.

Hine, Christine. 2000. *Virtual Ethnography*. London: Sage.

Jackson, Jean. 1990. "I Am a Fieldnote": Fieldnotes as a Symbol of Professional Identity. In *Fieldnotes: The Makings of Anthropology*, edited by Roger Sanjek, 3–33. Ithaca, N.Y.: Cornell University Press.

Jensen, Robert. 2007. The Digital Provide: Information (Technology), Market Performance, and Welfare in the South Indian Fisheries Sector. *The Quarterly Journal of Economics* 122 (3): 879–924.

Kimball, Solon, and William Partridge. 1979. *The Craft of Community Study: Fieldwork Dialogues*. Gainesville: University Presses of Florida.

Lutkehaus, Nancy. 1990. Refractions of Reality: On the Use of Other Ethnographers' Fieldnotes. In *Fieldnotes: The Makings of Anthropology*, edited by Roger Sanjek, 303–323. Ithaca, N.Y.: Cornell University Press.

Marcus, George E. 1998. *Ethnography Through Thick and Thin*. Princeton, N.J.: Princeton University Press.

Markham, Annette. 1998. *Life Online: Researching Real Experience in Virtual Space*. London: Sage.

Nardi, Bonnie. 2010. *My Life as a Night Elf Priest: An Anthropological Account of World of Warcraft*. Ann Arbor: University of Michigan Press.

Obbo, Christine. 1990. Adventures with Fieldnotes. In *Fieldnotes: The Makings of Anthropology*, edited by Roger Sanjek, 290–302. Ithaca, N.Y.: Cornell University Press.

Ottenberg, Simon. 1990. Thirty Years of Fieldnotes: Changing Relationships to the Text. In *Fieldnotes: The Makings of Anthropology*, edited by Roger Sanjek, 139–160. Ithaca, N.Y.: Cornell University Press.

Paccagnella, Luciano. 1997. Getting the Seats of Your Pants Dirty: Strategies for Ethnographic Research on Virtual Communities. *Journal of Computer-Mediated*

Communication 3 (1). Accessed February 15, 2015. http://onlinelibrary.wiley.com/doi/10.1111/j.1083-6101.1997.tb000 65.x/full.

Sanjek, Roger. 1990a. Fieldnotes and Others. In *Fieldnotes: The Makings of Anthropology*, edited by Roger Sanjek, 324–340. Ithaca, N.Y.: Cornell University Press.

———, editor. 1990b. *Fieldnotes: The Makings of Anthropology*. Ithaca, N.Y.: Cornell University Press.

Smith, Robert J. 1990. Hearing Voices, Joining the Chorus: Appropriating Someone Else's Fieldnotes. In *Fieldnotes: The Makings of Anthropology*, edited by Roger Sanjek, 356–370. Ithaca, N.Y.: Cornell University Press.

Taussig, Michael. 2011. *I Swear I Saw This: Drawings in Fieldwork Notebooks, Namely My Own*. Chicago: University of Chicago Press.

Taylor, T. L. 1999. Life in Virtual Worlds: Plural Existence, Multimodalities, and Other Online Research Challenges. *American Behavioral Scientist* 43 (3): 436–449.

Trouillot, Michel-Rolph. 2003. *Global Transformations: Anthropology and the Modern World*. New York: Palgrave Macmillan.

Chapter 9

Being in Fieldwork: Collaboration, Digital Media, and Ethnographic Practice

Heather A. Horst

The growth of interest in a range of new digital phenomena and terrains has expanded, provoking questioning, challenging, and redefinition of the possibilities and parameters for ethnographic practice and, especially, the practice of fieldwork. One of the central tenets of recent reflections on ethnography (especially anthropologically informed ethnographic practice) is the commitment to the rigor of the experience of "being in fieldwork" through participation in the worlds and milieux of research participants. As Sherry Ortner (1995) and a range of others have acknowledged in different forms and fashions, the "self as an instrument of knowing" remains a key tenet in anthropological fieldwork. Indeed, fieldwork in anthropology involves embodied forms of knowing and knowledge production and, in Konstantinos Retsikas's words, "the deployment of the fieldworker's body as a living, physical, sensing, and experiencing agent enmeshed in practical and intimate encounter" (2008: 127) within a range of spaces and places. This experiential and immersive commitment to engagement is often what sets anthropological ethnography apart from other disciplines and approaches. Yet, many of these theories of "being in fieldwork" hinge upon a single ethnographer or anthropologist as the center of the encounter.

As feminist anthropology and the reflexive turn in anthropology highlighted extensively in the 1990s, collaboration has always been part of ethnography, especially through our relationships with research assistants, participants, and "key informants," whose contributions often remain invisible to the final productions for a series of reasons, ranging from issues of privacy to exploitation (Sanjek 2014). Indeed, feminist ethnography has grappled with attempts to experiment with engaging research participants in writing and representing in ethnographic texts that explicitly seek to acknowledge the co-constitution and coproduction of knowledge in the field (Behar 1993). Yet such collaborations represent only one example of the different practices and patterns of collaboration in anthropology and its consequences for knowledge production.

This chapter explores the negotiations inherent in knowledge production and forms of "knowing" in collaborative, distributed, and interdisciplinary projects that privilege ethnography as an epistemological and methodological approach to knowing. More specifically, it explores the relationships between "traditional" forms of knowing and knowledge production and the processes of "being in fieldwork" in contemporary anthropology's complex and dynamic research environment, which is increasingly mediated through digital technologies, spaces, places, and artifacts (Horst and Miller 2012). Drawing from my participation on three ethnographic collaborations over the last decade, I reflect upon a shift from personalized, private experiences of fieldwork, wherein the individual self is the primary instrument of knowing, to a decentered self by which knowledge is constructed through different forms of interaction and mediated in and through digital interfaces and technology. I conclude with a brief discussion of the challenges of each mode of mediation and collaboration.

Digital Technology, Mediations, and Remediation

From the introduction of audio recorders, cameras, video recorders, and the laptop, technology has always been a part of the anthropological research endeavor, mediating our relationships, our memories, and the very construction of "the field" as a place, site, or network (Burrell 2009). Largely viewed as tools that facilitate and aid the process of fieldwork and the writing of ethnographic monographs, new digital media and technologies have spurred a range of debates about their roles in ethnographic research, both as objects of inquiry and as tools or techniques for research. Early work on newsgroups and online communities experimented with new forms of participation that considered the implications of conducting "virtual" or "online" ethnography, particularly efforts to respect the integrity of the endogenous categories of participants in these worlds (Hine 2000).

Early theorizing of "online" and "virtual worlds" often stressed the potential immateriality of the body for researchers who were imagined to carry out research from the "convenient" vantage point of their homes and offices. In addition to negating the corporeal dimensions of this process (eyestrain, neck and wrist pain, and other side effects), more recent work has returned our attention to the importance of the researcher's body and the experience of embodiment within our fieldwork experience. Boellstorff, for example, reveals how the research avatar in Second Life is the "locus of perception and sociality," one that cannot be understood as disembodied or disconnected from everyday practice or ways of knowing; moreover, he stresses the importance of context in understanding the role of the body while "being in fieldwork," noting that "virtual embodiment is always embodiment in a virtual place, and that this placeness of virtual worlds holds foundational implications for online corporeality" (2011: 510; see also Boellstorff 2008).

In a number of the collaborative ethnographic projects I have been engaged in over the past decade, we have developed mechanisms for creating and retaining embodied forms of knowing through perception and sociality, often through digital media and technology. During our research on the use of mobile phones among low-income Jamaicans in 2004 (Horst and Miller 2006), we used digital media and technology (particularly the Internet) to facilitate the four Ts—tours, time (or temporality), translations, and texts—that structure collaborative, ethnographic research.

To illustrate, Daniel Miller and I began our research together in rural Jamaica in January 2004. Because I had been living in and visiting this area of rural Jamaica for a decade, our household questionnaires utilized *tours* of local sites and key people. After this first visit, Miller came to Jamaica two additional *times* during the middle and end of the fieldwork, during which we developed a practice of coproducing fieldnotes via audio recording our immediate notes and reactions to interviews and other interactions; these supplemented our individual fieldnotes. We also started a process of "downloading" and, in effect, *translating* and archiving my experiences in Jamaica prior to the fieldwork period. Translation also involved extensive discussions on the differences between Jamaica and Trinidad, where Miller has carried out research (see Miller and Slater 2000).

Between Miller's visits (in January, July, and December 2004), we continued, through email, to circulate *texts*, such as fieldnotes, interview transcripts, and regulatory reports accessed in the United Kingdom. During the later visits, we continued to carry out tours to introduce Miller to key people and places that he had read about in my fieldnotes, transcribed conversations, and summaries. Through these techniques, Miller was able to attain a sense of "being in fieldwork" via the different modalities through which he was introduced to and came to know particular places, people, and events. As with other forms of episodic fieldwork (Postill 2011; Whyte 2013),[1] the structured process of phasing the research, engaging in a process of translation, and developing "tours" enhanced my own efforts to articulate and translate ideas, thoughts, and experiences.

A dramatic change in the accessibility and affordability of digital media technology occurred in the five years between the research on mobile phones in Jamaica and a new project on mobile phones that I began with Erin Taylor in 2010, which expanded the use of digital media and technology as a form of mediation for "being in fieldwork." The project was designed[2] to explore the impact of the changing telecommunications landscape for Haitian migrants living in the Haiti–Dominican Republic border zone who have access to two different telecommunications networks.

As with my previous research with Miller, Taylor and I utilized the four Ts to structure our research collaboration. In this case, however, I was the distant self who was experiencing "being in fieldwork" through multiple mediations. For example, throughout the research, I was able to use Skype (audio only) during fieldwork to call Taylor's local mobile in the Dominican Republic, usually every day or every other day in the evening. This also meant that I could sensorially experience "being in the field" through sound and other background noises and could listen to and discuss her daily activities and events, often prior to Taylor's writing of fieldnotes. This process, which occurred during the critical early phases of fieldwork, enabled us to identify, in close to synchronous *time*, new questions and themes and to draw comparisons with places and experiences from my previous fieldwork on mobile phones in Jamaica and from Taylor's knowledge of the urban Dominican Republic (instances of *translation*). She also uploaded photographs and videos while in the field, which we discussed and exchanged notes about during her fieldwork (examples of *text*). During the time I was situated geographically in the field in 2012, while conducting our portable kit study (Horst and Taylor 2014), Taylor took me on a *tour* of the field as she had constructed it, introducing me to places and people I had read about in fieldnotes, observed in pictures, or heard in the background on our Skype calls. Together, the tours, translations, texts, and the temporal dimensions of our research became a way through which I came to "know" the field through a variety of mediations.[3]

In these two, relatively small, research "teams," which consisted of two core people with a shared (although sometimes different) understanding of anthropological forms of ethnography, collaborative research continued to privilege the ethnographic mode of knowing through the self (or, more precisely, two selves) as an embodied form of knowledge production, one that in the face of geographic distance can be mediated by digital devices and technology. These engagements situated digital media and technology as channels through which a distant fieldworker comes to know and maintain relationships with "the field," as well as with the other researcher who directly constructs the field. In essence, digital media and technology become a form of mediation.

Yet "being in fieldwork" through digital media and technology is also a form of remediation. As Bolter and Grusin observe, "What is new about new media is therefore also old and familiar: that they promise the new by remediating what has gone before" (2000: 14). Here, older, face-to-face practices of both collaboration and "being in fieldwork" are being reshaped and represented by new practices in different forms. This presents the possibility of extending and, in the case of social media, even amplifying "being in fieldwork" as people move across different spaces and platforms (Postill and Pink 2012). However, as others in this volume note (in particular, Burrell, Chapter 8), the use of digital media and technology as proxies for physical and sensory colocation present challenges for the realization of "knowing" in the classic sense of "being in fieldwork" epitomized by such figures as Malinowski and Geertz.

Knowing Beyond the Self

In the previous section, I focused upon the ways in which digital media and technology present anthropologists and other ethnographers with possibilities for mediated forms of collaboration, particularly from a distance, that are attuned to a more traditional sense of "being in fieldwork" in anthropology. Although these issues remain pertinent to the emergent practices of anthropology, a raft of new research endeavors has emerged that often includes interdisciplinary teams, "audiences" for research outside of the discipline of anthropology (and/or academia generally), and an interest in comparison and contextualization on a broader scale. Although, arguably, applied anthropologists and others in fields such as science studies (Barry, Born, and Weszkalnys 2008; Suchman et al. 1999) have engaged in nontraditional forms of collaboration for some time, there is a growing recognition of "the imperative and impulse to collaborate," as George Marcus (2012: 433) characterizes this shift. Referring to these collaborative "third spaces" (Fischer 2003; Marcus 2012, 2013), Michael Fischer argues that here "anthropology's challenge is to develop translation and mediation tools for helping make visible the difference of interests, access, power, needs, desire, and philosophical perspective" (Fischer 2003: 3). As Marcus's (2012) recent work tracing the emergence of collaborations in these third spaces suggests, the experience of "being in fieldwork," the production of fieldnotes, and forms of knowing are being redefined and moving the margins to the center of the anthropological project.

Between 2005 and 2008, I was involved as a postdoctoral researcher in one such third space: "Kids' Informal Learning with Digital Media: An Ethnographic Investigation of Innovative Knowledge Cultures," or the Digital Youth Project, a collaborative research effort funded by the John D. and Catherine T. MacArthur Foundation. Led by Peter Lyman, Mizuko Ito, Michael Carter, and Barrie Thorne, the project began as a broad-based study of young people's new media usage and the everyday, informal learning in these new spaces. The twenty-eight researchers involved in the project were affiliated with one of the two organizing institutions, the University of California, Berkeley (UC Berkeley), and the University of Southern California (USC). Institutionally, I moved during the project from USC to UC Berkeley in light of the geographic focus of my research in Silicon Valley; subsequently, I participated in the weekly meetings at UC Berkeley as well as continuing to attend monthly meetings at USC in Los Angeles in person or via phone.

The project involved utilization of shared research instruments (such as a background questionnaire), disposition toward ethnography as the primary way of "knowing," and two additional approaches to studying engagement with new media. The first of these approaches focused upon knowing through engaging with young people in their everyday lives and then following "the action" to the various digital media and technology they were using. The second approach focused upon participation in social network sites, interests groups, and online communities and then following participants offline and/or across other online research sites. At the outset of the project, there was an understanding that fieldnotes and material would be shared across the team, although the exact mechanisms for this were not defined until later in the research project.

In the autumn of 2007, I flew from the San Francisco Bay area to Los Angeles to participate in a two-day meeting with my fellow researchers: two principal investigators, four postdocs, and eight graduate student-, masters-, and Ph.D.-level research assistants who were based at USC and UC Berkeley. Tooled out with our various laptops and mobiles, we assumed our positions around a long conference table, pulling out an array of devices, power cords, and other paraphernalia. Once settled in, we kicked off our meeting by creating a Google doc and inviting all members of the team to enter notes and edit this shared document. We also logged into a shared wiki space, where a group of us had already started to develop "codes" based on our "case studies," including my research on the relationships to media and technology among families living in Silicon Valley (see Horst 2009, 2012) and a smaller study of Neopets with Mimi Ito and Laura Robinson. As in every other meeting we held throughout the project, we also established a "backchannel," where people could pose questions or other issues that might not be "heard" during this large group meeting. A smaller group of us also logged onto IM to further "backchannel" our reactions to the discussions.

After a lengthy discussion about the expected outcomes of the project (a final report, coauthored book, and public forum), we began focusing upon a few themes and questions. What did we mean by "youth"? Should we be using "youth," "young people," or the more colloquial term, "kids"? How should we describe kids' identities in relation to technology in a language that reflected the practices we saw collectively? Given the shifts in the discussion, we decided to turn to the "identity" wiki page, where many of us had uploaded direct quotes from interviews, excerpts of fieldnotes, and descriptions of pictures, videos, and other materials. Rather than reading from our individual screens, one person decided to connect to the projector to make it easier for everyone in the room to see the main document. A few people added more material based on the discussions, but we eventually decided to discourage having too many of us on the wiki at once for fear of losing edits and, by extension, traces of those changes; the Google doc became a backup for some of this new material.

As the discussion turned to the range of identity practices posted on the wiki, one Ph.D. student commented that the research from a former M.A.[4]

who had stopped working on the project a year earlier had not been integrated into the wiki. Thinking the former researcher still had the transcriptions of the interview and the discussion he was remembering, the Ph.D. student sent her an email asking her to confirm his memory of the transcript and conversation, which had been held during one of the weekly meetings in Berkeley. He also asked if she was comfortable with the use of her case study as an exemplar of this kind of identity practice. A few minutes later, the former researcher was logged into IM and made a few comments that the Ph.D. researcher subsequently read, copied, and pasted into the backchannel for discussion. In this IM conversation, the former researcher also agreed to write up her case study for inclusion in the co-authored book (Ito et al. 2010).

After a few hours of discussion of different notions of identity, "geek" emerged as the term most often used by kids for those with technical proficiency. However, a few of us were reluctant to use the word "geek" because it suggested a reification or stereotype—the notion of an individual tech user or a signal for rich, Asian, or white kids—something the research team had been actively trying to avoid in characterizing their research findings. During our backchannel and informal conversations, when we started to discuss practice and participation across the diverse range of youth we had encountered, a few people working in less privileged and ethnically diverse locations described examples of kids who had become deeply immersed in amateur music, video making, online gaming communities, and so on. The team finally agreed upon "geeking out" (not "geeks") as a working term to describe young people who were deeply involved in these activities.

The other two "genres of participation" we had identified proved to be more difficult to name concisely, but a day later we agreed upon one more working term—"hanging out"—to describe those who devoted long hours to social network sites, gaming with others, and messaging. The third term, which eventually crystalized as "messing around"—to designate extensive individual exploration via the Internet—took more collaborative writing, reviewing, coding, and time (Ito et al. 2010). This process was scheduled on a shared Google calendar, and suggestions circulated via the wiki, email, and the project staff mailing list.

In many ways, the series of discussions was the beginning of collective "analysis" for the project, a moment where we could stop and take stock of the material we had produced over the past few years. Yet this was also one of only a few times that our dynamic and spatially dispersed research team was able to come together (in person or via conference call) to make sense of what had been occurring in our primary fieldwork "on the ground," whether that ground meant schools, afterschool programs, homes, or online spaces such as gaming guilds, vlogging communities, or social network sites. Moreover, and my personal reflections upon this experience of collaboration suggest, there was ongoing temporality embedded within the project. Many individuals changed their academic status during the life of the project, from undergraduate to graduate research assistant; master's degree to Ph.D. candidate; and postdoctoral scholar to assistant professor. Other researchers moved on from the team or became more centrally enmeshed in different, concurrent projects.

Beyond the changing constitution of the research team, the broader realization we shared was that an understanding of the range of everyday experiences of youth using digital media and technology, and of their informal learning processes, could not be reduced to any individual "case study," as we came to term the several different research sites in the Digital Youth Project. The challenge was to bring the series of individual project sites into one shared or, as we called it, "federated" conversation. This began at the regular meetings. Rarely recorded or archived, these discussions of "being in fieldwork" among research team members became a shared knowledge bank that was reopened and referred back to in subsequent meetings and for the generation of interim reports. In addition, a few people emerged as the "mediators" or "spokespersons" for the project by familiarizing themselves with the entire study, making sure project results were archived, and staying in touch with people who had moved on but who were still viewed as "owning" a case study in the project, with the responsibility of undertaking a final review of how the material presented to the team was represented.

In the second year of the project, we also began posting "Stories from the Field" on the project's public website (http://digitalyouth.ischool.berkeley .edu/) to share experiences and insights consolidated during regular meetings. There were several researchers who worked together on particular facets of the research, especially those that involved schools or afterschool programs. In my case, other researchers with expertise relevant to better understanding of one of my project participants sometimes came along to an interview or diary study session. In most instances, researchers shared and archived all or part of their de-identified fieldnotes, interview transcripts, and other materials via our online collaboration site, including the wiki based at USC.

Given the collective, relational nature of our research approach, I eventually came to see the engagement with project wikis, backchannels, Google docs, shared calendars, internal mailing lists, Word docs, tracked changes, websites, conference calls, and formal and informal meetings as another form of "being in fieldwork." The interactions in and through these various meetings and platforms became ways of knowing and relating to other people involved in the research endeavor and to their findings. In such projects, the self is no longer the central instrument of knowing; instead, the experience of knowing emerges through interactions between material objects, platforms, and spaces that have been collected or created throughout the collective and coordinated research process (Nafus and anderson 2009; Suchman et al. 1999). These spaces also come to constitute an experience of "being in fieldwork" and are fundamentally as important to the very constitution of "fields" as they are spaces for analysis.

Copresence and Relational Scales

To take this argument a step further, I want to explore how "being in fieldwork" can be scrutinized through an alternative lens from ethnographic approaches outside of the discipline of anthropology. Science studies scholar Anne Beaulieu's (2010) discussion of copresence provides a useful framework for reflecting on the different forms of "being in fieldwork" carried out in the Digital Youth Project and other large-scale collaborations wherein the process of "being in fieldwork" cannot be confined to an individual, a location, or a form of mediation.

Drawing a distinction between colocation and copresence, Beaulieu stresses the fluid and processual nature of fieldwork and of the very definition of the fields that we create and inhabit. As she describes it, developing a relationship of copresence is "a very active form of 'field-making.' The field is constituted in the interaction. The field is not a container or background in which interaction takes place, and a certain lack of stability of the 'field' could be considered a potential loss of adopting this approach" (2010: 464).

Beaulieu further notes that the "condition of co-presence" challenges ethnographic genres of analysis and production, opening up a space for a more nuanced discussion of changing practices of ethnography across sites, spaces, time, and research team members. Rather than portraying these

mediations and experiences of research as a pale attempt to capture colocation, Beaulieu introduces the notion of copresence as another way to conceptualize the multiplicities and temporalities of "being in fieldwork" and
the associated processes of knowledge production.

Whether the collaboration is "federated," as in the case of the Digital
Youth Project, or more systematically comparative, such as in the Global
Social Media Impact Study (http://www.ucl.ac.uk/global-social-media), it is
the connection or relational process that remains central to any collaborative (and arguably any ethnographic) enterprise. As Marilyn Strathern
(1999) has argued, fieldwork has always involved the ethnographer making
her- or himself open to entering into relationships with others. The findings, data, or materials we gather always reflect these relationships and, in
many ways, they are what makes the material meaningful. Whereas more
traditional anthropological projects often focus upon the relationships in
their primary fieldsites, individual researchers in the kinds of large-scale
collaborations I have been discussing must come to terms first with their
field relationships in their "primary" research and then, as well, with their
relationships with the broader research teams where the ethnographer is,
effectively, the representative of (often even fused with) the perspectives
and analysis of his or her particular field research experience.

In these situations, individual fieldworkers bear, primarily, the responsibility for the issues of rapport, representation, and experience of "being in
fieldwork" in their individual or collective research sites, issues of the sort
that have preoccupied anthropology in the post–*Writing Culture* (Clifford
and Marcus 1986) era. Their second relationship with the research material
and the research team comes through interactions in phone calls, instant
messaging conversations, reading and posting in wikis, face-to-face meetings, and blog posts. Making the material and the primary experience of
"being in fieldwork" accessible to others effectively opens the individuals
who "represent" their case study to other relationships and reflections
affecting fieldwork results and conclusions. This also reflects a process of
moving from fieldnotes that directly inform the writing of the text to "certain accessible, if not public, forms of concept work and critique in the
protracted phased segments of many fieldwork projects today" (Marcus
2012: 430).

The new relationships and interactions that are formed between
research projects, ethnographers, and the constituent case studies can vary
in scale and scope. In some instances, these become visible in perspectives,

criticism, and reflection that feed back into the analysis of each primary study. However, this is a second order effect of such projects. As Marcus characterizes "third spaces" such as the Digital Youth Project, "the creation of knowledge in the sense of fieldwork itself—partial to the traditional hypothesis of fieldwork—is displaced for innovations in collegial collaboration. This is a true diminution of the individualist project and its ideologies" (2013). This kind of collegial collaboration became evident in the Digital Youth Project and in our discussion of the overlay of structural inequalities tied to the concept "geek" (versus "geeking out"). The sharing of material from our collective fieldwork sites substantiated a murkier picture of digital engagements and structural challenges and reinforced our commitment to ethnography and comparison across many sites. Such efforts can result in the formation of relationships, ideas, and concepts that are new or, at the very least, surprising, and could not have been articulated in the same form, or with the same analytical vitality, outside the collective endeavor.

At the same time, the extension of "being in fieldwork" also raises ethical concerns about the sites and boundaries of research. For example, the discussion of the Digital Youth Project is based upon my own reflections of learning about working on a large, collaborative endeavor of this scale. But because the project itself was not understood at the outset as an object of inquiry (which would in turn require negotiations of permissions and possibly even a formal ethics submission), my ability to write about the experience has involved developing an ethics of the politics of representation that, in the spirit of the project, included requests for feedback from colleagues on the project. It also inspired considered reflections on the ethics of retrospectively making public what might otherwise remain the private domain of the project members.

Conclusion

This chapter has explored how ethnographic collaborations are challenging our understanding and research models of "being in fieldwork." It highlights multiple forms of collaborative research, ranging from the small-scale collaborations of two researchers to larger teams. Presenting three examples of collaborative projects, I described how small-scale projects can use digital media and technology to maintain the goals and aspirations of more traditional ethnography by mediating relationships between individual researchers, research sites, and the practice of "being in fieldwork." Although case studies in large-scale ethnographic projects may also use such methods to enable the completion of the primary ethnography, my focus upon comparison across multiple case studies revealed how digital media, technology, and collaborative relational spaces can be used not only in mediating relationships with the field or fieldsite but also can be focused on creating forms of copresences that facilitate the creation and appreciation of relations or connections between different sites.

For many small research teams, practices such as taking collaborators on tours, sharing texts and other research material, translating conversations and events, and phasing fieldwork in time (the four Ts) become ways through which experiences are mediated, and the experience of "being in fieldwork" can infuse collaborative ethnographic research. The challenge in mediated experiences in such fieldwork is that they must create a sense of copresence that can augment and even reframe the experience of "being in fieldwork." Without this mediated framework, fieldwork in and through digital media and technology is merely a remediation.

In large-scale collaborations, rather than a mediation of "on the ground" research, there is often a shifting of the locus of knowledge from the single ethnographer to a collaborative, external, visible, and moving object or focus. Here, the novel forms of collaboration shape everything from archiving practices to the tenor of weekly meetings to the sense of "ownership" in research. What becomes recognized as knowledge is constructed in these spaces and is open to those who choose to participate in or to enter into relationships with others and their research material. There is a movement from the locus of "being in fieldwork" in various locations, sites, and spaces to a notion of "being in fieldwork" through copresence via collective meetings, analysis sessions, and the production of material artifacts (Nafus and anderson 2009) and written results.

Still, as in primary ethnographic research, what is viewed as important or relevant in collaborative efforts is formed through the quality of the relationships and the work to keep the connections "alive," and this may fail when individual goals and aspirations are prioritized or the spirit of collegiality is not reciprocated. Even more important, although the research team (and the broader field) certainly benefits from more explicit discussions about the process and conditions of knowledge production, there are distinct challenges involved in navigating the ethics and the power dynamics between colleague-collaborator and fieldwork relationship. Anthropology's increasing collaborative and comparative research will require continuous rethinking of the multiple practices and contexts of "being in fieldwork" over time, space, and scales.

Acknowledgments

This chapter would not have been possible without the goodwill of my colleagues and collaborators as well as the constructive comments of Becky Herr-Stephenson, Mimi Ito, Daniel Miller, and Sarah Pink. I bear all responsibility for any errors, gaps, or leaps in logic.

Notes

1. Episodic fieldwork is the form of engagement that most academic anthropologists practice, particularly after their first fieldwork experience. Along with facilitating the aspiration of long-term engagement for anthropologists committed to a particular place or people, it has been shaped by the structural conditions of academia and funding for research and travel funds.

2. In the aftermath of the earthquake of 2010, the original funded project shifted to research on the introduction of mobile money and involved another core researcher, Espelencia Baptiste (see Taylor and Horst 2014).

3. Although I will not discuss this extensively, there is another layer of translations in and through the institutions through which research is conducted and funded. In this case, the institutional review board process and the funding for the project (an Institute for Money, Technology and Financial Inclusion grant) took some time to manage, given the earthquake that took place in January 2010, days after the project funding was awarded.

4. As noted in the text, I have disguised the identities of the researchers, as my account of events may not be shared among all members of the research team.

Bibliography

Andrew Barry, Georgina Born, and Gisa Weszkalnys. 2008. Logics of Interdisciplinarity. *Economy and Society* 37 (1): 20–49.

Beaulieu, Anne. 2010. Research Note: From Co-location to Co-presence: Shifts in the Use of Ethnography for the Study of Knowledge. *Social Studies of Science* 40: 453–470.

Behar, Ruth. 1993. *Translated Woman: Crossing the Border with Esperanza's Story*. Boston: Beacon Press.

Boellstorff, Tom. 2008. *Coming of Age in Second Life: An Anthropologist Explores the Virtually Human*. Princeton, N.J.: Princeton University Press.

———. 2011. Placing the Virtual Body: Avatar, Chora, Cypherg. In *A Companion to the Anthropology of the Body and Embodiment*, edited by Frances E. Mascia-Lees, 504–520. New York: Wiley-Blackwell.

Bolter, Jay David, and Richard Grusin. 2000. *Remediation: Understanding New Media*. Cambridge, Mass.: MIT Press.

Burrell, Jenna. 2009. The Field Site as a Network: A Strategy for Locating Ethnographic Research. *Field Methods* 21 (2): 181–199.

Clifford, James, and George E. Marcus, editors. 1986. *Writing Culture: The Poetics and Politics of Ethnography*. Berkeley: University of California Press.

Fischer, Michael M. J. 2003. *Emergent Forms of Life and the Anthropological Voice*. Durham, N.C.: Duke University Press.

Hine, Christine. 2000. *Virtual Ethnography*. London: Sage.

Horst, Heather A. 2009. Aesthetics of the Self: Digital Mediations. In *Anthropology and the Individual: A Material Culture Perspective*, edited by Daniel Miller, 99–114. Oxford: Berg.

———. 2012. New Media Technologies in Everyday Life. In *Digital Anthropology*, edited by Heather A. Horst and Daniel Miller, 61–79. New York: Berg.

———, and Daniel Miller. 2006. *The Cell Phone: An Anthropology of Communication*. New York: Berg.

———, and Daniel Miller, editors. 2012. *Digital Anthropology*. New York: Berg.

———, and Erin B. Taylor. 2014. The Role of Mobile Phones in the Mediation of Border Crossings: A Study of Haiti and the Dominican Republic. *The Anthropology Journal of Australia* 25 (2): 155–170.

Ito, Mizuko, Sonja Baumer, Matteo Bittanti, danah boyd, Rachel Cody, Rebecca Herr-Stephenson, Heather A. Horst, Patricia G. Lange, Dilan Mahendran, Katynka Z. Martinez, C. J. Pascoe, Dan Perkel, Laura Robinson, Christo Sims, and Lisa Tripp. 2010. *Hanging Out, Messing Around, and Geeking Out: Kids Living and Learning with New Media*. Cambridge, Mass.: MIT Press.

Marcus, George E. 2012. The Legacies of *Writing Culture* and the Near Future of the Ethnographic Form. *Cultural Anthropology* 27 (30): 427–446.

———. 2013. Experimental Forms for the Expression of Norms in the Ethnography of the Contemporary. *HAU: Journal of Ethnographic Theory* 3 (2): 197–217. Accessed February 16, 2015. http://www.haujournal.org/index.php/hau/article/view/hau3 .2.011/757.

Miller, Daniel, and Don Slater. 2000. *The Internet: An Ethnographic Approach*. Oxford: Berg.

Nafus, Dawn, and ken anderson. 2009. Writing on Walls: The Materiality of Social Memory in Corporate Research. In *Ethnography and the Corporate Encounter: Reflections on Research in and of Corporations*, edited by Melissa Cefkin, 137–157. New York: Berghahn.

Ortner, Sherry. 1995. Resistance and the Problem of Ethnographic Refusal. *Comparative Studies in Society and History* 37 (1): 173–193.

Postill, John. 2011. *Localizing the Internet: An Anthropological Account*. Oxford: Berghahn.

———, and Sarah Pink. 2012. Social Media Ethnography: The Digital Researcher in a Messy Web. *Media International Australia* 145: 123–134.

Retsikas, Konstantinos. 2008. Knowledge from the Body: Fieldwork, Power and the Acquisition of a New Self. In *Knowing How to Know: Fieldwork and the Ethnographic Present*, edited by Narmala Halstead, Eric Hirsch, and Judith Okeley, 110–129. London: Berghahn.

Sanjek, Roger. 2014. *Ethnography in Today's World: Color Full Before Color Blind*. Philadelphia: University of Pennsylvania Press.

Strathern, Marilyn. 1999. *Property, Substance and Effect: Anthropological Essays on Persons and Things*. London: Athlone Press.

Suchman, Lucy, Jeanette Blomberg, Julian Orr, and Randall Trigg. 1999. Reconstructing Technologies as Social Practice. *American Behavioral Scientist* 43 (3): 392–408.

Taylor, Erin, and Heather Horst. 2014. The Aesthetics of Mobile Money Platforms in Haiti. In *The Routledge Companion to Mobile Media*, edited by Gerald Goggin and Larissa Hjorth, 462–471. London: Routledge.

Whyte, Michael. 2013. Episodic Fieldwork, Updating, and Sociability. *Social Analysis* 57 (1): 110–121.

Williams, Raymond. 1977. *Marxism and Literature: From Medium to Social Practice*. Oxford: Oxford University Press.

PART IV

ONLINE FIELDWORK AND FIELDNOTES

Chapter 10

New York Parenting Discussion Boards: eFieldnotes for New Research Frontiers

Susan W. Tratner

This chapter describes the fieldnotes produced and used in an online research project. My fieldwork on UrbanBaby (urbanbaby.com) and YouBeMom (youbemom.com), two New York City parenting websites, began in July 2012 and extended through 2014. These two online communities are part of the continuing expansion of the Internet for personal communication among people who share common interests but may never meet in person. According to the Pew Research Center's Internet & American Life Project, by 2010, some 85 percent of people in the United States have used the Internet, and the number who reported that they participated in chat rooms or online discussions, such as on the two websites considered here, was 22 percent (Rainie 2012).

Anthropological research conducted online has been viewed with suspicion by many in the discipline, even in recent years. As the 2000s began, Maximilian Forte's (2002) survey of the top fifty U.S. anthropology departments found that almost 30 percent explicitly rejected the idea of an anthropology of cyberspace as an important research arena. As more communities of various kinds have expressed themselves electronically, however, and as more uniquely online cultures have emerged and developed, the acceptance of virtual ethnography has increased. Methodological questions related to this research terrain have begun to be discussed and answers offered.

Online Communities and Virtual Ethnography

Howard Rheingold (2000) was among the first researchers to describe a virtual or online community of geographically dispersed individuals who have a common interest and use the technologies of the Internet to communicate with each other. Rheingold's research on Whole Earth Lectronic Link (WELL) provided a first-person description of what it was like to participate in this world. Jenny Preece (2000) also helped conceptualize these Internet communities of people who participate because of a shared concern, purpose, or need and interact through their individual initiatives and contributions. Even earlier, studies of text-based discussions and online games, or multiuser dungeons (MUDs), including those of Morningstar and Farmer (1991) and Curtis (1997) on LambdaMOO, were contextualized by the intriguing propositions of Sherry Turkle (1995) about the changes that technologically mediated communication were having on our identities and interpersonal connections.

In 1996, the term "virtual ethnography" entered the research lexicon more widely via a journal article by Bruce Mason. It is probably best associated, however, with Christine Hine (2000), who wrote the first methodological guidebook for anthropological "virtual" research. Her work is widely cited, along with the germinal fieldwork-based discussion of virtual ethnography in Daniel Miller and Don Slater's (2000) study of Internet use in Trinidad, in which they showed how the "global" Internet becomes "local" to this island. Heather Horst and Miller's later research (2006) on the cell or mobile phone in Jamaica offered another detailed look at how digital technology was actually used and that it was used differently in various parts of the developed and developing world. Bonnie Nardi's (2010) discussion of online game play in the context of the multiuser World of Warcraft provided an excellent example of how to combine online with offline ethnographic research about a virtual community, here focused on various modes of inter-user contact related to this medieval fantasy world. More recently, Tom Boellstorff, Nardi, Celia Pearce, and T. L. Taylor have produced a jointly written volume (2012) providing guidance in pursuing *Ethnography and Virtual Worlds*.

The two online communities discussed in this chapter are organized primarily through discussion boards. Online discussion or bulletin boards involve the posting of messages that are typically displayed in a "threaded" fashion, in which the first message starts the thread and responses to this original "post" appear placed beneath it. In this way, new posts that discuss or reply to the original message are associated directly with that original post. The discussion boards examined in this chapter are all asynchronous, meaning that participants do not have to be present online together (Preece, Maloney-Krichmar, and Abras 2003). A community member can post a statement or question, log off, come back online in a few hours, and see the responses.

Online Parenting Communities

A variety of online communities have been studied since the 1990s. The WELL community is the best known, due to Rheingold's pioneering research. He described the emergence of this community as helpful and organic, with an original motto of "What it is is up to us" (2000: 31). Rheingold was involved in a variety of the WELL's discussion boards and reported extensively on the parenting portion of one of the original online communities. Many parenting websites, such as Babycenter and iVillage in the United States and ParentNET in England, are considered to be positive, uplifting, and emotionally safe spaces where parents can better understand the roles they play and receive peer help and support from other parents (Dworkin, Connell, and Doty 2013; Sarkadi and Bremberg 2005). Each of these communities has its own "netiquette," through which long-time users of the discussion board employ various means to let new users, or "newbies," find out "how things work around here."

It is difficult to accurately count the number of parenting-related websites available in 2014, but millions likely exist. The users are primarily women. In Sarkadi and Bremberg's (2005) survey of Sweden's largest parenting website, for example, 96 percent of the respondents were female; these women had a mean age of 30.6 and were of above average Swedish education levels but below average income figures.

Some authors, such as Brady and Guerin (2010), suggest that parenting websites are seen as valuable because they provide knowledge and confidence to mothers as they embark on this new stage in life. Previous generations of mothers, they argue, had stronger familial and social networks to rely on for both knowledge and support, but in modern European and American life, these family-based supports are not available. Gibson and Hanson (2013: 314) advance two factors that explain "the story of new mothers and technology" and the widespread use of discussion boards. The first is a mother's improved confidence in her new role through the reception of advice and support as she adjusts to being a new member of the "club" of parents. The second factor is the ability of the woman to preserve a bit of the "old me," which a new mother often feels she is losing with the arrival of a baby, accompanying bodily changes, and her changed role in the family. A mother's online connection to the world outside the home while she meets the needs of the new family member can be critical, even if it is through a parenting website. In line with this conclusion, Sarkadi and Bremberg (2005) found that the more frequent users of the sites they studied scored higher on measures of social support, indicating that the online social connection was significant to frequent users.

The importance of the "been there, done that" factor, of information and support from people already dealing with the same parenting problems, appeared to be valuable to the mothers studied by Madge and O'Conner (2006). Their research suggested that the Internet has replaced even the new mother's own mother, as well as mothers in their "real life" or offline interactions, as the primary source of parenting-related knowledge. Not only do the discussion boards provide information and convenience, they also offer a wider "range of audience" (Madge and O'Conner 2006: 205). Through this enhanced "range," one can obtain a variety of opinions quickly from people who have previously been through what a new mother is experiencing. Moreover, the website user providing information enjoys the satisfaction of being an expert who offers a useful answer. As Rheingold phrases it, "a virtual community is like a living encyclopedia [that] can help their members cope with information overload" (2000: 46).

Obtaining information or support online appears to have certain advantages over offline conversation. In such offline interactions, the participating parents must find mutually acceptable times to communicate, in spite of often unpredictable schedules of activities, naps, diaper changes, feedings, and their infants' mercurial moods. Online resources circumvent these scheduling issues, as well as other geographical and logistical barriers (see Coulson, Buchanan, and Aubeeluck 2007). The online discussion boards provide needed information, support, and mental stimulation at the precise time an individual is able to access it, without having to disrupt the baby or other children's routines. Depending on how one feels that day, it is a readily accessible pool of parenting information or snark (sarcastic comment), available with the click of a mouse when mom takes a moment to herself. Mothers know that "synchronously or asynchronously, the sun never sets on the virtual community" (Healy 1997: 60).

Although many parenting websites existing in cyberspace appear to be separated from a tangible, physical reality "out there," they often have clear, spatially grounded moorings: as Schwanen, Dijst, and Kwan put it, "the Internet cannot be separated from its geographical context" (2006: 586). Sites that start as regional resources may become nationwide ones, or vice versa, and they are marked by physically locatable regimes, norms, and cultures. In this way, "cyberspace" can operate to consolidate and reinforce cultural norms that are spatially specific "on the ground." This is clearly the case in the two New York City websites I studied. Here, such issues as the real estate market, weather conditions, politics, and the process of getting children into desirable school programs were rooted in location and geography.

Anonymity

Anthropological tradition holds that we must protect the informants and communities in which we work. Many researchers remove identifying information and create pseudonyms for physical locations and individuals in their written or publically presented work. In the case of these two research sites, however, in 2013 a character on the television show *30 Rock* referred to a mean, anonymous parenting board in New York City, and within an hour both YouBeMom and UrbanBaby were identified online as the likely basis of the joke. As all online participants enjoy anonymity on the sites themselves and as numbers of readers of this chapter might readily identify the sites, I have decided to use their two actual names. Other researchers of online communities have made the same decision, including Boellstorff (2008), Coleman (2013), and Nardi (2010).

Both discussion boards operate with complete anonymity. Aside from those participants who choose to sign their posts with self-designated "monikers," there are no required user names, no handles, no avatars, no signs or indications of who or even how many different people are participating by messaging at a particular moment or in a particular thread. This has a significant impact on communication. Although the theoretical questions discussed by Goffman (1959) of how one chooses to present herself or himself are relevant, there is nonetheless a lack of any "reliable" or "conventional" identifying signals. Judith Donath (2007) suggests that this can cause such postings to be unreliable overall and that, indeed, one must assume that every post on an anonymous site is potentially unreliable.

The anonymous nature of the two sites was an impediment in my research, as it was nearly impossible in most cases to trace the postings of any individual participant or to follow up with any such person. I had no way of identifying or contacting her or him. Similarly, an anonymous site fails to provide information about a post's responding participants. There is no available knowledge about the educational or professional background of any participant unless it is volunteered. One participant does not know whether another participant is a member of their own family, a PTA president, a friend of their teenaged daughter, or a sixty-five-year-old self-professed troll (disruptive user).

There were clearly times that posts were for "lulz"—the chance to intentionally violate expectations and norms of everyday life. Nonetheless, this complete anonymity is useful to a parent participant for a number of reasons, particularly the creation of a "safe space" within which one may discuss highly personal, controversial, or even mundane topics. Anonymity can help expose issues and provide information for anthropologists as well (Schoenebeck 2013).

A Short History of UrbanBaby and YouBeMom

UrbanBaby (UB) was founded in August 1999 by a married couple: Susan Maloney, a former *Esquire* magazine editor, and John Maloney, president of the website Tumblr. It was designed to be a site that provided information to expectant and new parents throughout the United States. The portion of the site that became most popular was the message board, which remains anonymous and is primarily New York–centric (Nussbaum 2006). The site was sold to CNET, an American media website, in 2006. CNET was itself sold to CBS in 2008.

Over time, UB became very popular. In 2013, it was ranked the number 134,699 most popular website in the United States, and it has reached as high as number 63,435 in 2008 (Alexa.com 2013; DigDo 2013). With this popularity came notoriety as well. The website *Gothamist* reported that UB is a "must read if you're about to have a kid in the five bouroughs [sic]"

(Chung 2004). Other posts on *Gothamist* (Feldmar 2012) and *Gawker* (2003) generally have been more scathing than sympathetic. UB has been called "a collective id" of certain groups of New York City mothers in *New York Magazine* (Nussbaum 2006); it was said to "have some of the worst human behavior I've seen in my life" by actor Tina Fey (Michael K. 2013), and to be an "urban snake pit" by *New York Times* columnist Ginia Bellafante (2012). Yet UB is famous not only for the snark; it is also widely viewed as one of the few free and authoritative sources of information regarding New York City preschools and kindergartens, including their ultracompetitive application processes.

In 2008, there was a reorganization of the UB website layout (Kaufman 2008), a change radical enough that some users of the site were unhappy. One such couple, who have wished to remain private and whose names are not commonly known, created YouBeMom (YBM), a new, competing site using a layout similar to UB's original design. Following this, UB became known as the go-to site for informational searches and longer discussions, and YBM emerged as the place to discuss topics using shorter and pithier postings. Some people are users of only one board, but others go back and forth depending on the topic or their mood.

UB remains more asynchronous than YBM, where nearly simultaneous posts and responses more frequently occur. If the initial participant on YBM does not post a reply to a response within a few minutes, that initial participant will later have to post a follow-up question in order to get people's attention again. As a result, on YBM, communication on the board with other people typically occurs in a rapid succession of messages, even if it is technically an asynchronous board that contains stored threads for review at a later time.

Unlike Rheingold's (2000) or Madge and O'Connor's (2006) characterizations of the online parenting discussion boards they studied as supportive spaces, UB and YBM are sites where mothers also post openly about the negative aspects of their marriages, family, jobs, friends, and children. In terms of Erving Goffman's core ideas in *The Presentation of Self in Everyday Life* (1959), we can think of such social network sites as Babycenter or Facebook as the "stage," the portion of these women's lives where everyone is nice, their marriages are strong, their children are smart and well-behaved, and they love their jobs as wife and mother. In contrast, UB and YBM are the "backstage," the places where they can feel freer to express negative emotions, fears, and anxieties. As Schoenebeck (2013) points out, anonymity, as it is afforded by these two sites, allows for "disinhibition": participants can self-disclose or act out online because there is a complete separation between offline and online presentations of self.

An Online Research Project

My exposure to the two websites was initially as a participant mother. I found UrbanBaby when looking for information regarding the ultracompetitive process of applying to preschools, the same entry point as many other people involved with these bulletin boards. After a few years of increasing participation with both sites and their discussion boards, I realized that I had stumbled upon a well-defined fieldwork site. I then started planning formal research.

Initially, I was interested in observing online discussions using Judith Warner's concepts about parenting "in the age of anxiety" (2006) and in determining how anonymity, as a double-edged sword of freedom and viciousness, operated for women who are often subjected to the confinement of gendered communication norms (Tannen 1994). I began to participate in message threads both as a member of the community—asking questions and responding to posts—and as an explicit researcher—posing questions directly, openly eliciting data, and requesting offline interviews.

As other researchers (Boelstorff 2008; Rheingold 2000) have stated, it is difficult to describe yourself as doing "anthropological research" if you are sitting at a computer and typing back and forth with invisible people. It is equally difficult to defend this to friends and family members who know that you were active in these online communities before you had formulated your research interests.

My research had two parts. The first was the participant observation of the two online communities UB and YBM. The second was interviews with users of the websites. Beginning in 2012, I went online multiple times a day to "check in" on the two sites. Often, there was a common theme being discussed on both sites—Halloween costumes, school vacation plans, or a national or local news story—that developed along a relatively predictable path. As UB is asynchronous and people do not expect to communicate in real time, the discussions moved more slowly, even though there was more traffic overall. Consequently, I found myself monitoring YBM more consistently. YBM members often did not provide a reference to the site's official "most discussed" or "most liked" post pages, an indication that communication was more (but not entirely) synchronous than on UB.

In addition to observing and participating in message threads, I asked specific and pointed questions. I gave myself a "moniker" or nickname, "anthropologistmom," both as a means of informing the participants that I was present as a researcher of the community and as a way of answering some expected questions. I also created an email account, anthropologistmom@hotmail.com, to allow individual respondents to contact me directly, and I encouraged those who might be hesitant to do so to first create their own anonymous email accounts.

This resulted in some problems when people sent me an initial email. I would send back an informed consent document and this response from me would either startle them, or they might neglect to use their new anonymous account when answering me. IRB regulations were, in general, unclear in regard to online public spaces as locations of research. My university's IRB approval document did not require informed consent for the online community portion of my research, but I felt that it was an important ethical step to provide such a document.

I also conducted offline verbal interviews by telephone and in person with people who identified themselves to me as members or users of the two websites. Some were with people whom I met offline and who mentioned that they used one of these sites. But I also interviewed people who responded to my requests for interviews posted on the sites themselves.

One of the challenges of fieldwork with this particular population is their "Fight Club" rules. The phrase comes from the 1999 movie *Fight Club* and its frequently repeated line: "The first rule of Fight Club is: you do not talk about Fight Club." These women hold the same view. They do not talk about their engagement with these websites IRL (in real life). There are three main reasons. First, they want to believe that they are intellectually and morally superior to the reputed "trainwreck" or "Jerry Springeresque," aspects of these sites. Second, they do not want to admit having enough spare time to engage with these sites in a city where keeping busy with multiple activities has social cachet. Third, there appeared to be a common fear that telling people you use the site might inhibit you from posting any personal information or views that might "out" or identify you.

With people who wanted to preserve their anonymity, I conducted telephone interviews and used a buffer number, from freeconferencecall.com, that my interviewee could call anonymously. This method allowed the interviewees to have fewer worries about being "outed" on the site itself. In addition, freeconferencecall.com audiotaped our interview while I typed notes on my laptop computer as the interview transpired. When the interview concluded, I could then download the interview audiofile to include in my fieldnote records. I could also still access the audiotape whenever I wished through the freeconferencecall.com server.

Headnotes

To use Simon Ottenberg's (1990) conceptualization, all anthropological research produces "headnotes." My five years of experience with one of the parenting sites has produced rich memories, impressions, and experiences that have and will continue to inform my work. These headnotes are the backbone of my research and fieldnotes. For example, I am familiar with various nicknames or monikers of such people as "Congo," "PICU mom," "Sandwich dad," "Gay Uncle," and "Inmate Mom." And having experienced five annual cycles of holidays, summer camp, vacations, and school applications, I have acquired extensive headnotes about the wider worlds of these two communities.

Scratchnotes

Scratchnotes are the quick notes taken at the time of ongoing participant observation and that are designed to provide as soon as possible a record of what has happened. They consist of shorthand, key words, and brief impressions (Ottenberg 1990; Sanjek 1990). Figure 10.1 is a page of these scratchnotes that were composed while I was doing online participant observation on the two sites themselves.

This page includes a variety of topics that were either of interest to a significant number of UB or YBM site users or that reflect cultural themes of interest to me. With each scratchnote, I include a URL link to one of the two websites so I can access a complete transcript of what was happening online and revisit this fuller context myself.

In the process of writing this chapter, I came to recognize that this method of note-taking and storage has a significant risk. If either online site decides to eliminate old threads, or the site shuts down, I will lose a

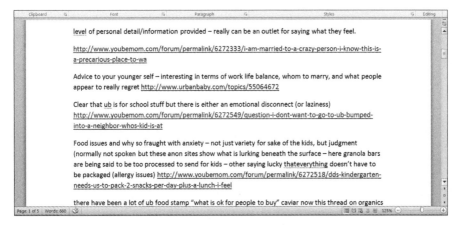

Figure 10.1. Susan W. Tratner's scratchnotes. Screenshot by Susan W. Tratner.

significant portion of my total fieldnotes. To prevent this situation, I had to balance the desire to continue my research with the need to take screenshots of every URL I had referred to in my nearly two years of fieldwork.

Interviews

My research is both online and offline, and all of it is stored in electronic format. The interviews I conducted were taped on a small microcassette recorder in face-to-face situations or recorded via the technology service freeconferencecall.com when I was doing telephone interviews. My interviews, therefore, are stored either on recorded tapes or on digital audio files. Both provide verbatim records of what respondents and I actually said. I have not transcribed most of my interviews, but because I am a fast typist, my electronic fieldnotes taken during interviews are relatively close to a complete transcription.

The digital audio file option is an excellent way to complete an interview when you are at a distance from the person you are interviewing or, in my case, when she is only available from one to three p.m. during her child's nap, or she is willing to participate in the research but wants to keep "Fight Club rules" and not be identified or meet in person. As other authors in this volume discuss (Schrooten, Chapter 5; Slama, Chapter 6), audio files

Figure 10.2. Susan W. Tratner's fieldnotes. Screenshot by Susan W. Tratner.

can also become a valuable record for our interlocutors, as well as for ourselves as researchers, in the future.

Online Site Links and Threads

The major portion of my fieldnotes is what could be called extended scratchnotes: my short descriptions and responses recorded while following online message board postings, with a direct URL link to a message thread. As there is no separate archiving or (to date) removal of old posts by the two sites, the links provide a permanent verbatim record of what transpired on a particular day regarding a particular topic. The official system of thread organization on the UB website is numerical—each thread is given a unique number that is attached to the end of each post. On the YBM site, both a number and the first few words of the original post constitute the permanent name for the thread (see the URLs in Figure 10.2).

In my fieldnotes, I describe or illustrate the thread's content and indicate the reason why I decided to collect that thread for my research. I try

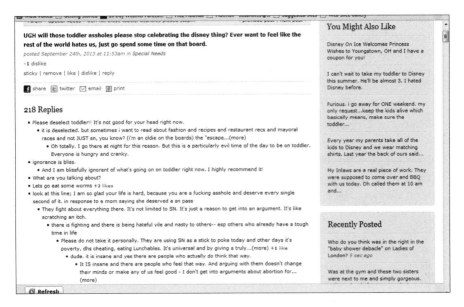

Figure 10.3. YouBeMom thread segment. Screenshot by Susan W. Tratner.

to provide some context about the thread for myself as well as some initial analysis and any preliminary connection to larger themes that I have observed come up before. The example in Figure 10.2 is part of my field-notes from a single day where the topic of special needs kids was being talked about in the context of Disney World.

A complete thread itself, however, is often also useful for further research and analytical purposes. Figure 10.3 is one segment of the complete thread regarding the way that mothers of special needs children were feeling attacked by other members of the same board.

Differing responses and subtle nuance can be observed when reviewing a complete thread. As in James Spradley and Brenda Mann's (1979) classic analysis of "How to Ask for a Drink," online community members display various styles of presentation and modes of negotiation of cultural and gendered communication that can garner either support or derision. I have seen posts on very sensitive topics, including spousal infidelity, that have been phrased in such a way as to suggest that the responding online group has turned on the original poster and has found fault with her or him, even "flaming" (sharply criticizing, see Urban Dictionary 2014a) the original poster in a nasty manner in which insult becomes more important than reasoned argument. The exact wording of a multiuser thread, therefore, can be critical for a proper analysis of meaning, and many complete thread posts are included in my fieldnotes.

Thematic Organization

I review my scratchnotes, together with online commentary and relevant threads, in order to identify topics that are illustrative of more general cultural themes. These range across common domains and topics, including judgments about "sanctimommy-ness," the "mommy wars," discussions of class and race, school-related issues, urban folklore, and points of interest on various annual cycles. (A "sanctimommy" is someone who is overly invested in parenting and usually derisive of those who are looser about raising children; see UrbanDictionary.com 2014.) This level of involvement in every aspect of parenting has led to side taking on a variety of parenting issues such as circumcision, breast versus formula feeding, and working versus stay-at-home parenting. It has been branded the "mommy wars."

In order to provide an organizational structure, I create a new, more complete Microsoft Word document for each theme or topic, combining scratchnotes, links and accompanying descriptions, and reflections from headnotes. For example, one of the more hotly contested topics on UB and YBM is the issue of "class" and who is "middle class" in the greater New York area. On almost a weekly basis, one or both sites has a sizable thread in which someone asserts that they are either "middle class" or "just barely getting by" on an income of between two hundred thousand and five hundred thousand dollars. This topic is guaranteed to garner a long and usually vitriolic thread of posts. Figure 10.4 is a screenshot from my Word document on this topic.

I have also prepared lists of linguistic usages and terms as a way of organizing my notes into thematic documents. Some of this is based on the analyses of gendered communication and argument culture by Deborah Tannen (1994, 1998) and the work of Jones and Schieffelin (2009). One of my thematic groupings is a variation of means-ends semantical lists based on Spradley's (1979) domain analysis. Figure 10.5 is an example of my thematic organization in which I have itemized certain indirect insults

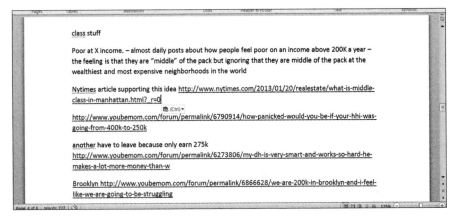

Figure 10.4. Susan W. Tratner's organized structure on "class." Screenshot by Susan W. Tratner.

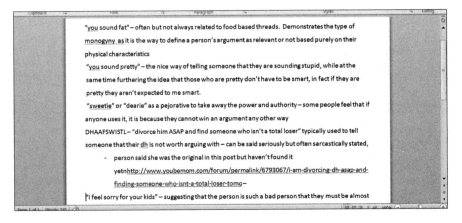

Figure 10.5. Susan W. Tratner's thematic organization of insults. Screenshot by Susan W. Tratner.

found on the two discussion boards. This builds on the research of Bernstein et al. on 4chan in that the online language is offensive, funny, open, and creative as well as "pushing the bounds of propriety" (2011: 53). (In fact, the list in Figure 10.5 is somewhat sanitized for general consumption; it actually includes various formal and colloquial anatomical references.)

Changing Technologies

One of the changing circumstances in studying online cultures or, indeed, in conducting any research that involves online access is the increasing accessibility of wireless Internet connections. The speed and ubiquity afforded through mobile devices appears to be shrinking the digital divide between the fieldworker and the field. At least 88 percent of Americans have a cell phone, and six in ten adults go online wirelessly with a cell phone, e-book reader, or laptop or tablet computer (Zickuhr and Smith 2012: 2). This indicates that not only the participants and informants in the cultures we study but also the researchers themselves are likely to be using a variety of digital devices.

This was certainly true in my case. I started my interactions with the two websites in 2012 using a laptop computer on our home wireless network and a desktop computer in my Empire State College office. I maintained my fieldnotes in Word documents at both locations, frequently emailing and downloading them from one computer to another. At first, I used long file names ending in "_v01" and eventually reaching "_v12" extensions, until I decided to simplify my work by having separate "fieldnotes" files on each computer.

When I started to use a smartphone, the challenges of coordinating my fieldnotes increased. I would type "sticky," "save," or "watch" posts as I followed and interacted with the two sites on this mobile phone, which I carried everywhere, and would also send myself text messages with observations, explanations, and other research-related information. Then, when I obtained an iPad in the middle of my first year of fieldwork, I used the "scratch pad" function on that device to add to my fieldnote archive.

All this resulted in four different sets of extended scratchnotes entered on four different devices. Obviously, I did not want to repeat any already recorded fieldwork data or analysis. I managed this by "unsticky-ing" or "unwatching" a post when I had entered the information in my fieldnote files.

I have tried to keep my fieldnotes backed up in various ways. Although I admire those who blog their fieldnotes (Petterson 2013; Wang 2012), I have relied mainly on the somewhat old-fashioned procedure of emailing fieldnotes to my Hotmail account periodically. There I can "search" my own email in order to find what I am looking for, being careful to use only the most recent version of each fieldnote file.

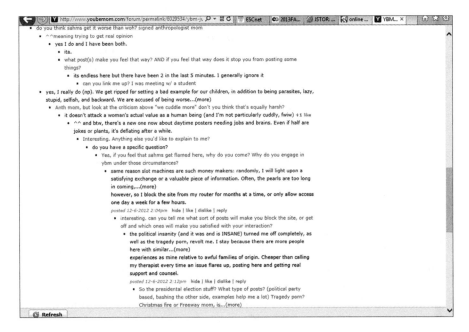

Figure 10.6. YouBeMom message board thread. Screenshot by Susan W. Tratner.

Changes in technologies, or outdated back-up systems, are a significant risk for electronic fieldnotes. Imagine a lifetime of fieldnotes collected on five-inch floppy disks without a useful reader. Imagine losing texted scratchnotes when changing telephones or telephone services. In my case, during my fieldwork I moved from one physical phone to another and became distressed to learn that months of texted scratchnotes would not be automatically transferred to my new phone. The old phone now serves only as a digital notebook for this research project.

The Ethnographer's Voice

One of the unanticipated insights that I have noted during my online fieldwork is that my voice is fully evident throughout the research. A significant portion of my scratchnotes refers to hyperlinks to online message board threads in which I participated (see Figure 10.6). Unlike face-to-face verbal interviews, moreover, my fieldwork errors or missteps are visible in these communications and preserved openly for all who may view the website. If I asked a question well or poorly, or if I asked double-barreled or leading questions, the evidence is there. If I misused vocabulary; was chided, derided, or "flamed" for violating assumed norms; or if people stopped communicating with me when I identified myself as an anthropological researcher, my mistakes or failings became a matter of public record. I have no ability to filter out or hide negative responses and must leave my errors and rejections online for as long as they exist on the two websites.

Such visibility was less evident in the era before digital audiotaping of interviews and before various other forms of efieldnotes. Anthropologists have always been present in the interviews they have conducted, but only after audiotaping became more common and the technology simpler to carry and use could it become obvious to others accessing their fieldnote records exactly what had been said or not said by a researcher. Although it remained less likely that later scholars would pour through analog audiotapes, researchers had a second opportunity to improve (or omit) their poorly posed questions when they typed and edited interview transcriptions.

Due to the anonymous nature of online interactions, however, I will never be able to re-ask questions or to follow up online interactions with informants with any degree of certainty that the person I am interacting with now is the same person I was interacting with online just hours or minutes prior.

Conclusion

The ever-expanding reach of electronic communication and Internet-enabled devices suggests that online ethnographic research and, therefore, efieldnotes will continue to expand their presence in anthropological fieldwork. This chapter has identified some various forms that fieldnotes can take in one research project, as well as some possible pitfalls and solutions.

Bibliography

Alexa: An Amazon.com Company. 2015. Site Overview: urbanbaby.com. Accessed February 18, 2015. http://www.alexa.com/siteinfo/urbanbaby.com.

Bellafante, Ginia. 2012. Judgement Day for the Kindergarten Set. *New York Times*, February 17. Accessed February 18, 2015. http://www.nytimes.com/2012/02/19/nyregion/an-admissions-decision-that-brings-more-agony.html.

Bernstein, Michael S., Andrés Monroy-Hernández, Drew Harry, Paul André, Katrina Panovich, and Gregory G. Vargas. 2011. 4chan and/b/: An Analysis of Anonymity and Ephemerality in a Large Online Community. In *Proceedings of the Fifth International Conference on Weblogs and Social Media*, 50–57. Menlo Park, CA: AAAI Press. Accessed February 18, 2015. http://www.aaai.org/ocs/index.php/ICWSM/ICWSM11/paper/viewFile/2873/4398.

Boellstorff, Tom. 2008. *Coming of Age in Second Life: An Anthropologist Explores the Virtually Human*. Princeton, N.J.: Princeton University Press.

———, Bonnie Nardi, Celia Pearce, and T. L. Taylor. 2012. *Ethnography and Virtual Worlds: A Handbook of Method*. Princeton, N.J.: Princeton University Press.

Brady, Ellen, and Suzanne Guerin. 2010. "Not the Romantic, All Happy, Coochy Coo Experience": A Qualitative Analysis of Interactions on an Irish Parenting Web Site. *Family Relations* 59: 14–27.

Chung, Jen. 2004. NYC to Parents: Watch Your Baby! *Gothamist*, August 30. Accessed February 18, 2015. http://gothamist.com/2004/08/30/nyc_to_parents_watch_your_baby.php.

Coleman, E. Gabriella. 2013. *Coding Freedom: The Ethics and Aesthetics of Hacking*. Princeton, N.J.: Princeton University Press.

Coulson, Neil, Heather Buchanan, and Aimee Aubeeluck. 2007. Social Support in Cyberspace: A Content Analysis of Communication Within a Huntington's Disease Online Support Group. *Patient Education and Counseling* 68 (2): 173–178.

Curtis, Pavel. 1997. Mudding: Social Phenomena in Text-Based Virtual Realities. In *Culture of the Internet*, edited by Sara Kiesler, 121–142. Mahwah, N.J.: Lawrence Erlbaum.

Dig.do—Domain Information About Top Sites. 2013. Domain: urbanbaby.com. Accessed February 18, 2015. http://dig.do/urbanbaby.com.

Donath, Judith. 2007. Signals in Social Supernets. *Journal of Computer-Mediated Communication* 13 (1): 231–251.

Dworkin, Jodi, Jessica Connell, and Jennifer Doty. 2013. A Literature Review of Parents' Online Behavior. *Cyberpsychology: Journal of Psychosocial Research on Cyberspace* 7 (2): 1–10.

Feldmar, James. 2012. UrbanBaby Income Thread Will Make You Feel Horrible About Life. *Gothamist*, January 4. Accessed February 18, 2015. http://gothamist.com/2012/01/04/urbanbaby_income_thread_will_make_y.php.

Forte, Maximilian. 2002. Another Revolution Missed: Anthropology of Cyberspace. *Anthropology News* 43 (9): 20–21.

Gawker. 2003. UrbanBaby. May 2. Accessed February 18, 2015. http://gawker.com/012121/urbanbaby.

Goffman, Erving. 1959. *The Presentation of Self in Everyday Life*. New York: Doubleday.

Healy, Dave. 1997. Cyberspace and Place: The Internet as Middle Landscape on the Electronic Frontier. In *Internet Culture*, edited by David Porter, 55–68. New York: Routledge.

Hine, Christine. 2000. *Virtual Ethnography*. London: Sage.

Horst, Heather, and Daniel Miller. 2006. *The Cell Phone: An Anthropology of Communication*. Oxford: Berg.

Jones, Graham, and Bambi Schieffelin. 2009. Enquoting Voices, Accomplishing Talk: Uses of Be + Like in Instant Messaging. *Language and Communication* 29: 77–113.

K., Michael. 2013. Tina Fey Says Mommy Message Boards Are a Cesspool of Disgusting Foolery. *dlisted*, March 7. Accessed February 18, 2015. http://dlisted.com/2013/03/07/tina-fey-says-mommy-message-boards-are-cesspool-disgusting-foolery/.

Kaufman, Joanne. 2008. Urban Baby Lessons: Don't Mess with Mom's Chat. *New York Times*, May 19. Accessed February 18, 2015. http://www.nytimes.com/2008/05/19/business/19baby.html?_r = 0.

Madge, Clare, and Henrietta O'Conner. 2006. Parenting Gone Wired: Empowerment of New Mothers on the Internet? *Social and Cultural Geography* 7 (2): 199–220. Accessed March 18, 2014. http://hdl.handle.net/2382/1403 (page discontinued).

Mason, Bruce. 1996. Moving Toward Virtual Ethnography. *American Folklore Society News* 25 (2): 4–5.

Miller, Daniel, and Don Slater. 2000. *The Internet: An Ethnographic Approach*. Oxford: Berg.

Morningstar, Chip, and F. Randall Farmer. 1991. The Lessons of Lucasfilm's Habitat. In *Cyberspace: First Steps*, edited by Michael Benedikt, 273–302. Cambridge, Mass.: MIT Press.

Nardi, Bonnie. 2010. *My Life as a Night Elf Priest: An Anthropological Account of World of Warcraft*. Ann Arbor: University of Michigan Press.

Nussbaum, Emily. 2006. Mothers Anonymous. *New York Magazine*, July 24. Accessed February 18, 2015. http://www.emilynussbaum.com/new_york/2006/07/urban baby.php.

Ottenberg, Simon. 1990. Thirty Years of Fieldnotes: Changing Relationships to the Text. In *Fieldnotes: The Makings of Anthropology*, edited by Roger Sanjek, 273–289. Ithaca, N.Y.: Cornell University Press.

Petterson, Lene. 2013. Video Blogging Ethnographic Field Notes. *Popular Anthropology Magazine* 1 (4): 35–38. Accessed February 18, 2015. http://www.academia.edu/3820856/Video_blogging_ethnographic_field_notes.

Preece, Jenny. 2000. *Online Communities: Designing Usability, Supporting Sociability*. Chichester, U.K.: Wiley.

———, Diane Maloney-Krichmar, and Chadia Abras. 2003. *History and Emergence of Online Communities*. Draft. Accessed February 18, 2015. http://www.itu.dk/people/khhp/speciale/videnskabelige%20artikler/Preece_2003%20-%20DRAFT%20History%20and%20emergence%20of%20online%20communities.pdf.

Rainie, Lee. 2012. Changes to the Way We Identify Internet Users. "PewResearch-Center: Internet, Science & Tech." Accessed February 18, 2015. http://www.pew internet.org/2012/10/03/changes-to-the-way-we-identify-internet-users/.

Rheingold, Howard. 2000. *The Virtual Community: Homesteading on the Electronic Frontier.* 2nd edition. Cambridge, Mass.: MIT Press.

Sanjek, Roger. 1990. A Vocabulary for Fieldnotes. In *Fieldnotes: The Makings of Anthropology,* edited by Roger Sanjek, 92–138. Ithaca, N.Y.: Cornell University Press.

Sarkadi, Anna, and Sven Bremberg. 2005. Socially Unbiased Parenting Support on the Internet: A Cross-Sectional Study of Users of a Large Swedish Parenting Website. *Child: Care, Health and Development* 31 (1): 43–52.

Schwanen, Tim, Martin Dijst, and Mei-Po Kwan. 2006. Introduction: The Internet, Changing Mobilities, and Urban Dynamics. *Urban Geography* 27 (7): 585–589.

Schoenebeck, Sarita Yardi. 2013. The Secret Life of Online Moms: Anonymity and Disinhibition on YouBeMom.com. In *Proceedings of the Seventh International Conference on Weblogs and Social Media in Seventh International AAAI Conference on Weblogs and Social Media,* 555–562. Accessed February 18, 2015. http://www.aaai .org/ocs/index.php/ICWSM/ICWSM13/paper/view/5973/6395.

Spradley, James. 1979. *The Ethnographic Interview.* Belmont, Calif.: Wadsworth.

———, and Brenda Mann. 1975. *The Cocktail Waitress: Woman's Work in a Man's World.* Long Grove, Ill.: Waveland Press.

Tannen, Deborah. 1994. *Talking from 9 to 5.* New York: HarperCollins.

———. 1998. *Argument Culture.* New York: Ballantine Books.

Turkle, Sherry. 1995. *Life on the Screen: Identity in the Age of the Internet.* New York: Simon and Schuster.

Urban Dictionary. 2004a. Flaming. Accessed February 18, 2015. http://www.urbandic tionary.com/define.php?term = flaming.

———. 2004b. Sanctimommy. Accessed February 18, 2015. http://www.urbandiction ary.com/define.php?term = sanctimommy.

Wang, Tricia. 2012. Writing Live Fieldnotes: Towards a More Open Ethnography. *Ethnography Matters,* August 2. Accessed February 18, 2015. http://ethnography matters.net/2012/08/02/writing-live-fieldnotes-towards-a-more-open-ethnography/.

Warner, Judith. 2006. *Perfect Madness: Motherhood in the Age of Anxiety.* New York: Riverhead.

Zickuhr, Kathryn, and Aaron Smith. 2012. Digital Differences. "PewResearchCenter: Internet, Science & Tech." Accessed February 18, 2015. http://pewinternet.org/ Reports/2012/Digital-differences.aspx.

Chapter 11

When Fieldnotes Seem to Write Themselves: Ethnography Online

Bonnie A. Nardi

This chapter concerns how I came to rethink what constitutes fieldnotes. I discuss changes in the production of fieldnotes afforded by digital technologies, using the concept of affordances from J. J. Gibson's perceptual psychology (1979). Kaptelinin and Nardi (2012) broaden Gibson's notion to include culture, noting that affordances are the "action possibilities offered by the environment to the actor" that mediate cultural experience (967). This chapter analyzes the expansion of action possibilities that digital tools underwrite. I draw from my study of an online video game and from two studies conducted by my students: Caitlin Lustig's research on the Bitcoin community in which she participated in an online forum (Lustig and Nardi 2015), and Nicole Crenshaw's study of video gaming, in which she collected data on a forum (Crenshaw and Nardi 2014). I describe how the written texts produced in forums and chat discourse in video games constitute a form of fieldnotes.

Fieldnotes and Texts

I use the word "text" in its humblest, most ecumenical sense to indicate a collection of words written to be read by someone. I do not think, in this digital age, we can deny the status of text to the billions of words committed to pixels by insisting that a text must, for example, be fixed and "important" (see discussion of Ricoeur by Bond [1990: 275]), or that a text cannot involve dialogue. At websites such as 4chan, words are written to be read and then deliberately discarded, sometimes within seconds (Bernstein et al. 2011). Such texts are hardly fixed, yet millions of people read them. Online forums and games generate lively dialogues that develop as writers and readers interact through the written word. Words are the chief "primitives," in the computer science sense, of Internet activity, and a free and open notion of "text" is imperative if one is going to embrace the diverse, evolving nature of writing.

Online, people produce words in massive quantities. The principal purpose of an online forum is to produce words for others to read. It is through writing that a forum creates and sustains itself as participants ask questions, offer opinions, provide information, give advice, make jokes, reflect on activities of interest, comment on others' posts, and sometimes write merely to provoke (Shelton et al. 2015). Online texts belong to the present as well as to an indeterminate future in which unknown audiences may read them. Textual activity relies on the smooth production, distribution, evaluation, and archiving of words—capacities afforded by digital technologies.

What is the status of online forum and chat texts for the ethnographer? Can they be considered fieldnotes? We usually take fieldnotes to be words crafted by the ethnographer himself or herself. But there is no reason that must always be the case. Others, such as local assistants, have long written voluminous fieldnotes accepted and used by anthropologists (Sanjek 1990, 2014). We may, then, understand forum and chat texts as fieldnotes—high-fidelity representations of the events and ideas pertinent to ongoing activity in a social group that the ethnographer is studying. These fieldnotes appear to "write themselves," as the natives produce activity through writing. This writing can be harvested by the ethnographer to define, frame, and inform anthropological accounts. Like conventional fieldnotes, online texts are "raw" in that they must be organized, analyzed, understood, contextualized, and "written up."

Online texts lack the ethnographer's musings and impressions, but they nonetheless faithfully record events of interest. I can think of few other activities that anthropologists study in which the activity itself is, coextensively, a set of readable, usually very rich fieldnotes. Instead of the ethnographer producing an account such as "Joe said he did not agree with Sam, and Sam countered with a story from his experience as a participant in an Open Source community," the exact words of the exchange are digitally recorded. Just as fieldnotes can be "scratchnotes," "headnotes," or "fuller descriptive fieldnotes" (Ottenberg 1990; Sanjek 2014), we may find other distinctive kinds of fieldnotes useful, such as, in the present discussion, fieldnotes that write themselves. The pervasiveness of the Internet and its crucial importance to contemporary culture and society situate online texts as key loci of data. The activity of collecting and analyzing online texts is central to the evolution of ethnographic practice.

Are online texts of the sort I am talking about better regarded as "documents"? While theoretically, a document is any record (Buckland 1991), anthropologically speaking, "document analysis" generally concerns documents produced for predetermined purposes (such as a letter of introduction or a draft of an academic paper or a blog), or, at least I would argue that we should see it that way. The emergent exchanges within online forums and chat are fundamentally conversational, reactive, and interactive. Few would argue that an everyday conversation is a document. Forum posts and chat utterances respond to what has come before in the online discourse and occur in a speeded-up, intertextual mode in which comments and replies emanently reference one another.

Forum and chat texts differ from conventional documents in that they embed, completely within themselves, readers' assessments. Upon reading words online, participants form judgments, expressing their evaluations through a variety of affordances (which vary across sites) such as replies, votes, comments, likes, retweets, shares, favorites, +1s, karma points, views, virtual gifts, virtual tip jars, and actual monetary tips. These ubiquitous evaluative tokens become part of the texts, and they impart, to the audience and to ethnographers, a strong sense of the content of interest and value to the audience. Fieldnotes "write themselves," revealing participants' preferences, interests, and decisions regarding allocations of scarce resources of attention.

Qua fieldnotes, online texts possess high fidelity and coherence. The texts make clear who is saying what and when they said it. A topic or thread will eventually close, with no further words written. The record is, therefore, complete. It is almost as though we had bridged the gap Borges wrote of in his story "On Exactitude in Science," in which cartographers attempt to treat their maps as "point for point" reality:

In that Empire, the Art of Cartography attained such Perfection that the map of a single Province occupied the entirety of a City, and the map of the Empire, the entirety of a Province. In time, those Unconscionable Maps no longer satisfied, and the Cartographers Guilds struck a Map of the Empire whose size was that of the Empire, and which coincided point for point with it. The following Generations, who were not so fond of the Study of Cartography as their Forebears had been, saw that that vast Map was Useless, and not without some Pitilessness was it, that they delivered it up to the Inclemencies of Sun and Winters. In the Deserts of the West, still today, there are Tattered Ruins of that Map, inhabited by Animals and Beggars; in all the Land there is no other Relic of the Disciplines of Geography. (Borges 1999: 325; first published 1946)

Interestingly for ethnographers, digital technology changes the end of the story. Maps need not be abandoned; they are far from useless. Rather than generating overwhelming complexity, the point-for-point fidelity of digital texts is manageable because of the limited extent of the texts and the power of the digital tools available to manage them. My claims about completeness refer specifically to the record of events texts provide, not to the entire data set that could be generated through the diverse palette of methods anthropologists deploy (see Boellstorff et al. 2012).

Incompleteness awaits elsewhere—as with all fieldnotes, those that write themselves will never be fully analyzed and written up as published work. The anthropologist feels somewhat sad about the partial realization of the work—about the untold stories that remain trapped forever within the raw notes (see Sanjek 2014).

I turn now to consideration of the ethnographer's interactions with participants who natively produce fieldnotes. As in any ethnographic encounter, fieldnotes come into being through social relations the ethnographer establishes with study participants. What do those relations look like online?

A Survey Becomes a Conversation

Let us begin the discussion with consideration of that most quotidian of research instruments, the survey. Online tools make it remarkably easy to conduct surveys. Posting a survey to a forum can be a good way of gathering data and establishing a presence. Doing so is oddly like arriving in a remote village to begin anthropological research. Such research often commences with the time-honored tradition of an inaugural census to meet people and initiate the process of building rapport, as well as attending to the practical matter of finding out how many people live in the village (see Malinowski 1922). Posting an online survey can accomplish similar goals; the survey publicizes the ethnographer's presence and requests participants' cooperation. When presented tactfully, online surveys can summon considerable good will and engage participants in conversation with the ethnographer. Unlike conventional surveys conducted by calling a random sample of people on the phone, or by standing in a mall asking questions, an online survey presented in an established forum taps into existing social relationships, interests, and habits of communication.

For example, to study the Bitcoin community, Caitlin Lustig posted a survey on the main Bitcoin forum. Bitcoin is a legal cryptocurrency operating without government regulation or support. Its online forums attract libertarians, anarchists, people who believe in alternative infrastructure, and speculators seeking to diversify portfolios. The Bitcoin community is articulate, educated, outspoken, and determined to preserve the anonymity of its members in accordance with values of independence and autonomy. The survey immediately piqued forum members' interest.

Aware of the kinds of people she was dealing with, Lustig had been careful to follow forum protocol, setting up an account in the "newbie" area of the forum before presenting the survey. She introduced herself, gave her real name, explained the nature of the research, and identified her subject position as a graduate student. Because many sensational stories about Bitcoin have been written by mainstream media, focusing on, for example, Bitcoin's use in the illegal drug trade, some forum members heralded Lustig's announcement of the survey as a positive event that might foster another perspective, one they hoped would be more legitimate and representative of the community at large. Forum members were thus enthusiastic about the research and promoted the survey through posts such as the following:

> What is important is that there is more work in the public sphere that makes Bitcoin more normal in the eyes of the uninitiated. This

Figure 11.1. "Natives" with bitcoins. Screenshot by Bonnie A. Nardi.

is just one step in that direction. Maybe the results get published and hit Google. Maybe 6 months later some writer trying to find a story to sell reads the survey results, then contacts Ms. Lustig. And we get an opinion being considered that is more informed than so many of the morons currently opining on Bitcoin. . . . This is still the beginning. The potential of Bitcoin will only be realized when there is sufficient awareness, knowledge, and accessibility.

Although Lustig did not use the words anthropologist, ethnographer, or participant observation in her introduction, forum members were quick to catch an anthropological vibe, and one wag Photoshopped bitcoins into an image of "natives," and posted it on the forum (see Figure 11.1). Many forum members found the image humorous, and the post added to Lustig's presence on the website.

Unlike our usual fieldwork, in which participants quietly support the research through participation and good will but would be unlikely to generate discussion about a survey, online forums are typically reactive and vocal. Lustig received many encouraging comments about the survey, such as

I don't usually take the time to participate in surveys, but FWIW [for what it's worth] I think this one was very well-thought out. I'm interested in the results and I hope she gets a lot of responses.

Alright, great, I'm looking forward to the analysis. I'd imagine that most people who filled in the survey are reasonably balanced people, politically and geographically diverse, but hey, no point in me trying to guess the findings!

One forum member promoted the survey in a post, and his approval and publicity increased the response rate. The post explained that Lustig seemed sincere in her attempts to understand the community and that cooperation would be beneficial. Many members commented in turn to encourage others to take the survey. Consistent with the Bitcoin community's value of reasoned discourse, members offered specific reasons to complete the survey: it was well designed and could be completed quickly, Lustig's findings could help outsiders form a more positive view of the Bitcoin community, and the posters themselves were looking forward to the results. The promotional post also included the forum member's own answers to the survey, which may have encouraged others to fill it out because they could preview the questions. The affordances of digital technology are clearly at play here in participants' ability to speak to an assembled audience, voice opinions, and give advice, as well as show the particulars of their own participation in research activity.

Conversations stimulated by an online survey reveal a good deal about participants' educational backgrounds, their opinions about research in general, and their eagerness to discover what research can tell them about their own communities and activities. Lustig received several email "reminders" from Bitcoin community members that they were looking forward to the results of her work. She was also given a gift of bitcoins to reward her efforts, marking her legitimacy in the community. As in village life, where small exchanges are part of everyday activity, so it is in the Bitcoin community, and members occasionally give tips for good posts. Lustig received ฿0.05 bitcoins (7.50 USD) from a well-wisher. The gift and the unsolicited (but very welcome) help of the interested person who promoted the work are reminiscent of traditional, small-scale ethnographic work. Lustig remarked in an email to me, "This experience [studying the Bitcoin community] seems to suggest that we can still draw a lot from traditional ethnographic studies when thinking about online communities." I could not agree more, and it is a tribute to ethnographic practice that it continues to provide effective tools and techniques for studies in our dramatically changing world.

For a study of the video game Guild Wars 2, Nicole Crenshaw posted a survey on avatar personality on a forum called reddit (spelled lowercase). This popular forum is organized into a collection of "subreddits," that is, subforums devoted to specific topics. Posting to the /r/GuildWars2 subreddit was a foolproof way to locate study participants interested in and knowledgeable about the game. As a highly trafficked website, reddit is increasingly useful for research. In January 2014, it ranked twenty-seventh in the United States and seventy-second globally, with billions of page views. Within a short time, Crenshaw's survey had been taken by more than a thousand participants.

In the forum conversations about the research, participants asked many questions and felt comfortable posing even somewhat tangential queries. Crenshaw used such questions as an opportunity to establish rapport through friendly replies. For example, a participant asked why the survey question on marital status was worded in a particular way. (See Figure 11.2, a screenshot I include so readers can see what the subreddit looked like.)

A nice dialog between Crenshaw and the participant ensued, in which the participant appreciated that Crenshaw took the question seriously. Her congenial response was public to others, demonstrating good will toward, and care for, those participating in the study. Crenshaw received a gift of game "gold" (virtual currency to buy game items in the game economy) in response to the survey, delivered through the Guild Wars 2 email system. The player sent an email message along with the gold commending Crenshaw for studying the community:

> Hi,
> I just wanted to compliment you on your fascinating post. :) Thanks so much for taking an interest in the community and compiling these surveys and then crunching the numbers! A daunting task, I'm sure, but the results sure were fun to read :)

Sometimes participants' questions concerned technical aspects of research practice. Many forum participants were curious about the nuts and bolts of Crenshaw's methods. She had mentioned that interviews

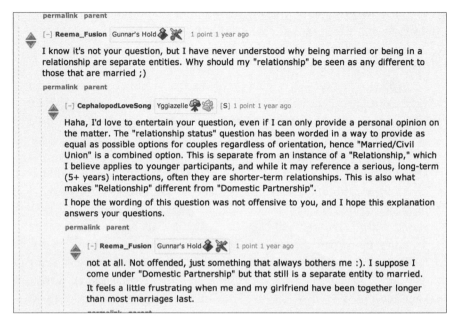

Figure 11.2. Conversation on a subreddit. Screenshot by Bonnie A. Nardi.

would follow the survey. One participant asked: "So how long does it take to transcribe an interview? Do you really take it all down, or just the good bits?"

That Lustig and Crenshaw's surveys stirred interest and approval can be attributed in no small measure to careful preparation of the survey questions. Crenshaw had extensive knowledge of Guild Wars 2 and its culture from playing the game and reading forums and other materials, and Lustig made a thorough study of the history of Bitcoin, including an investigation of the complicated technology on which it is built. Ethnographers often do not get credit for the precision with which we design research instruments; perhaps as we take our work online and leverage the affordances of digital technology, we will find increased appreciation from the assembled publics to whom we are able to speak. Crenshaw and Lustig received many positive comments on their surveys, although surveys are not usually thought of as terribly interesting. Three of Crenshaw's forum members wrote, for example:

[Poster One:] Nice questions indeed. I'm really curious what you, we or "the people" can learn from this survey. Will you share some insights with us when you've processed it?

[Poster Two:] Much better survey than the others ones posted here! =D Doesn't feel condescending, for once~

[Poster Three, replying to Poster Two:] I agree, this survey didn't feel like a chore. It was relaxing opening up about my character creation process.

Best of luck on your research study!

Another participant, an alum of our university, the University of California, Irvine (UCI), wrote in the uninhibited, ironic style of much online discourse:

UCI alumn ZOT ZOT MOTHERFUCKERS!!!!
. . . okay filling out the survey now

("Zot," to explain, is the sound UCI's animal mascot, an anteater, makes.)

Participants' digital inquiries, commentaries, and exuberant enthusiasm about research can, even as they generate rich fieldnotes, also serve in the interest of what the National Science Foundation calls "broader impacts." Texts discussing the research activity itself may accomplish quite a lot: raising the salience and visibility of research, stimulating discussion of how and why research is actually conducted, and allowing for public discourse about what has been learned and why it is important. These opportunities for outreach are readily available online and are especially important for anthropology, as our work often receives less public attention and recognition than that of other fields.

Pushback

Of course, anything can happen as we conduct research online, just as it can offline. My students' experiences were positive, but there is never a guarantee of success in any ethnographic endeavor. Online conventions of frankness and directness, along with the ease of communication afforded by digital technologies, may open conversations in which participants challenge the ethnographer in quite direct ways. For example, at first, Lustig was met with suspicion from a few forum members. This response was not surprising, given that Bitcoin is a cryptocurrency, and many in the community are zealous about maintaining individual anonymity. One person posted that the community would be watching Lustig, writing: "Hello Caitie Lustig, we are currently monitoring and researching your activities on the forum." Another put up a picture of her that he found on the Internet, presumably in an attempt to verify that she was the person she claimed to be and not an agent of the National Security Agency or a similar organization. These events were isolated incidents (and the latter action was actually in support of Lustig, although it also stands as a nod to the general wariness of the Bitcoin community). But it is easy to see how suspicions could escalate into rejection of the researcher and the research. Indeed, some ethnographers have experienced sufficient hostility from participants in online venues that they decide to go elsewhere.

Challenges to ethnographers are not new; in traditional fieldwork, ethnographers have been presumed to be witches, ghosts, spies, missionaries, government agents, and various other miscreants. Online, we must be careful to remember that everything we say is recorded and shareable and can be revisited by participants. From a pedagogical viewpoint, senior researchers should be mindful that being told one is being "monitored," or receiving similar comments, can be unnerving to fledging ethnographers. Part of our role is to anticipate such situations and help students prepare to respond, knowing that the affordances of digital technology mean that online responses are part of a permanent record. Members of educated publics who participate in online forums are, in fact, very likely to be watching. And writing. Because writing is the central activity of online forums, it is natural for study participants to write down what they observe and think. And that may include reactions to what the ethnographer is doing!

Participants in online forums are not shy about offering opinions on how the research is being conducted. We may find ourselves challenged by study participants in ways we are not used to. Participants often have Ph.D.s themselves. In Crenshaw's study, many comments offering both encouragement for the research and friendly critique of the study methods appeared on the subreddit. Participants wrote things such as

Seems to me you could get a better response by not limiting yourself to US :)

Cool survey! One small suggestion: education level on PhD should just say doctorate or terminal degree instead of PhD to accommodate people with MDs, JDs, etc.

Several questions related to the topic of sampling came up, and Crenshaw quickly developed a FAQ about this question and a few other issues that repeatedly arose. She included the following explanation about the sample design:

I had anticipated mostly US-based players, which is why the server list question only has the NA [North American] servers. I myself am US based, hence the census terms (this prevents any messy legal issues with referring to certain races as X, Y, or Z). However, I don't discourage input from anyone! If I do get more EU players, I can shift my analysis with that in mind. I just apologize that it's not as EU friendly as NA friendly.

Bitcoin participants asked Lustig about her methods and requested responses to specific questions. The crucial post with the completed survey became a place where people could go to raise concerns. Lustig participated in the conversation, answering methodological questions and offering explanations. When trying to address a concern that a participant raised with respect to his opinion that she needed to be "very careful about what conclusions to draw from the survey," she explained her methods further and attempted to provide as much detail as she could. Online venues are uniquely vulnerable to public conversations about the ethnographer's methods, and although such exchanges make for great fieldnotes, they keep the ethnographer on her toes. Educated study participants in offline settings may also ask about, and question, study methods, but generally there is not a great deal in the way of public forums for discussion. Exceptions exist, of course, such as when pitching prospective research to, for instance, a hospital or research lab, where prospective study participants would likely discuss methods in some detail in a collective setting when deciding whether to grant access to the site. In online forums, public challenges, some friendly, some not, are the norm, not the exception. One silver lining is that students learn to articulate their methods and strategies early in their careers!

In venues where words are everything, ethnographers must craft theirs carefully. In introducing herself and presenting the research, Lustig decided that she did not want to say that she was "observing" the community, because it might connote surveillance, an undesirable activity for the Bitcoin community. She explained instead that she would be supplementing the survey data with interviews and by spending time on the forum.

Seeing Fieldnotes Differently: My Experience Studying World of Warcraft

I have in some sense recast the usual notion of fieldnotes in this chapter, at least to the extent that I have not accepted that fieldnotes must typically be "personal, parochial, subjective" (Bond 1990: 274). I amplify the notion of "fieldnotes" to include natively inscribed happenings in the field that are automatically recorded in computer files and coextensive with the activity under study. Allowing this amplification seems consistent with Jackson's earlier (1990) empirical research on how field researchers define fieldnotes. In the mid-1980s, she interviewed seventy field researchers, mostly "card-carrying anthropologists," as she put it, and reported that definitions of fieldnotes varied enough among her interviewees that we cannot plausibly argue that there exists a single, fixed definition upon which the research community agrees. Consistent with ethnography's natural flexibility, field-notes are a pliant medium, responding to the needs of the particular venues in which the ethnography is being conducted.

I did not always see it this way. I subscribed to a conventional view of fieldnotes as something an ethnographer wrote. This belief eroded when I studied the video game World of Warcraft, a popular title played all over the world (see Nardi 2010). One of the first things I noticed when entering this unfamiliar environment (I had never played a video game) was the function /chatlog—a command within the game to record text chat and game events in a file stored outside the game. I had merely to type the magic word (and it felt very magical indeed after all the fieldnotes I had written by hand over the years), and a legible, error-free, timestamped, computerized version of chat and game events appeared in my World of Warcraft directory. Everything players typed was recorded. Records of game events were more selective, having been predefined by the game designer, but they still provided good context.

World of Warcraft chatlogs look like this:

7/23 20:17:20.982 Experience gained: 3200.
7/23 20:17:36.349 [Guild] Innika: ding
7/23 20:17:45.039 [Guild] Angelstears: grats Innika
7/23 20:17:49.484 [Guild] Naysmith: grats
7/23 20:17:50.087 [Guild] Phlod: grats
7/23 20:17:50.153 Holzmer cheers at you.
7/23 20:17:50.541 [Guild] Fizzler: gras
7/23 20:17:52.284 Holzmer claps excitedly for you.
7/23 20:17:57.981 Holzmer is very happy with you!
7/23 20:17:57.702 You wave at Holzmer.
7/23 20:18:03.491 [Guild] Seraphis: grats
7/23 20:18:05.949 Holzmer congratulates you.
7/23 20:18:09.361 You thank Holzmer.

In this chatlog, my character Innika has just achieved a new level in the game ("ding") after having earned 3200 experience points, an event the game automatically records. My guildmates (club members) congratulate me through typing words ("grats") and typing brief game commands that print automated messages such as "Holzmer congratulates you."

As these chatlogs began to pile up (ominously so, as I was playing fifteen to twenty hours a week), I began to see them in a new light. They were a key record of what had happened while I was playing—they were, in short, fieldnotes. These fieldnotes were afforded by a capacity of the game software to capture participants' words in a complete record of what they had written. The Borgesian map hove into view—there was no difference between the words in my chatlogs and the words I saw typed into the chat window while I was playing. The words were those of naturally occurring dialogs communicated in the native medium—chat—of online video games.

I consulted the chatlogs often. I used quotes from them in my papers, and I conducted a quantitative analysis of how quickly players answered each other's questions, an analysis in which I calculated times to the second (Nardi, Ly, and Harris 2007). I could make such calculations easily because I had timestamps (out to the millisecond) for every utterance. I was not writing the fieldnotes myself, but they served the same purpose as my own handwritten notes had in previous studies. The chatlogs were, in many ways, more exact and precise.

I recognized right away, though, that a certain important class of chat utterances was not being captured: the private messages other players received and sent to each other that were taking place around me. Only my own "whispers," and those I received from others, were included in the chatlog. Big data approaches that claim to analyze "complete" records of video game activity lack a critical source of player expression (and should never be advertised as complete). It is in whispers that people gossip, complain, flirt, build teams, educate one another, create social bonds, and perform many crucial communicative acts. In the following exchange, for example, I leave my moribund guild and join a new one, invited by a previous member of my soon to be erstwhile guild:

> 2/7 17:57:03.588 To Lirimaer: how's your new guild going?
> 2/7 17:57:31.595 Lirimaer whispers: Good, I just got promoted to the high council. We have over 30 level 60's.
> 2/7 17:57:37.521 Lirimaer whispers: I'm now in charge of guild events =)
> 2/7 17:58:08.339 To Lirimaer: that's great!
> 2/7 17:58:48.170 Lirimaer whispers: want to join? seeming the brotherhood [the old guild] is like dead now = P
> 2/7 17:59:11.026 To Lirimaer: sure but i thought you had to be a [level] 40.
> 2/7 17:59:35.534 Lirimaer whispers: I joined stargazers. Started as the lowest rank, now im one of the leaders = D
> 2/7 18:00:09.751 To Lirimaer: ok. sure i need a new guild. it's a little lonely here. that's great that you've come up in stargazers :)
> 2/7 18:00:19.982 Lirimaer whispers: =) thanks.

As I progressed in the game I began to "raid," a team activity requiring tight coordination. Raiding is supported by a voicechat channel used to direct and manage the action. Raiding prompted a return to old-school fieldnotes—I had no audio record like what I was getting for text with / chatlog. The digital record was far from complete. Writing things down was somewhat difficult during raiding because there is no place for a spectator in a raid, and I was only allowed into the raid because I could perform my role. (For readers who are gamers and might be interested, I was a healing priest, sometimes specced holy and sometimes discipline.) The performance kept my fingers busy on the keyboard. I learned to take notes about the audio conversations and raid events when the raid was regrouping after a defeat. Fortunately for my research, defeats are common in raiding, especially when raiders are learning a new contest, so I managed to find time. I had to commit as much to memory as possible during the action so I could write it down when the moment came.

I divided my attention between performing my in-game role and watching for events of anthropological interest (a skill all participant observers gain over time). I also had the chatlogs of player conversation during the raid and key raid events that were automatically recorded. My analyses of World of Warcraft have thus been informed by chatlogs, discussions with participants about their private messages, and the fieldnotes I wrote about audio conversations and events not captured by /chatlog. The World of Warcraft fieldnotes are a mélange of natively produced/automatically recorded notes and the usual handcrafted "personal, parochial, subjective" fieldnotes of traditional ethnography.

Though I completed the primary data collection in 2009, I still find myself going back to the chatlogs when I need data for a theory paper or to look up a detail for a lecture. My handcrafted notes are less vivid and detailed, and I have to try harder to rebuild the context in my mind. If we come to privilege fieldnotes that write themselves, it may be because they say more than we can, an outcome of the ease with which digital technology affords the recording of our every word and a good many of our actions.

Conclusion

Despite the quasi-Borgesian maps produced by fieldnotes that write themselves, it is, nonetheless, the special burden of anthropology to remind science that we do not yet live in a world in which digital records are a complete reflection of who we are and what we do. At the same time, it appears that a new reality may be forming, with the possibility that we are indeed heading toward a world in which we will be substantially defined by our digital activity. This world is prefigured by developments such as the uptake of wearable technologies, the turn to microwork and crowdsourcing, and a shift to autonomous, self-contained online activity such as that of the Bitcoin community and online video games.

Anthropology should be alert to the rich possibilities for ethnographic inquiry these ventures present, paying special attention to the affordances of the technologies that undergird them. Perhaps even more kinds of field-notes will emerge as we investigate technologies such as Oculus Rift, a commercial virtual reality system; Corning's architectural-digital glass; and the suite of technologies producing the "quantified self." The great thing about ethnography is that it does not commit to methodological orthodoxy, as Jackson's card-carrying anthropologists told her back in the 1980s. Ethnography is well positioned to encounter and make sense of what our life and times are becoming in a rush of change.

Bibliography

Bernstein, Michael, Andres Monroy-Hernández, Drew Harry, Paul André, Katrina Panovich, and Greg Vargas. 2011. 4chan and /b/: An Analysis of Anonymity and Ephemerality in a Large Online Community. *Proceedings of the Fifth International AAAI Conference on Weblogs and Social Media*, 50–57. Accessed February 19, 2015. http://projects.csail.mit.edu/chanthropology/4chan.pdf.

Boellstorff, Tom, Bonnie Nardi, Celia Pearce, and T. L. Taylor. 2012. *Ethnography and Virtual Worlds: A Handbook of Method*. Princeton, N.J.: Princeton University Press.

Bond, George C. 1990. Fieldnotes: Researches in Past Occurrences. In *Fieldnotes: The Makings of Anthropology*, edited by Roger Sanjek, 273–289. Ithaca, N.Y.: Cornell University Press.

Borges, Jorge Luis. 1999. *Collected Fictions*. New York: Penguin. First published 1946.

Buckland, Michael. 1991. *Information and Information Systems*. New York: Greenwood Press.

Crenshaw, Nicole and Bonnie Nardi. 2014. What's in a Name? Naming Practices in Online Video Games. *Proceedings CHIPlay*. 67–76.

Gibson, James J. 1979. *The Ecological Approach to Visual Perception*. Boston, Mass.: Houghton Mifflin.

Jackson, Jean E. 1990. "I Am a Fieldnote": Fieldnotes as a Symbol of Professional Identity. In *Fieldnotes: The Makings of Anthropology*, edited by Roger Sanjek, 3–33. Ithaca, N.Y.: Cornell University Press.

Kaptelinin, Victor and Bonnie Nardi. 2012. *Activity Theory in HCI Research: Fundamentals and Reflections*. San Rafael: Morgan & Claypool.

Lustig, Caitlin and Nardi, Bonnie 2015. Algorithmic Authority: The Case of Bitcoin. *Proceedings HICSS 2015*, 743–752.

Malinowski, Bronislaw. 1922. *Argonauts of the Western Pacific*. New York: E. P. Dutton.

Nardi, Bonnie. 2010. *My Life as a Night Elf Priest: An Anthropological Account of World of Warcraft*. Ann Arbor: University of Michigan Press.

————, Stella Ly, and Justin Harris. 2007. Learning Conversations in World of War-craft. In *Proceedings of the 40th Annual Hawaii International Conference on Systems Science,* 79–88. Accessed February 19, 2015. http://darrouzet-nardi.net/bonnie/pdf/Nardi-HICSS.pdf.

Ottenberg, Simon. 1990. Thirty Years of Fieldnotes: Changing Relationships to the Text. In *Fieldnotes: The Makings of Anthropology,* edited by Roger Sanjek, 139–160. Ithaca, N.Y.: Cornell University Press.

Sanjek, Roger, editor. 1990. *Fieldnotes: The Makings of Anthropology.* Ithaca, N.Y.: Cornell University Press.

————. 2014. *Ethnography in Today's World: Color Full Before Color Blind.* Philadelphia: University of Pennsylvania Press.

Shelton, M., Katherine Lo, and Bonnie Nardi. In press. Online Media Forums as Separate Social Lives: A Qualitative Study of Disclosure Within and Beyond Reddit.

Chapter 12

The Ethnography of Inscriptive Speech

Graham M. Jones and Bambi B. Schieffelin

Fugacious, yet we take the dream
As pure, inscriptive speech. . . .
—John Falk, "Scribing"

For most cultural anthropologists, fieldnotes are the paradigmatic form of data to emerge from participant observation research. While limited direct quotation from fieldnotes is not uncommon in anthropological texts, the relationship between original ethnographic data and published ethnographic scholarship is usually obscured by processes of organizing, collating, interpreting, editing, and rewriting. Although they also produce and use fieldnotes, linguistic anthropologists generate another form of entextualized data that is itself iconic of their subfield: the transcript. Like fieldnotes, transcripts are primary objects of analysis, but unlike fieldnotes, they are at least partially reproduced in a majority of linguistic anthropological publications (often over editors' protests), reflecting the value researchers place on the meticulous analysis of verbal patterns and interactional processes.

Publishing transcripts is an index of the considerable time and effort linguistic anthropologists invest in generating textual representations of audio- or video-recorded interactions, often with fine-grained detail of features such as pauses, self-corrections, or overlaps between speakers. This degree of micro-level detail is itself a persuasive form of verisimilitude. Beginning with Elinor Ochs (1979), numerous scholars have shown how, in one way or another, transcripts—far from offering direct, transparent access to "real" interaction—involve interpretation, convention, artifice, and ideology (Edwards 2003; Roberts 1997). For instance, transcribers make politically laden decisions about either aligning transcriptions of talk to the standards of written language or adapting the written word to capture the sound of speech—decisions that affect how readers view the status of speakers and their discourse (Bucholtz 2000).

Duranti (2006: 306) points out that transcription involves a movement from "a technology-mediated inscription" (a recorded artifact) to a "technology-mediated representation" (a written artifact), reminding us that "this is not a small achievement, and considerable technological, methodological, and theoretical efforts have gone into making it possible." Because transcripts are representations, he argues, "they can only give us, through a combination of symbolic, iconic, and indexical signs, a restricted, selected perspective—a stance, a point of view, often with an attitude. . . . Transcripts have properties of models. It is such model-like properties that can allow us to argue through them and about them. It is their model-like properties that make them good to think with" (309).

In the context of this volume's inquiry into the implications of digital technologies for ethnographic praxis, we reflect on a form of technology-mediated inscription that can itself be used as a transcript with minimal subsequent manipulation. For the purpose of studying text-based channels of digital communication such as instant messaging (IM) or chatting—which participants themselves often classify as forms of conversational *talk* and describe with the metalanguage of *speech* (Jones and Schieffelin 2009)—researchers can, where practically and ethically feasible, operationalize the technology-mediated inscriptions generated in and by the conversation itself as the functional equivalent of a written transcript. We propose to call these sui generis quasi-transcripts "inscripts." These byproducts of inscriptive speech are not models of talk. They are talk.

In discussing the relationship between inscription and transcription, Duranti (2006: 305) invokes the work of philosopher Paul Ricoeur. A further examination of Ricoeur's account of the difference between speaking and writing may be useful in light of relatively novel digital inscriptive technologies of the sort we consider here. Ricoeur (1973, 1976) argues that inscription objectifies discourse, removing it from the context of the speech event, in which meaning is dialogically co-constructed. It is precisely this alienation of discourse through writing, however, that makes readership possible as a mode of textual appropriation. Technologies of synchronous, text-based computer-mediated communication (which may have been hard for Ricoeur to imagine four decades ago) seem to challenge his close association of inscription and alienation: IM and chat, particularly when they are culturally valued as a form of talk, offer the potential for relatively non-alienated writing; they often constitute something very much like a co-constructed speech event through writing. At the same time, the traces that these conversations leave behind in the form of inscripts certainly are detachable from the originating speech event, posing for would-be ethnographers the same hermeneutic challenge of overcoming distantiation as the literary works Ricoeur alludes to. This alienability is a precondition for analysis.

Inscripts offer analysts entextualizations of talk produced by interactional partners who engage in conversation while themselves attending reflexively to the materiality (see Shankar and Cavanaugh 2012) of the typewritten word. Recording and transcribing otherwise ephemeral talk enables interpretation by slowing down perception. Like face-to-face talk, computer-mediated conversation can be fast-paced and of only momentary interest to participants. But it is not ephemeral. It leaves lasting traces, stored indefinitely, that are potentially accessible to researchers. What's more, these traces are, in principle, exhaustive: inscripts contain most of the signifying material—graphemes, fonts, punctuation, time intervals—available to interactional partners.

This exhaustiveness should not be taken to indicate that these self-generating transcripts avoid the epistemological perils of researcher-generated transcripts. Context remains a crucial and problematic issue. Possessing an inscript in no way confers relevant contextual information—such as cultural background knowledge or the personal history of conversational partners—necessary to interpret it. Moreover, the use of inscripts as ethnographic data depends on a process of selection, as do transcripts: "the act of choosing a segment of life to transcribe implies decisions about the significance of the strip of talk or the speech event, which, in turn, implies that the talk or event has been interpreted from some point of view" (Green, Franquiz, and Dixon 1997: 173). As exhaustive as the inscriptive protocols are in digital communications, some features still escape recording: for instance, notifications that a particular message has been seen or that another user is typing can convey important paralinguistic information in a conversation (see, for example, Rodriguez 2012) but are generally not recorded in chatlogs. Finally, reproducing computer-mediated talk in scholarly publications (as in the case of this chapter) often involves changes in font, layout, and mode of interface that may inadvertently affect content.

With these caveats, we want to explore some of the interesting properties of working with inscripts as opposed to transcripts. Inscripts provide entextualized conversational data without the mediating activity of a third-party transcriber or transcription software. Rather, conversationalists inscribe their own entextualized utterances, the exchange of which constitutes a cumulative log of turns. Of particular interest is the way that participants themselves orient to the entextualization format. Their active, reflexive involvement in the writerly choices—analogous to the deliberate processes of selection and combination through which transcribers produce transcripts—generate inscripts that can, in turn, be analyzed for evidence of communicative competence and semiotic ideologies. We have previously used inscripts alongside transcripts from the same speaker pool to compare stylistic variation across spoken and written channels of communication (Jones and Schieffelin 2009). Here, we examine three themes specifically pertinent to the research with and on text-based compter-mediated communication (CMC): ethnopoetics, reflexivity, and circulation.

The Ethnopoetics of Inscriptive Speech

The area of ethnopoetics represents a useful point of reference in our formulation of an approach to inscripts. Hymes (1994) conceptualizes ethnopoetics as an inquiry into the structural conventions of verbal artistry, arguing that language researchers too often transcribe oral narrative in a paragraph form (likening it to canonical prose narrative) that distorts speakers' deliberate organizational decisions. "Any presentation of a narrative on the page," he writes, "implies a hypothesis as to its form. . . . Presentation in terms of lines and verses makes visible the shaping artistry of narrators. . . . The reading is slowed, which makes it far more possible to perceive repetition, parallelism, and succession. . . . Such analysis contributes to a general theory of the competence and practices involved in oral narrative itself" (340–341).

Criticizing the inaccuracies of third-party transcription, Hymes argues for an approach to studying oral narrative in terms of the speakers' own implicit strategies for organization through lines and verses. Inscriptive speech makes many of these decisions manifest. As we have argued else-where (Jones, Schieffelin, and Smith 2011), in chat-based conversations, speakers artfully manage line breaks with a stroke of the return key, using the poetic convention of enjambment to coordinate structure and modulate meaning. In the following example, drawn from an IM chat between two young women (for which time stamps were not provided), the first speaker narrates a previous conversation. She uses line breaks (lines 1 and 5) to differentiate her voice as a narrator and the voices of the characters—including herself—whose speech she reports. This "shaping artistry" (as Hymes puts it) makes the parallelism between the speech of contrasting voices manifest in the structure of the story. In line 3, a line break functions to close the frame of reported speech, allowing the narrator to comment derisively on the reported utterance, "hahaha."

Example 1 (IM 2007)

1 chicachevere123: cause he was like
2 chicachevere123: i can live without sex
3 chicachevere123: i don't need it
4 chicachevere123: hahaha
5 chicachevere123: i was like
6 dreamalittledream: whaaaaat
7 chicachevere123: yeah if we're dating
8 chicachevere123: that's gonna cause problems

The line breaks here are (very effectively) doing the work of quotation marks, periods, commas, capitalization, and paragraphing to coordinate the mimetic representation of a narrated conversation. Importantly, they offer an approach to textual organization that is stylistically consistent with the conventions of a medium in which speakers do not see each other's words as they are typed but only when they are sent through a push of the return key. Here, shortness of utterances is a way of holding the floor and main-taining interest, particularly in the context of a morally charged narrative such as this. Note that in line 6, the addressee of this narrative interjects an assessment of the speech reported in lines 2–3, breaking into the frame of reported speech that the narrator establishes in line 5. The narrator's following utterance appears to both respond to this contribution ("yeah") and continue with the report of her own utterance ("if we're dating. . . ."); alternately, her "yeah" could be read as a discourse marker, establishing a contrastive stance within the reporting frame.

In the previous example, a narrator uses quotative *like* as a device for reporting the speech of herself and others (*he was like* . . . .; *I was like* . . . .). This device has been widely associated with adding vividness to storytelling, because it allows storytellers to dramatically reenact speakers' roles rather than directly reporting or indirectly describing their utterances (see, for example, Buchstaller 2003). The increasing presence of quotative *like* in English-language chat (Jones and Schieffelin 2009; Tagliamonte and Denis 2008) may reflect lag time as speakers develop conventions necessary for achieving such mimetic vividness in written communication—overcoming the "meditational barrier" (Bauman 2010) of the typewritten form. The following example, collected in 2006, points to the development of conventions for typographically representing utterances with an expressivity approximating spoken renditions of constructed dialogues. Here, a narrator uses quotative *like* to relay a story about her boyfriend Zachary "zoning out," in her terms.

Example 2 (IM 2006)

 1 FuManChewy (9:56:26 PM): im like, zachary u okay?
 2 FuManChewy (9:56:27 PM): zachary?
 3 FuManChewy (9:56:34 PM): ZACHARY?
 4 FuManChewy (9:56:39 PM): omg wtf
 5 [. . .]
 6 FuManChewy (9:57:45 PM): i kept askign him if he was okay
 7 FuManChewy (9:57:49 PM): and he was like im fine
 8 FuManChewy (9:57:59 PM): then i realized he wasn't paying attention
 9 FuManChewy (9:58:03 PM): and im like, are u paying attention
10 FuManChewy (9:58:04 PM): ?
11 FuManChewy (9:58:09 PM): and he's like, i'm not even gonna lie
12 FuManChewy (9:58:10 PM): nope
13 FuManChewy (9:58:19 PM): and i was like !!!!! bastard!

The narrator uses quotative *like* five times in the short excerpt (lines 1, 7, 9, 11, 13) from her story illustrating Zachary's inconsiderate inattentiveness. In lines 1–3, line breaks add vividness to the story. Each break indicates a pause in speech, conveying both the prosody of storytelling and mirroring the passage of time in the reported event (note the elapse of seven seconds between lines 2 and 3 and five seconds between lines 3 and 4). A variation from lower to upper case (lines 2–3) amplifies the mounting urgency—and probably increased volume—of the speech reported. In line 4, the narrator uses two conventionalized CMC initialisms, "omg" (oh my God) and "wtf" (what the fuck), to encode her reported thought in the same quotative frame. Several lines later, FuManChewy reports her frustration toward Zachary, enquoting a repeated mark of punctuation ("!!!!!") as an iconic representation of her attitude or stance, which is in turn followed by her verbalized assessment of him: "bastard!"

The artful use of iconic paralinguistic features such as line breaks, capitalization, and punctuation, along with evocative medialectal features such as initialisms, allow the narrator to achieve heightened vividness in her typewritten report of a spoken conversation. Indeed, these spontaneously produced reported dialogues are themselves kinds of transcripts done from memory. Just as anthropologists and sociolinguists have used transcriptions to study the language ideologies of both native transcription assistants (Haviland 1996) and scholarly transcribers (Bucholtz 2007), inscripts reflect language and media ideologies emergent in the process of written communication (Jones 2014). Of course, enacting ideologies of any sort does not make people cultural automata. In the following section, we consider more closely how inscripts can reveal the high degree of reflexivity—taken as a hallmark of both speakers' self-awareness and the ability of language to refer to itself—involved in spontaneous inscriptive speech.

Reflexivity in Inscriptive Speech

Every act of communication can be considered as an instance of entextualization, in which a message is articulated using codes and conventions in a particular referential context and transmitted through a communicative channel between an addresser and an addressee (Bauman and Briggs 1990). All entextualizations exhibit choices not only in production format but also in message formatting. In this section, we explore how the specificity of mediating channels affects the entextualization process, emphasizing the reflexive ability of language to refer to itself or, more broadly, for signs to refer to other signs. Common forms of reflexivity include metalanguage—talk about the form and function of talk—and expressions such as citations or quotations in which one statement or text refers to another. Methodologically, reflexivity is a useful way to get at explicit or implicit understandings of how communication works or should work in a particular setting.

We examine two inscripts of Internet relay chat (IRC), a form of synchronous, polyadic, typewritten communication in which users logged in to a particular channel exchange text-based messages (like instant messaging but with potentially many users). Our inscripts are drawn from conversation on a channel used by computer hackers to discuss the programing language COBOL (and other peripheral interests). Gabriella Coleman (2012) calls IRC "the central nervous system of so many geek and hacker interactions." The inscripts we analyze reflect what Coleman identifies as "a form of charismatic sociality quite common on IRC where cleverness, cunning, and playfulness garner attention and sometimes, even respect" in a way that exceeds the instrumental exchange of knowledge in which participants also engage.

Both these examples concern the entry of a new participant into the "multi-layered, multi-threaded, somewhat chaotic, and often quite playful" (Coleman 2012) state of IRC talk. In the first example, the new entrant violates norms of politeness, occasioning sanctions from two other participants.

Example 3 (IRC 2010)

1 03:04:41 ƒ BEAN has joined #cobol
2 03:05:05 everyone idle?
3 03:05:23 ?ecsss
4 03:05:24 ecsss enter channel say something stupid
5 03:05:25 ?ecaq
6 03:05:26 ecaq enter channel ask question

In line 1, an automatic announcement indicates that user BEAN has logged into the channel. Because other users may be logged on but not attending to the channel, after twenty-four seconds of inactivity, BEAN posts the question "everyone idle?" After eighteen seconds, BEAN receives two responses in rapid succession that involve the use of a feature of the channel called a "bot." A bot is an automated program that acts as an IRC user in certain circumstances, responding to particular utterance prompts with reciprocal turns. The bot in this example, skybot, maintains a dictionary specific to this channel that channel users themselves update with terms and definitions relevant to channel topics. As in lines 3 and 5, a user can initiate a "lookup" by entering a question mark followed by the query term. Skybot responds with a definition.

In this case, user pov queries the initialism "ecsss" which skybot defines as "enter channel say something stupid." Almost simultaneously, user Aguirre queries the initialism "ecaq," which skybot defines as "enter channel ask question." These initialisms both characterize the opening turn of a user who has newly joined an IRC channel. Note that they both name speech acts: *saying* and *asking*, respectively. As far as we have been able to determine, they are unique to the specific website that hosts this particular channel, if not to the channel itself. In their referential specificity, these initialisms are calibrated to the particular communicative context of IRC conversation. They index and encode communicative norms of this particular speech community, namely that, upon joining the channel, a user should enter conversation in a contextually relevant manner. Conversation on the channel is never-ending, and an indeterminate number of users remain perpetually logged in, yet there are no technical restrictions concerning who can talk when. In this context, opening turns that are not contextually relevant to ongoing talk represent a breach of turn-taking etiquette.

It is crucial to note that users pov and Aguirre do not merely respond "ecsss" or "ecaq" to BEAN's objectionable turn. Their queries animate (Goffman 1979) responses that are authored by skybot but that have also already been authored by the users who entered these terms into skybot's dictionary. This results in a kind of heteroglossia (Bakhtin 1992)—the presence of multiple voices in a single utterance—that is characteristic of all speech but that becomes particularly striking in online communication. These turns also produce a kind of indirection comparable to Mitchell-Kernan's (1972) account of "signifying and marking." Just as Mitchell-Kernan famously argues, the entextualization of assessments in this example constitutes a kind of verbal artistry, one that presupposes the particular conjuncture of a shared metacommunicative code, a shared referential frame, and communicative competence in a particular mode of interaction.

In our second example, a participant in the same channel uses skybot in a way that reflects a normative understanding of conventional turn-taking procedures and mastery of the metacommunicative code associated with the assessing communicative behavior on the channel. He or she also shows an intertextual awareness of the use of skybot for indirectly sanctioning violations of turn-taking etiquette but uses all of these features in a context-defining rather than a context-defined manner.

Example 4 (IRC 2010)

1 21:16:11—> tim has joined #cobol
2 [. . .]
3 21:16:19 ?ecpl
4 21:16:19 ecpl = enter channel paste link
5 21:16:20 http://www.youtube.com/watch?v = zkd5dJIVjgM

In this example, user tim joins the IRC channel, apparently with the intention of sharing a link to a YouTube video. Anticipating negative reactions from other users, she or he enters a skybot query for the initialism "ecpl," which skybot defines as "enter channel paste link." Here the skybot query serves as a presequence, announcing the sharing of a link in violation of the preferred procedure of establishing contextual relevance in opening turns.

The link leads to a video from the children's program *Sesame Street* that parodies an Old Spice deodorant commercial popular online. In it, the Muppet Grover proclaims, "Anything is possible when you smell like a monster." The link itself serves as a contextualization cue, keying tim's opening turns as humorous. In contrast to our first IRC example, in which users retrospectively classify another user's turn as a violation of turn-taking conventions, here, tim prospectively announces an impending violation of turn-taking conventions, using the skybot lookup in a way that mirrors the indirection exhibited in the previous example. There is no subsequent commentary on these opening moves, suggesting that, at least in this conversation, anything is indeed possible if you smell like a monster.

These two IRC examples illustrate the crucial dimension of the entextualization process that John Lucy (1999: 214) refers to as "implicit reflexivity." Implicit reflexivity describes the way in which entextualizations index the speaker's activities of selection and combination, which are a fundamental part of utterance formation. Implicit reflexivity also concerns the materiality of the message form, which is an important feature in considering mediated entextualizations. These two IRC examples illustrate the general way that entextualizations index, through implicit reflexivity, the particular conditions of mediation in which and through which they are produced. Entextualizations bear the traces of a process of selection: the choice of channel, addressee, referential contexts, and communicative codes. They also bear the traces of combinatory processes, whereby speakers weave various elements together in articulating a message. Implicit reflexivity indexes the technical specificity of the production format (for instance, the functionality of the skybot lookup in these examples). It also indexes social factors, such as the communities of speech and practice that intersect with particular media and that espouse evolving communicative norms. Finally, implicit reflexivity also concerns cultural factors, such as the generic conventions and intertextual references necessary for the poetic elaboration of expressive entextualizations.

The entextualization of talk in IRC generates inscripts as an inevitable by-product. Dimensions of implicit reflexivity evident in participants' inscriptions suggest how awareness of the constraints and opportunities of this particular channel enter into the production of talk. That this talk is written by speakers gives it particular value as evidence of the way members of a particular speech community (or subculture) approach the process of inscription and play with a channel's affordance. The examples in this section are also evidence of speakers' shaping artistry and humorous speech play. In the following (and final) section we examine how inscriptions of digital communication can constitute objects of interest, amusement, and analysis for "native" speakers themselves by briefly considering some ways inscripts circulate online in the context of Internet culture.

The Traffic in Inscriptive Speech

Linguistic anthropologists are not the only ones interested in the textual vestiges of digital talk. For instance, text message conversations stored in cell phones can constitute potentially damaging evidence of illicit relationships (Archambault 2011) that can potentially be leveraged by mass media and criminal prosecutors (Squires 2011). Computer hackers have increasingly experimented with "the activist tactic of hacking to leak" (Coleman 2013: 226) politically incriminating emails. Numerous websites offer specialized niches for entertaining inscripts, for instance: "Autocorrect Fails," chatlogs featuring instances in which an automatic text-replacement feature—generally iPhone's—substitutes humorous, inappropriate content (see http://www.damnyouautocorrect.com) or chatlogs from websites like Omegle that connect pairs of anonymous strangers for the purposes of text-based, synchronous talk—and which are frequently "trolled" by Internet pranksters trying to sucker unwitting parties into aggravating interactions (see http://omeglesbest.tumblr.com).

In this context, we choose to focus (somewhat arbitrarily) on Creepy White Guys, a blog that recently went viral, spawning a short-lived Internet meme. According to KnowYourMeme.com (see http://knowyourmeme .com/memes/creepy-white-guys), an anonymous user—presumably an Asian woman—launched the Tumblr blog on February 2, 2014 to share screenshots of online interactions with white male suitors: "Every Asian girl who has ever tried online dating," she explained, "whether on POF, OKCupid, or Match has experienced it: messages from Creepy White Guys with Asian fetishes. I just got back into the dating scene and am already being bombarded with some absolutely horrifying messages. I've collected some of the best ones here, and I welcome any additions to my collection." The blog was eventually taken down, but not before a number of other Tumblr users responded to the blogger's invitation to share examples of their own. The content has now been archived in repositories of Internet memes such as Cheezburger.com, which is our source for the data discussed here (see http://cheezburger.com/247301). In the first chatlog archived on Cheezburger (Figure 12.1), a white male asks an Asian female addressee if she plays "Street Fighter much" because she looks like the Asian female character with "a tight body" in the video game. The woman responds sharply to this ill-conceived come-on.

In addition to the archived conversations originally posted on the Creepy White Guys blog, as of July 15, 2014, there were 158 comments about this topic—and the inscripts themselves—on the Cheezburger site. Of course, commentary on this topic proliferated elsewhere online (including Twitter, Facebook, and others), but here we focus only on the Cheezburger reactions. Participants in this forum heatedly disagreed about whether it is racist for white men to fetishize Asian women and whether it

Figure 12.1. "Creepy White Guys" Cheezburger chat log 1. Screenshot by Graham M. Jones and Bambi Schieffelin.

is racist for an Asian woman to single out only white men as "creepy." Of particular interest to us, however, is the way that they make stored conversations like the one in Figure 12.1 into "shared stance objects" (Du Bois 2007: 168), analyzing verbal features and interactional dynamics. Some participants even comment on the inappropriateness or appositeness of particular turns, as in Figure 12.2.

Others positively and negatively assess the character of speakers in the original inscript, with reference to particular utterances—both the putatively "creepy" white guys (Figure 12.3), and their female Asian addressees, who have themselves posted the conversations online (Figure 12.4).

The following example (Figure 12.5) reflects a sentiment that some of our undergraduate students have often echoed: given the prurient entertainment value of conversations like these, it is not unimaginable that the

Figure 12.2. "Creepy White Guys" Cheezburger chat log 2. Screenshot by Graham M. Jones and Bambi Schieffelin.

Figure 12.3. "Creepy White Guys" Cheezburger chat log 3. Screenshot by Graham M. Jones and Bambi Schieffelin.

Figure 12.4. "Creepy White Guys" Cheezburger chat log 4. Screenshot by Graham M. Jones and Bambi Schieffelin.

"creepy white guys" are in fact "trolling" (that is, playing a joke on) the addressees. The ease of doctoring, fabricating, or otherwise falsifying chat-logs gives further reason for regarding the veracity of such inscripts with some suspicion: perhaps the blogger is herself a troll. Uncertainties about the origin of these conversations—when one does not know the partici-pants and has no further data about their practices—certainly necessitate

zeemumu
2 Months Ago

There's a nagging thought in the back of my mind telling me that most of these are trolls and were either made for the purpose of being uploaded to that blog or the person posting them was gullible.

Like   Reply

Figure 12.5. "Creepy White Guys" Cheezburger chat log 5. Screenshot by Graham M. Jones and Bambi Schieffelin.

circumspection in approaching them as anything like ethnographic evidence. Nevertheless, the plausibility of these interactions in the eyes of most commentators and the scrutiny that they occasion—be they authentic or fictitious—is suggestive of the interest that inscripts hold for many nonspecialists outside the field of anthropology.

Users of digital media are, of course, increasingly aware of the potential of inscripts to circulate—and awareness of future retrievability may even enter into the composition process, as with hashtags or other user-appended metadata. The poignancy of Creepy White Guys derives in part from suitors' apparent naiveté (or, more precisely, lack of reflexivity) about how their words could be repurposed as incriminating evidence. As users have become more savvy about the potential consequences of the alienability of inscripts in recent years (Holson 2010), new media have emerged that—at least in theory—engineer ephemerality into digital talk. A spate of "ephemeral messaging" apps allows people to send messages that evanesce, irretrievably, after they are viewed (Olson 2013). Snapchat, a service specializing in photo messages (potentially with added text), epitomizes such products. According to one of the cofounders: "What Snapchat said was if we try to model conversations as they occur they're largely ephemeral. We may try to write down and save the really special moments, but by and large we just try to let everything go. . . . I think it feels crumby to have to market yourself all day long; the whole notion of a personal brand got very, very popular and still persists today, as people manage all their profiles" (Warman 2013). An ethnographic approach to such a form of digital communication in which inscription does not generate inscripts might involve recourse to a secondary medium of recording (as with the ethnography of spoken conversation): taking screenshots of Snapchat messages or using a third-party app specifically designed to archive Snapchat content.

Conclusion

Dominic Boyer has challenged anthropologists to "reflect on how our research imagination, our research designs and methods, and our modes of analyzing and representing the world around us are adjusting to new informational and communicational circumstances" (2013: 175). In this context, we have sought to raise questions about how the technological ability to store digital speech events may shape our own theoretical projects. Transforming ephemeral communicative events into objects of indefinite preservation and nomothetic analysis impacts our ideas as anthropologists about what language is (Bauman 2011). Transcripts—and now inscripts—allow us to extract speech, reinterpret and recontextualize it, and circulate it to audiences far removed from its original source, thus giving utterances a temporal and historical dimension perhaps unintended by those who produced them.

Yet intentions here are extremely difficult to sort out. Perhaps speakers' awareness of the relative permanence or impermanence of talk indeed does lead them to intentionally shape the form of the utterances we analyze. This points to a larger issue. We have drawn examples from interactional settings ranging from relatively private (and presumably sincere) to relatively public, where anonymity creates uncertainty about speakers' projects, demanding that we as analysts of the medium approach information with the utmost epistemological caution. In other words, when participants themselves cannot be quite sure *whom* or, in the case of conversations involving bots or similar entities that generate automatic responses, *what* they are interacting with, it becomes difficult to maintain some of linguistic anthropology's cherished assumptions about the centrality of intentional speaking subjects and intersubjective awareness to speech events (compare Du Bois 1993).

Perhaps Bakhtin offers a way forward. "Language is not a neutral medium that passes freely and easily into the private property of the speaker's intentions," he writes (1992: 294). "It is populated—overpopulated with the intentions of others. Expropriating it, forcing it to submit to one's own intentions and accents, is a difficult and complicated task." The online traffic in inscripts is a reminder that reflexive activities of recontextualizing verbal materials are not unique to anthropologists. Digital communications may facilitate such reflexivity, giving speakers new instruments for manipulating, analyzing, and recirculating discursive material. But digital communications are certainly not necessary for speakers to relay information about previous speech events to each other or recycle previous speech for other purposes. Repurposing can extend the lives of all utterances—be they oral or inscriptive—and reflects the inherently intertextual—or, in Bakhtin's terms, "heteroglossic," "dialogic," and "polyphonic"—nature of language in society.

Bibliography

Archambault, Julie Soleil. 2011. Breaking up "Because of the Phone" and the Transformative Potential of Information in Southern Mozambique. *New Media & Society* 13 (3): 444–456.

Bakhtin, Mikhail M. 1992. *The Dialogic Imagination: Four Essays*. Austin: University of Texas Press.

Bauman, Richard. 2010. "It's Not a Telescope, It's a Telephone": Encounters with the Telephone on Early Commercial Sound Recordings. In *Language Ideologies and Media Discourse: Texts, Practices, Politics*, edited by Sally Johnson and Tommaso M. Milani, 252–273. New York: Continuum.

———. 2011. "Better than Any Monument": Envisioning Museums of the Spoken Word. *Museum Anthropology Review* 5 (1–2): 1–13.

———, and Charles L. Briggs. 1990. Poetics and Performances as Critical Perspectives on Language and Social Life. *Annual Review of Anthropology* 19: 59–88.

Boyer, Dominic. 2013. *The Life Informatic: Newsmaking in the Digital Era*. Ithaca, N.Y.: Cornell University Press.

Bucholtz, Mary. 2000. The Politics of Transcription. *Journal of Pragmatics* 32: 1439–1465.

———. 2007. Variation in Transcription. *Discourse Studies* 9 (6): 784–808.

Buchstaller, Isabelle. 2003. The Co-Occurrence of Quotatives with Mimetic Performances. *Edinburgh Working Papers in Applied Linguistics* 12: 1–8.

Coleman, E. Gabriella. 2012. Am I Anonymous? *Limn* 2. Accessed February 20, 2015. http://limn.it/am-i-anonymous/.

———. 2013. Anonymous and the Politics of Leaking. In *Beyond WikiLeaks: Implications for the Future of Communications, Journalism and Society*, edited by Benedetta Brevini, Arne Hintz, and Patrick McCurdy, 209–228. New York: Palgrave Macmillan.

Du Bois, John W. 1993. Meaning Without Intention: Lessons From Divination. In *Responsibility and Evidence in Oral Discourse*, edited by Jane Hill and Judith T. Irvine, 48–71. Cambridge: Cambridge University Press.

————. 2007. The Stance Triangle. In *Stancetaking in Discourse: Subjectivity, Evaluation, Interaction*, edited by Robert Englebretson, 139–182. Philadelphia: John Benjamins.

Duranti, Alessandro. 2006. Transcripts, Like Shadows on a Wall. *Mind, Culture, and Activity* 13 (4): 301–310.

Edwards, Jane. 2003. The Transcription of Discourse. In *The Handbook of Discourse Analysis*, edited by Deborah Schiffrin, Deborah Tannen, and Heidi E. Hamilton, 321–348. Malden, Mass.: Blackwell.

Falk, John L. 2000. *Snow and Other Guises*. Toronto: Guernica Editions.

Goffman, Erving. 1979. Footing. *Semiotica* 25: 1–29.

Green, Judith, Maria Franquiz, and Carol Dixon. 1997. The Myth of the Objective Transcript: Transcribing as a Situated Act. *TESOL Quarterly* 31 (1): 172–176.

Haviland, John B. 1996. Texts from Talk in Tzotzil. In *Natural Histories of Discourse*, edited by Michael Silverstein and Greg Urban, 45–78. Chicago: University of Chicago Press.

Holson, Laura M. 2010. Tell-All Generation Learns to Keep Things Offline. *The New York Times*, May 8. Accessed February 20, 2015. http://www.nytimes.com/2010/05/09/fashion/09privacy.html?_r = 0.

Hymes, Dell. 1994. Ethnopoetics, Oral-Formulaic Theory, and Editing Texts. *Oral Tradition* 9 (2): 330–370.

Jones, Graham M. 2014. Reported Speech as an Authentication Tactic in Computer-Mediated Communication. In *Indexing Authenticity: Sociolinguistic Perspectives*, edited by Thiemo Breyer, Véronique Lacoste, and Jakob Leimgruber, 188–208. Berlin: De Gruyter.

————, and Bambi B. Schieffelin. 2009. Enquoting Voices, Accomplishing Talk: Uses of *Be + Like* in Instant Messaging. *Language & Communication* 29 (1): 77–113.

————, Bambi B. Schieffelin, and Rachel E. Smith. 2011. When Friends Who Talk Together Stalk Together: Online Gossip As Metacommunication. In *Digital Discourse: Language in the New Media*, edited by Crispin Thurlow and Kristine Mroczek, 26–47. New York: Oxford University Press.

Lucy, John. 1999. Reflexivity. *Journal of Linguistic Anthropology* 9 (1–2): 212–215.

Mitchell-Kernan, Claudia. 1972. Signifying and Marking: Two Afro-American Speech Acts. In *Directions in Sociolinguistics: The Ethnography of Communication*, edited by John J. Gumperz and Dell Hymes, 161–179. New York: Holt, Rinehart & Winston.

Ochs, Elinor. 1979. Transcription as Theory. In *Developmental Pragmatics*, edited by Elinor Ochs and Bambi B. Schieffelin, 43–72. New York: Academic Press.

Olson, Parmy. 2013. Delete by Default: Why More Snapchat-like Messaging Is on Its Way. *Forbes.com*, November 22. Accessed February 20, 2015. http://www.forbes.com/sites/parmyolson/2013/11/22/delete-by-default-why-more-snapchat-like-messaging-is-on-its-way/.

Ricoeur, Paul. 1973. The Model of the Text: Meaningful Action Considered as a Text. *New Literary History* 5 (1): 91–117.

———. 1976. *Interpretation Theory: Discourse and the Surplus of Meaning.* Fort Worth: Texas Christian University Press.

Roberts, Delia. 1997. Transcribing Talk: Issues of Representation. *TESOL Quarterly* 31 (1): 167–171.

Rodriguez, Salvador. 2012. Facebook Message "Seen" Feature Could Create Awkward Situations. *Los Angeles Times*, June 5. Accessed February 20, 2015. http://articles .latimes.com/2012/jun/05/business/la-fi-tn-facebook-seen-feature-20120531.

Shankar, Shalini, and Jillian R. Cavanaugh. 2012. Language and Materiality in Global Capitalism. *Annual Review of Anthropology* 41: 355–369.

Squires, Lauren. 2011. Voicing "Sexy Text": Heteroglossia and Erasure in TV News Broadcast Representations of Detroit's Text Message Scandal. In *Digital Discourse: Language in the New Media*, edited by Crispin Thurlow and Kristine Mroczek, 3–25. Oxford: Oxford University Press.

Tagliamonte, Sali A., and Derek Denis. 2008. Linguistic Ruin? LOL! Instant Messaging and Teen Language. *American Speech* 83 (1): 3–34.

Warman, Matt. 2013. Snapchat's Evan Spiegel: "Deleting Should Be the Default." *The Telegraph*, November 16. Accessed February 20, 2015. http://www.telegraph .co.uk/technology/social-media/10452668/Snapchats-Evan-Spiegel-Deleting-should -be-the-default.html.

PART V

WIDENING COMPLEXITIES AND CONTEXTS

Chapter 13

Preservation, Sharing, and Technological Challenges of Longitudinal Research in the Digital Age

Lisa Cliggett

Imagine this moment: You have driven high into the mountains, catching glimpses of the sparkling bay below. You have parked on the steep drive, climbed the two flights of wooden stairs, gazed from the front porch at the bridge across the bay, and now you stand in the hallway. She invites you into her office. Softly lit, with worn Asian rugs under your feet, the office walls tilt at you, with shelves, filing cabinets, and boxes stacked high. Within those shelves, filing cabinets, and boxes lie a treasure you have imagined, but not yet seen—forty years of stories, details, and background about the people and families with whom you have just lived for the past two years. It is the history, knowledge, and context that an elder passes on to the next generation. And at some point it hits you—there are at least five hundred thousand sheets of paper here, about one hundred linear feet of boxes, notes, images, diaries . . . DATA.

Fifteen years later, you stare at the computer screen, lists of folder names with dates, locations and family names in the title, attempting to give order to this massive collection of interrelated information. These electronic folders contain all the fieldnotes, interviews, recordings, photos, and maps you've accumulated over the many field seasons since your first foray into ethnographic research with one community.

Reflecting on her office with its tilting walls, and on your own packed hard drive, you sit paralyzed with the weight of data management on your shoulders.

*   *   *

Although my experience described in that first scenario—in which I first met Elizabeth Colson at her house high in the Berkeley hills—offered the promise of discovery and possibility to a newly minted anthropologist, the combination of both of those scenarios was more an experience of "Oh no, what have I gotten into?"

Make no mistake—having the unexpected opportunity to join in the long-term Gwembe Tonga Research Project (GTRP) has been my professional good fortune and passion. But on the day that I walked into Elizabeth's home office, I did not imagine the technological, logistical, ethical, and professional challenges that lay ahead in working within a longitudinal and collaborative framework. Not the least of these challenges is just that thing that so excited me on that crisp fall day in 1996: the data.

In this chapter, I reflect on my experience of being drawn down the rabbit hole of data linkage and management. I consider what it means to be part of a collaborative project and how that membership influences our relationships to the data we produce. I also discuss challenges in making our data useful and accessible, for our research team and for others who may have interest in the knowledge we have generated (by "we" I mean qualitative researchers broadly, not just anthropologists). In discussing issues of archiving, particularly digital archiving, for our project and for other qualitative researchers, I highlight key issues of concern—including confidentiality and ethnographic context. Ultimately, I suggest that, given the fragility of digital data, disciplinary concerns about knowledge preservation, and recent funding mandates, we all must seriously consider digital archiving as part of our research methodology. Perhaps one way to explore our position vis-à-vis digital archiving is to think more concretely about the different "values" of our data, an idea I explore at the end of this chapter.

When I began my field research and career path, I never imagined that spreadsheets of file details, data maps, hard drives, and digital backups would play such a central role in my day-to-day professional life (indeed, I think none of us in the cusp digital generation would have predicted the digital dominance in our lives), but honestly, data management was nothing I ever thought about as I developed my research methodology, analytical lens, and writing style. Now, every fieldnote I write, every interview I do, and every map or image I create becomes one more digital item to be managed—and not just for the immediate or near future. Because I play a role in a longitudinal project, I now think of the durability of every bit (and byte) of data I create (or my students and colleagues create) and its future digital life.

Perspectives on Longitudinal Research

The basis of a longitudinal project in which we follow a community over time—the single most important detail—is the ability to link data from one season to the next, from one time frame to both past and future time frames. Unless we can do that, what might be a longitudinal project becomes merely a chronological series of research projects in the same fieldsite, among the same communities. Each discreet project might offer insight, but the chance to reveal deeper insight about processes over time dwindles with every missed linkage.

Elizabeth Colson and Thayer (Ted) Scudder understood this challenge, at least by their second field visit to the Gwembe Valley. In 1962, they returned to conduct "the after" portion of their study on the impacts of forced relocation on Gwembe Tonga populations that were resettled in 1958 by the damming of the Middle Zambezi River and the creation of Lake Kariba. Elizabeth and Ted's key to linkages over time, which I think of as their project's Rosetta Stone, was the village "checklist," in which each individual was identified by a "relational code." The code included the original household number Elizabeth and Ted assigned in 1956 and codes for marital relationship and generation. An example of this coding system can be seen in Figure 13.1. Under number 6.1.5, the code "SIN22W1-S1W1D2 stands for "SIN" village, household number 22's (male head's) first wife's first son's first wife's second daughter. Although the code is certainly cumbersome and adheres to a particular notion of "family" and "household," it does articulate some specific relationships—at least for straightforward marital and reproductive connections (more complicated

Mrd:
1. SIN 22W1S1W1 M█████. 1943. Mufumu. Std IV.
   Mrd: 1) KA█████, eloped 1961.
   Their children:
   1. E█████, M. Feb. 1963-1966.
   2. SIN 22W1S1W1D1 CH█████████████ F.
      June 10, 1965. Form II, Mazabuka. Works
      World Vision 1992. Mrd: 1) SIN 27W2S3
      Sh█████ Ci█████, AP 1986.
      No child by 1992.
   3. SIN 22W1S1W1S1 ED████ SI█████, M.
      Feb. 2, 1968. Grade 6, 1982. May 1992
      hunting work. Lives F's homestead. Mrd
      1. J███, D of Si█████ of Ma█████,
         Nov 14, 1988,
         1. C█████, M. 1 Nov 1991.
   4. Miscarriage. April 1970.
   5. SIN 22W1S1W1D2 B███, F. April 26, 1971.
      Grade 7. Mrd: 1) Do███, S of N██
      Chakasala Dec 8, 1990. Lives N██ V.
      No children in 1992.
   6. SIN 22W1S1W1S2 BA█████, M. April 17, 1974.
      Gr 7 1991, 1992 repeating.
   7. SIN 22W1S1W1S3 A███, M. Dec 23, 1976.
      Gr 5 1992.
   8. SIN 22W1S1W1S4 SI█████, M. Sept 17,
      1979. Grade 4, 1992.
   9. Ch█████ M. FE1982-JL1983.
   10. Mu█████, F. JA 1985. Grade 1 1992.
   11. Fa███ M. Dec 1990. OK 1992.
2. SIN 18W1D1 K███, 1952-86. Mufumu D of 18.
   Mrd 1969, div. 1972.d. 86. See her number.
3. SIN 22W1S1W2 DI█████ BE█████, 1955. Munsaka
   of Jumbo. Mrd: 1) KA█████, eloped Sept 6,
   1972. Their children:
   1. SIN 22W1S1W2D1 RE███ KA█████, F. Sept
      16, 1973. Grade 7 last. Mrd:
      1. SN 47W2S2 Ph███ Mp█████, S of G███,
         16 January 1992. No child yet 1992.
      Then long interval with no pregnancy until
      treatment at Monze hospital
   2. SIN 22W1S1W2D2 IN█████ (T███), F.
      March 4, 1978. Gr 6 1992. Lived Ndola
      with 'MB' Tr███ and in Livingstone with
      with MB 'Sc███ 1992 Si█████.
   3. SIN 22W1S1W2D3 KE███, F. Sept 2, 1980.
      Gr 2 1992.
   4. Mu█████ F. AP 22, 1983. Grade 1, 1992.
   5. Ag███ He███, F. OC 1985. No sch 1992.
   6. Ga███ F. July 1988. OK 1992.
   7. Ast███ F. Nov 1990. Still nursing 1992.

Figure 13.1. Sample of a GTRP checklist. Used with permission of Elizabeth Colson and Thayer Scudder.

extended family or dependent relationships within households require more narrative explanations). Somewhat surprisingly, these codes have reemerged in my archiving work as a general way to identify kinship lines when I anonymize data, as discussed below.

The checklist became a soft-cover bound book (much like a hard copy Ph.D. dissertation) listing all the families in a given village and all of their descendants, marriages, divorces, deaths, migrations, and other notable life events. Each fieldwork season produced new pages as family histories were updated. When I first arrived in the Gwembe Valley in 1994, I carried with me this kinship Rosetta Stone for the villages where I was to live and work (see Cliggett 2005). That data-set linked me to forty years of Elizabeth and Ted's work.

The village checklists document social relationships over time, but it is the fieldnotes, interviews, maps, and other qualitative data that constitute the "thick description" (Geertz 1973) that anthropologists seek (see Figures 13.2 and 13.3). Elizabeth and Ted recognized the importance of linkages over time in this arena as well, but in the non–digital age, the tools to enact such linkages were more cumbersome. To start with, all data were hard copy—typewritten fieldnotes and interviews, hand-drawn maps, hard print photos. In the process of typing up their notes and interviews, they also inserted content codes, so that a first level of analysis occurred at the moment of data creation. Together, they developed a coherent coding system by which they could then *manually* index and file the narrative and other data, thus creating the five hundred thousand sheets of paper that filled the tilting walls of Elizabeth's office. They typed their fieldnotes in triplicate, with carbon paper between each sheet—some five sheets of material to pound through as they typed. They each received a set of the other's notes, and they deposited the third set with what was then the Rhodes-Livingstone Institute (now the Institute of Economic and Social Research at the University of Zambia). From the beginning, Elizabeth and Ted saw their research as collaborative and open.

Filing, indexing, and maintaining a searchable order of the hard-copy material required Elizabeth and Ted's committed and diligent labor. Beyond that logistical and technical management of data, the analysis and synthesis of that hard-copy material required equally committed and diligent labor in order to produce well-grounded and ethnographically informed findings—*all without the aid of computers* (although punch cards were used in the 1980s to work with a set of census material). By the 1990s,

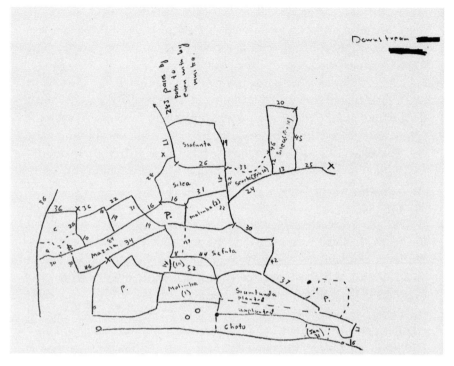

Figure 13.2. Sample of a Scudder hand-drawn map. Used with permission of Thayer Scudder.

when Elizabeth and Ted began using computers to write their fieldnotes, the growing hard-copy longitudinal data archive they had created required analysis akin to historical or literary archival work.

And there lies the challenge of the current era and, certainly, my personal challenge. For Elizabeth and Ted, who carry their "headnotes" (Ottenberg 1990; Sanjek 1990) with them, digging through forty years of hard-copy fieldnotes may seem like visiting an old friend. For a newcomer to the project (even though I am not so new anymore), it can feel like an impossible task. Attempting to link people and events through time by using someone else's enormous amount of hard-copy data files can be more time-consuming and intellectually challenging than doing one's own field research (and there are a host of reasons why doing your own field research takes precedence, such as independent career development, tenure and promotion, and so on). In my own case, moreover, the multiple data sets from the many and continuing

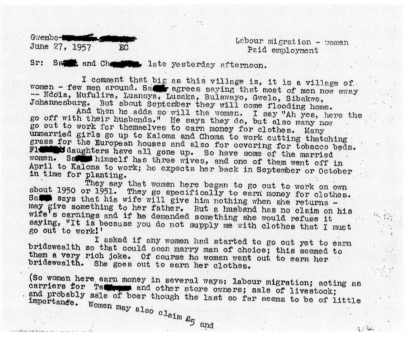

Figure 13.3. Sample of Colson fieldnotes. Used with permission of Elizabeth Colson.

fieldwork periods of my own Gwembe Tonga research, starting in 1994, have become their own unwieldy digital conglomeration.

It was these two realizations (about the GTRP hard-copy archive and my own increasingly chaotic digital mass of data) that drove me to explore possibilities for creating an ethnographically nuanced and interlinked digital archive—one in which data content is linked across data types and through time. The benefit to me and my other and newer colleagues (see Cliggett 2002) on the Gwembe Tonga Research Project should be obvious: if we could meaningfully access Elizabeth and Ted's five hundred thousand sheets of paper in a digital format, the search potential would be revolutionized. A search that requires one hundred hours of not even reading, but first simply identifying which chunks of notes, which days of observations, and which interviews to read could be condensed to searching for particular words or strings of words, dates, events, or peoples' names, leaving a majority of time for the *necessary* reflective reading, thinking, and interpreting. I stress *necessary* to make a point—digitizing data does not simplify the intellectual *thought work* required for good ethnography. Digitizing and computer tools facilitate the searching, not the thinking. Despite what some tech-oriented scholars may think or what critical ethnographers fear, technologies will never replace our human, nuanced, and trained analytical skills in producing good ethnography.

Beyond revolutionizing Elizabeth and Ted's data set, if we could better link their data to mine and those of the others who have worked among the same communities, thus making the entire GTRP data set electronically searchable in ethnographically significant ways, it would not only transform their research potential in that region of the world, it would have the additional potential to transform how we think more broadly about our anthropological methods and analysis. However, the concept of an interlinked digital ethnographic archive compels the asking of many questions (beyond simply "how?"). Since 2011, I have grappled with several of these questions. The remainder of this chapter explores these issues, using my work with the Gwembe Tonga Research Project data as the specific test case.

What Can a Digital Archive Do?

The challenges to digital data preservation, archiving, and sharing loom large, but there are equally as many benefits that are worth recognizing. The starting point for archiving is *preservation* of digital data. It sounds simple and obvious, but in fact, false assumptions about digital reliability and longevity are rampant. Obviously, threats such as fires and flooding equally affect digital or hard-copy data. To manage these dangers, we know we should back up our files to a location distant from our main computer—whether it is a personal external hard drive stored in a fire- and flood-proof location, a university server, or a cloud backup system. Of course, if we did a survey of anthropologists, it is likely that we would find that fewer than half would describe actively backing up their data to a remote storage space. (That is a point for a different discussion).

The less obvious threat to digital data is time. With time, we often lose track of our digital files, believing they are somewhere on our hard drive and that we can find them when needed. Also with time comes new hardware, new versions of software, and degradation of storage media. With each year and with each iteration of technical developments, we move one step farther from the original digital host of the data we created. In some cases, the whole software program may become defunct, which is what happened to my field data from 1994, written in the ancient WordStar software. In 2003, when I tried to access those files in order to consult them as I wrote my first ethnography (Cliggett 2005), I had the terrifying realization that I could not open them. Thanks to the information technology staff at my university, whom I refer to as my "IT heroes," the text from the files was retrieved; at least I could use the "find" tool in Microsoft Word to search for particular people and events. However, in extracting the text from the ancient program files, I had lost all the formatting (headers, underlining, italics, notes, and so on), which made skimming and reading the raw files a more difficult and slower process.

Since beginning work on this archiving project, I have heard many stories of data loss, both hard copy and digital, confirming that I am not alone in my experience of terror when I discovered that my files existed in a technological prehistory. At an archiving workshop in fall 2012, I learned of a Melanesianist scholar whose house, full of fifty years of data and artifacts, was flooded in one of the U.S. east coast hurricanes in 2011; all of that data was lost. Another colleague told me about survey data on economic and livelihood behavior in Belize that he collected in the 1980s, diligently entering it into state-of-the-art software. But after writing the report, he did not try to look at that data again until around 2008, when he realized it was lost in the technological cloud of obsolescence. And in the process of working on this volume, Roger Sanjek told me about his own Queens digital data, which were lost to the same technological phantoms. The fact is that our data, whether hard copy stored in our houses or electronically stashed in our computers, is fragile and at great risk of loss.

Technical obsolescence is one of the key issues raised by archivists and data preservation IT people when they argue for the importance of genuine data preservation—preservation that ensures that digital files can be accessed long into the future. The above stories of woe should at least alert us to the reality of data fragility and make us consider strategies for long-term data preservation, simply for our own access. The answer to the obsolescence problem is ensuring that files migrate forward into current standards of hardware and software, including system platforms and non-proprietary, long-term preservation formats (The National Archives of Australia has a good discussion of these issues at http://www.naa.gov.au/records-management/agency/preserve/e-preser vation/index. aspx). The growing "repository" movement in universities and other institutions seeks to address this need by serving as a secure digital space for data sets—managing multiple copies, ensuring migration to new standards over time, and using open-source formats for long-term access.

Beyond ensuring that our data is available to each of us for the long term, a digital archive also makes data easier to search, something I mentioned at the outset of this chapter. Creating an archive that allows linkage across data types and fieldwork periods means that with each new round of data collection, a researcher builds and adds to a growing body of knowledge. Not all anthropologists pursue field research with the same groups of people over time, but for those of us who do, having a systematic strategy for working with the entirety of data ensures that all data "have a voice" in our analyses. Without the power of searching through a linked set of data over time, even research with the same communities often becomes ethnographic snapshots rather than a full and rich view of lived experience and change over time.

The more controversial value of archiving ethnographic data, at least for many qualitative researchers, is the potential for data sharing and use by secondary researchers. In the next section, I discuss this issue in more detail. The fact is that by preserving our digital data for our own use, we also create the possibility that others may access it if we choose to allow such access.

Questions and Concerns in Digital Data Archiving

It may be obvious that exploring possibilities for an integrated ethnographic archive makes sense for a longitudinal collaborative project like that of the GTRP. Creating such archives for those who work alone or who work on shorter-term projects and then move to new venues with new study populations and new topics may not be as compelling. For those thinking, "Archiving? Nope, not for me," brace yourselves. There are movements about that may push all of us in directions we do not imagine. The 2011 National Science Foundation (NSF) and 2003 National Institutes of Health (NIH) mandates about data preservation and sharing are nothing to ignore. NSF's policy on data sharing specifically addresses "primary data" and "samples": "Investigators are expected to share with other researchers, at no more than incremental cost and within a reasonable time, the primary data, samples, physical collections and other supporting materials created or gathered in the course of work under NSF grants"; and further, "Grantees are expected to encourage and facilitate such sharing" (NSF 2011: D.4.b). Although those who do not conduct research within the structures of funded projects certainly have more flexibility in how they manage their data, funding agencies are becoming more attentive to what we do with our data once we have collected it.

There are many who dispute this call for increased data accessibility, citing legitimate concerns about confidentiality, protection of study populations, more intellectual and interpretive issues of ethnographic context, individualized knowledge (our "headnotes"), and the limited or potentially misapplied value of "raw" data for those not familiar with the research setting (AnthroDPA 2009; Kelty et al. 2008; Pienta, Alter, and Lyle 2009). These are all real issues, and I consider them below. However, compared to many other countries, the United States lags behind in this qualitative data preservation and sharing trend. U.S. funding agencies are in good company with international trends in scientific knowledge.[1] These mandates are here to stay, and quite likely they will become more stringent, with greater oversight to ensure compliance.

Protection of Study Communities, Confidentiality, and Privacy

The issues of confidentiality and protection of study communities have been the most important questions for me. To clarify, archiving and preserving data in any kind of institutional repository does not automatically translate to simple open and unrestricted access. First and foremost, institutional archives are about preservation of documents. Beyond that goal, there is a broader goal of making data available to other users. However, repositories *do* allow us to set controls on who accesses data, time frames for embargos, and other controls that ensure protection of human subjects. When we deposit our files in an archive, we work with staff there to set the terms of use—whether embargoed for thirty years, accessible only through approval, open access, or something in between (and if one repository does not offer those options, you can find others that do).

However, because of the historically collaborative and open nature of the Gwembe Tonga Research Project, I am forced to think more concretely about data sharing. From the beginning of my fieldwork, I knew that Ted and Elizabeth would likely see my fieldnotes—it was an inherent agreement when they offered to share their data with me. Consequently, from the outset, I wrote my fieldnotes and transcribed interviews expecting that at least two other people would see my work. Thus, I do not have the dilemma of mixed personal, diary-like commentary in the same text as "the data." I did have a journal where I wrote reflective and personal thoughts, and my letter writing often served a need for personal expression, but these are documents I choose not to include in the ethnographic archive I envision. As I think about the separation of "data" and personal thoughts in this digital era, it is hard for me to imagine that anyone writing notes in electronic form *would* mix the two. Digital files are so much more mobile than hard-copy files; to give someone a set of typed or handwritten fieldnotes requires an active task of copying and delivering. These days, we send email attachments or share a Dropbox folder with lightning speed. Once "out there," it is not possible to take sent or posted data away from the recipient or control where it goes next. For these reasons, I always talk with students about keeping very personal or sensitive material out of the main fieldnotes and interview data.

As for archiving, when I began thinking about creating a useable digital archive, one of the first things I considered was: "Who might look at this material?" My answer was, in principle, anyone. It could be my colleagues on the project, students, other anthropologists, other scholars, journalists, the public, and, not least, members of the communities where we have worked. In fact, this last has been one of the points in support of archiving. Proponents argue that the communities we have worked amidst for so long have a right to see the data we produce about their lives, not just the reports we write. In some cases, native peoples want access to ethnographic data to claim legal rights—to land or cultural integrity; in other cases, they seek information on historical aspects of their communities (Christen 2008; Leopold 2008; Russell 2005). The creation of a coherent digital record inherently offers the possibility of increasing access by any number of people to our ethnographic knowledge. With increased access, however, we are forced to think much more concretely about how we can protect the people and communities among whom we work.

Much has been written about the ethics of our data collection and about best practices to ensure the American Anthropological Association mandate of "do no harm." In the digital age and the current archiving landscape, we need to "do no harm" in quite different ways than we have previously. At the least, institutional review boards (IRBs) and ethics committees will need to revisit their requirements (such as destruction of data once analysis is complete) in light of the new funding policies, and researchers will need to update informed consent agreements and allow data to be used beyond a particular research project or purpose (see UK Data Archive 2015 for more discussion).

Some of the answers to this challenge fall in the terrain of anonymizing data more thoroughly and, certainly, of setting some restrictions on who can access what data or on omitting the most sensitive data. I have written elsewhere about practical steps in preparing qualitative data for archiving, including anonymizing (Cliggett 2013). More complicated are the questions about how to maintain context, including placement within larger family histories, when real people and place names have been changed. Unfortunately, in the case of the GTRP data, the issue of anonymizing sufficiently, particularly existing data sets, has become a real obstacle to building the kind of usable linked ethnographic archive that can trace families and events over time. If making an integrated ethnographic archive useful to secondary users, whether historians, students, or others, depends on capturing deep and meaningful context, how do we do that *while simultaneously* preserving confidentiality?

Maintaining Context and Building Knowledge

One element of context can be achieved by using qualitative data analysis software. With such tools, we can insert content coding, including cross-references to extended family and events, as well as analytical notes. The additional benefit of attaching these kinds of "tags" on an archived data set is the chance for a secondary user to build on existing analysis. For example, some of my first GTRP research examined family support for the elderly, including gifting between generations. With my data coded for that topic, another researcher might consider gifting more broadly, using my codes but also adding codes that offer new analysis.

Other secondary uses might include history of science studies, which could use existing codes to trace disciplinary trends in topics and theories. Of course, there are also more uncomfortable possibilities, such as those that emerged in the Malinowski diary furor, the Derek Freeman–Margaret

Mead controversy, or the still simmering "Darkness in Eldorado" case (Fernandez 2013; Glenn and Bartlett 2009; Malinowski 1989; Mandler 2013). Such cases of "outing" anthropologists, although famous, perhaps, are, in fact, few. More common are restudies and other projects that build on and celebrate our senior colleagues' work—certainly not as tabloid worthy but definitely more grounded in solid scholarship. Ultimately, in terms of knowledge building, the opportunity to use existing coding and build on it offers far more analytical power than starting from scratch with uncoded raw data.

However, after experimenting with various tactics for anonymizing a sample of my coded GTRP data while also maintaining person or place linkages—such as those ensuring that I am able to trace a particular person or family through time—I have not found a simple answer. It increasingly appears that until new software allows maintenance of existing coding and also includes anonymizing options, we will need to keep two archived copies of all of our GTRP data: one set, for project researchers who have approval to work with the data, will include robust context by maintaining full notations and names of people and places; the second set, for more open access, will need to be fully anonymized. This second version of the data will be less suitable for tracing links over time, and quite likely, it will lack the analytical power of the previous GTRP coding. This unsatisfactory solution is due to current limitations of various software, both qualitative data analysis software and anonymizing programs. Currently, this kind of software removes coding from any other software application as it processes a file. For future research, my hope is that we can implement one coding system for use in all of our narrative data, building on Elizabeth's original codes (which I mentioned when discussing longitudinal research). The codes would be attached to "the main characters" we work with and to the actual place names. But for the existing data sets, the current technical complications, along with the enormous labor involved to anonymize existing data, means using an alternative method.

While creating both an "open" and a "researchers'" archive is a cumbersome and labor-intensive solution to issues of confidentiality, context, and knowledge building, for the moment, it may be the most practical choice I have—that is, if I remain committed to having the data more openly accessible. At a political level, I do believe, in principle, that our data should be accessible; taxpayers have generously allowed me to do this work, the data is a kind of knowledge from which others can gain insight, and if the people who so graciously tolerated my endless questions and awkward presence would like to see what came of all that time they gave me, I believe, ultimately, that they should have access—as long as we "do no harm" in the broadest sense.

During my 2005 fieldwork season, I had a very real experience regarding our project data and the "do no harm" mandate. One of our recently hired, and relatively young, research assistants (RAs) was the son from a family who was in the original Gwembe Tonga cohort from 1958. One afternoon, I was working with him, going through the village "checklist" to identify people for interviews. When he came across his family's history, he wanted to read the checklist entries in detail, not just for his immediate family. As I watched him read the full family account, I saw his eyes grow wide and heard him catch his breath. He had read a fieldnote passage revealing that his mother, now in her mid-sixties, had been briefly married as a teenager, before she married his father. My RA was genuinely astonished, and I was caught off guard.

Two thoughts came to me at once: "Uh-oh, I didn't think about this possibility," and "Really? He didn't know his mother was married before?" Mind you, this is in a community where people talk openly about their fathers being witches, uncles stealing from community farm cooperatives, and siblings planning to elope with their lovers. After his initial surprise, he seemed to calm down, and we talked about the information in the checklist. He accepted the idea that as part of our project we write family histories as they happen and that over time we have compiled a long time-line of family life, including events that happened many decades ago. As startling as this incident was for both of us, I am lucky and grateful that my RA's discovery was not of some even more sensitive information and that my lesson did not come at a much greater cost.

However, both of my thoughts illustrate the reasons we need to be expansive in our definition of "do no harm." We really do not know about all the possibilities that could arise with insufficiently anonymized data being made public. We also cannot assume that any information that seems relatively innocuous to us is public knowledge in the communities where we work. As laborious as it can be, I would argue that anonymizing is the most important aspect of creating any kind of archive. And when anonymizing is not possible—as with most of the existing GTRP data—controlled access or time-limited embargoes are the only option.

What Is the Value of Data?

Beyond the issues of confidentiality and maintaining ethnographic context, I have pondered another terrain of questions since beginning this archiving adventure. When in our careers do we think about archiving our data? What kind of research activities and collaborations would push us toward archiving? Who do we think might want to see our data if we did archive? All of these together lead to broader and more ontological questions: What is the value of our data? Is our data valued differently by different people? And if our data does have value beyond our individual selves, whose responsibility is it to make it accessible?

As I said earlier in this chapter, I began my research knowing that at least a few others might look at the notes I write. Fairly quickly after I started my research path, I realized that my "raw material" would become part of a long and established body of fieldwork data. I also realized that my research trajectory would be influenced by the profound accumulated value of the entirety of GTRP data. Finding a way to make efficient use of all that data would transform my analytical processing work, as well as that of future GTRP research collaborators and of scholars interested in the project for any number of reasons. For me, the answers to bigger questions about the value of our work, and the value to whom, came to me through my experiences with the GTRP data.

For others, with vastly different research trajectories and with varying professional experiences, these questions may never arise or may emerge later, over time. Our fieldwork data certainly carries value in the immediate, short-term time frames of a specific research project and for its individual researchers. It is also possible that as scholars move through career stages and research agendas that may include other situations and sets of research subjects and professional colleagues, they may value their data differently.

In Figure 13.4, I try to envision how data might be valued at these different career stages and research-project social forms. On the horizontal, right-to-left axis, I list career trajectory points, from student through professional ranks to retirement and, further, to include research project histories, intellectual eras, knowledge building at disciplinary levels, and meta-knowledge about the history of disciplines and of science. On the horizontal front-to-back axis, I list research social arrangements, from individual researcher to research relations with colleagues and students and research teams and, ultimately, to currently unknown categories and groupings that

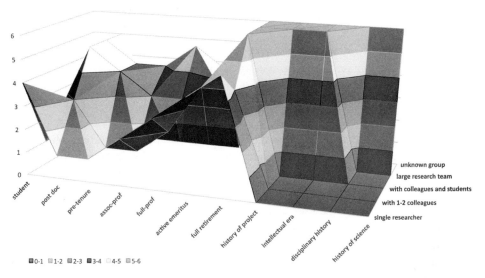

Figure 13.4. The value of data. Chart created by Lisa Cliggett.

may be identified by others in the future. The vertical axis approximates a value scale, with one the lowest value and five the highest. In this three-dimensional approximation, the value to ourselves and others of a given body of data varies with each moment in our (and our data's) professional pathway and with our (and the data's) position within a social organization of research tasks, users, and uses.

On this scale, we see an abrupt jump come retirement, whether or not a researcher has collaborated with others. As many senior anthropologists have described to me, and as the Wenner-Gren Historical Archives Program (http://www.wennergren.org/programs/historical-archives-program-hap) demonstrates, at retirement or after, including postmortem, there is a flurry of concern about what to do with a scholar's life work, including data and unpublished materials. It is as if the light bulb of value suddenly turns on.

Looking at the period early in career trajectories, we see students who value data due to anxieties about completing their degrees. Once on a tenure track path (if they secure such an academic position), data often take a back seat as they scramble to publish their work from their dissertations, prepare classes, and learn the ropes of academia. As new projects come their way, they begin thinking about and valuing data anew and, finally, with the great spike at retirement, do so again.

Solo researchers may begin by having less concern about their data's value to others, but as professional collegiality and research or publishing collaborations form, the collective value or appraisal of their data may increase. Certainly, when multiple researcher teams or "schools" produce data, value is high because the whole group may require transparency and access or may draw professional scrutiny. And beyond the work of a solo researcher or the life course of a research project, there are other groups of people who may have an interest in the products of that research, including interest in the original data. In the stages of professionally active retirement and beyond, for large research groups or teams and for wider professional groupings or "schools," data may hold profound value. This is the point at which the discipline, and scholars of science more broadly, may appreciate our data in a myriad of ways.

With fuller awareness of the multiplicity of values our data may acquire along these different personal and professional scales and trajectories, we can better consider how data should be managed at different points. In the case of the hard-copy data of retired or deceased scholars, boxing up all of those physical materials and depositing them in a university library or research archive may seem straightforward (if the librarians agree). How-ever, the cohort of senior scholars possessing primarily hard-copy materials will shrink as time goes on, and future scholarly cohorts with a majority of their data in digital form will grow. Libraries are already responding to the explosion of digital scholarship with digital libraries and repositories. As ethnographers producing fieldnotes, we have not responded so quickly. It is time to inject discussions of digital data preservation and management into the methods classes we teach and to instill in succeeding anthropologi-cal cohorts the notion that data management of qualitative research begins even before a researcher has any data.

Conclusion

One difference between hard copy and digital data is their visual presence: boxes and drawers of hard-copy material surround a person, as my opening description of Elizabeth's office suggests. Digital data, in contrast, burrow deep into our hard drives, sink into a university server, idle on a tiny flash drive or slim DVD in an office drawer, or disappear into the cloud. In these conditions, files get lost, become obsolete, or lose their analytical power, through lost linkages and codings, to their wider ethnographic context. The only way to avoid those mishaps is to become conscious of our data's value from the start of our research and take steps to ensure that our data is managed with that value in mind.

In this digital age, we are faced with an explosion of our own data, never mind the massive data in collaborative efforts. Individually, we have masses of photos, digital audio files, text data in digital form, digital spatial data, and digitally born data from blogs, virtual communities, and websites. We are producers of digital artifacts. As scholars concerned about the communities we study and the knowledge we produce, we should be equally concerned with the paths that our digital artifacts take in the world, which means being proactive in managing them.

Acknowledgments

I am grateful to many colleagues for the conversations that have stimulated my thoughts on this topic. Special thanks go to Roger Sanjek and Susan Tratner for organizing the meeting sessions leading up to this volume and for their insightful comments along the way. Colleagues Srimati Basu, Liz Faier, Diane King and Mark Whitaker commented on earlier versions of this chapter, for which I am extremely grateful. The work described here was supported by the NSF (BCS-1157418).

Note

1. See the Cessda website at http://www.cessda.net/, the UK Data Archive at http://www.data-archive.ac.uk/find/international-archives, and the Social Science Data Archives at http://www.sociosite.net/databases.php.

Bibliography

AnthroDataDPA. 2009. Report from Anthropological Workshop on Digital Preservation and Access. Joint NSF/Wenner-Gren Supported Workshop May 18–20, 2009. Accessed August 2, 2010. http://anthrodatadpa.org/addpa/ (site discontinued). Summary of workshop accessed March 18, 2015, http://anthrosciences.org/xwiki/bin/Resources/AnthroDataDPA.

Christen, Kimberly. 2008. Archival Challenges and Digital Solutions in Aboriginal Australia. *SAA Archaeological Record* 8 (2): 21–24.

Cliggett, Lisa. 2002. Multigenerations and Multidisciplines: Inheriting Fifty Years of Gwembe Tonga Research. In *Chronicling Cultures: Long-Term Field Research in*

Anthropology, edited by Robert V. Kemper and Anya Peterson Royce, 239–251. Walnut Creek, Calif.: AltaMira.

———. 2005. *Grains from Grass: Aging, Gender and Famine in Rural Africa*. Ithaca, N.Y.: Cornell University Press.

———. 2013. Qualitative Data Archiving in the Digital Age. *The Qualitative Report* 18 (24): 1–11. Accessed February 23, 2015. http://www.nova.edu/ssss/QR/QR18/cliggett1.pdf.

Fernandez, Oscar. 2013. Malinowski and the New Humanism. *History of the Human Sciences* 26: 70–87.

Geertz, Clifford. 1973. Thick Description: Toward an Interpretive Theory of Culture. In *The Interpretation of Cultures: Selected Essays*, 3–30. New York: Basic Books.

Glenn, David, and Thomas Bartlett. 2009. Rebuttal of Decade-Old Accusations Against Researchers Roils Anthropology Meeting Anew. *The Chronicle of Higher Education*, December 3. Accessed February 23, 2015. http://chronicle.com/article/Rebuttal-of-Decade-Old/49320/.

Kelty, Christopher, Michael Fischer, Alex Golub, Jason Jackson, Kimberly Christen, Michael Brown, and Tom Boellstorff. 2008. Anthropology of/in Circulation: The Future of Open Access and Scholarly Societies. *Cultural Anthropology* 23 (3): 559–588.

Leopold, Robert. 2008. The Second Life of Ethnographic Fieldnotes. *Ateliers du LESC* 32 (4). Accessed March 18, 2015. http://ateliers.revues.org/3132.

Malinowski, Bronislaw. 1989. *A Diary in the Strict Sense of the Term*. Palo Alto, Calif.: Stanford University Press. First published 1967.

Mandler, Peter. 2013. *Return from the Natives: How Margaret Mead Won the Second World War and Lost the Cold War*. New Haven, Conn.: Yale University Press.

NSF. 2011. Award and Administration Guide: Chapter VI—Other Post Award Requirements and Considerations. 11–1 January 2011. Accessed March 17, 2015. http://www.nsf.gov/pubs/policydocs/pappguide/nsf11001/aag_6.jsp

Ottenberg, Simon. 1990. Thirty Years of Fieldnotes: Changing Relationships to the Text. In *Fieldnotes: The Makings of Anthropology*, edited by Roger Sanjek, 139–160. Ithaca, N.Y.: Cornell University Press.

Pienta, Amy, George Alter, and Jered Lyle. 2009. The Enduring Value of Social Science Research: The Use and Reuse of Primary Research Data. ICPSR Working Papers 2010–11–22. Accessed February 23, 2015. http://deepblue.lib.umich.edu/bitstream/2027.42/78307/1/pienta_alter_lyle_100331.pdf .

Russell, Lynette. 2005. Indigenous Knowledge and Archives: Accessing Hidden History and Understandings. *Australian Academic and Research Libraries* 32 (2): 161–171.

Sanjek, Roger. 1990. On Ethnographic Validity. In *Fieldnotes: The Makings of Anthropology*, edited by Roger Sanjek, 385–418. Ithaca, N.Y.: Cornell University Press.

UK [United Kingdom] Data Archive. 2015. Create and Manage Data: Consent and Ethics. Accessed February 23, 2015. http://www.data-archive.ac.uk/create-manage/consent-ethics.

Chapter 14

Archiving Fieldnotes? Placing "Anthropological Records" Among Plural Digital Worlds

Rena Lederman

"Everyone is shifting to a digital world," Ms. Mueller said, "There may be room for pen and paper when putting up a sign or writing a birthday card, but for note taking and work, there's no way of reversing the current changes."

—Bilton (2014)

The goal of this volume is to understand "the making of anthropology" in increasingly digitized twenty-first-century environments and, in particular, to understand the transformation of fieldnoting since the publication of *Fieldnotes: The Makings of Anthropology* (Sanjek 1990). Taking that baseline seriously, the goal of this chapter is to find a fresh vantage from which to consider our object-in-motion. If *Fieldnotes* did nothing else, it demonstrated that—no matter whether they are considered materially, historically, functionally, relationally, affectively, or in terms of genre or form (among the angles assayed in that collection)—anthropological fieldnotes were never simple things nor was fieldnoting ever a standardized practice.

Whatever fieldnotes have been over the past century, the contemporary social and techno-material environments in which they are located are rapidly changing. Remapping these environments is necessary if we are to navigate them. Toward that end, this chapter adopts a "neo-Boasian" attitude (Bashkow 2008) or "negative strategy" (Strathern 1990). That is, I aim to understand our object by means of contrastive juxtapositions: with what are anthropological practices such as fieldnoting contrasted and conflated, by whom, in what contexts, and to what effects?

This chapter isolates a small cache of these questions for attention. Discussions concerning the archiving of anthropological records have been influenced by recent policy changes among major social and behavioral science (SBS) funders such as the National Science Foundation and National Institutes of Health. Policies mandating "data management plans" to ensure "timely access" to the primary data that funded projects produce—a practice common in the natural sciences—have oriented SBS discussions toward the mechanics of digital "data sharing" for "secondary analysis" (see Heaton 2012, who points out that this methodology is most closely associated with the use of "pre-existing statistical data"). Even anthropological advocates of archiving (such as Fowler 1995) have adopted this idiom ("datasets," "raw material of observation"). Although it may appear commonsense, unmarked, or general, this language references a distinctive research paradigm. The appearance of neutrality leaves the impression that there is, in effect, one "digital world" and one kind of archive.

Nevertheless, there are long-standing archival alternatives that, although not born digital, have been having their holdings digitized over the past couple of decades and that may accommodate common styles of fieldnoting (fieldnotes "in the narrow sense": see below) better than the SBS model. This chapter considers why that wider horizon has most often been obscured from view and why the fog is worth clearing.

Placing Fieldnotes in Plural Digital Worlds

There are many good reasons for preserving fieldnotes beyond the lifetimes of their makers. Indeed, the benefits of archiving anthropological research materials and other informal writing (or "gray literature") have been recognized and championed within anthropology since before digital media were the norm, although these media have vastly expanded our capacity to store and access both our own and one another's work (Silverman and Parezo 1995; see also Leopold 2008; Schmid 2008; Tuzin 1995; Winslow 2009).

For example, Sydel Silverman, former director of the Wenner-Gren Foundation for Anthropological Research, and several colleagues created the Council for the Preservation of Anthropological Records (CoPAR) to convince anthropologists to archive their fieldnotes and other research materials (Parezo, Fowler, and Silverman 2003; Silverman and Parezo 1995). CoPAR was promoted by the National Science Foundation's Anthropology Program (Winslow 2009) and funded by Wenner-Gren, but it initially sought funding from the National Endowment for the Humanities and drew on and developed connections with historiographic and humanistic archiving organizations and institutions, such as the Smithsonian Institution's National Anthropological Archives, whose website has links to the council's projects (http://www.anthropology.si .edu/naa/home/naahome.html).

Although it is unique for being devoted to the preservation of ethnographic fieldnotes, photographs, and related field material (Leopold 2008), the National Anthropological Archives are similar to many other repositories in the United States and elsewhere that are relied on by historians and other humanists. Conventional primary research of such scholars does not involve eliciting or creating sources: controversies during recent decades concerning Cultural Studies, an ethnographically inclined interdisciplinary movement in the humanities, made this conventional orientation even more clear. The same is true of longer-standing controversies in historical studies over "oral history" (see, for example, http://www.goethe.de/ins/za/ prj/wom/orh/enindex.htm), a field devoted to recording the testimony of eyewitness participants in events, with the purpose of supplementing existing document collections (see, for example, http://www.oralhistory.org/ about/do-oral-history/). Their hybrid methodology is why oral history projects, such as Mass Observation in the United Kingdom, are not infrequently mentioned alongside critical discussions of the SBS database archiving model (see Parry and Mauthner 2004). In conventional historiography, elicited information is problematic: the primary research of most historians involves working with pre-existing written sources and other artifacts created by the normal activities of people whose lives they seek to understand. The detective work of searching out sources in formal repositories and private stashes, which enables historians eventually to piece together a story and evoke past worlds, is a creative challenge that they meet with the help of knowledgeable archivists (Darnton 1984: 4; Lucas 1981).

In contrast, for social and behavioral scientists accustomed to creating and controlling their own datasets, "working with documents" supplements their typical "firsthand" survey interviewing and experimental research: it may, for example, involve asking research participants to keep diaries or make drawings (Gibson and Brown 2012). Recently, social and behavioral scientists have also been using "found" sources. Indeed, "data mining" of social media sites such as Facebook, Twitter, and Google Maps ("big data")—which involves working with preexisting materials generated in the course of everyday life in twenty-first-century digital worlds—bears a certain resemblance to historiographic primary research. Nevertheless, social and behavioral scientists have tended to privilege data creation by means of study designs that define research conditions over which the investigator has specified forms of control. Repositories designed for SBS research styles include, for example, those accessible through the Inter-University Consortium for Political and Social Research (ICPSR, established in 1962 and centered in the United States at the University of Michigan); in the United Kingdom, they include the Economic and Social Data Service (ESDS dates from 2004) and Qualidata, specializing in qualitative source material (established in 1994; see http://www.socresonline.org.uk/1/3/qualidata.html).

Developing this comparison, we can use the tags "datasets" and "documents" to index two research and archiving cultures whose differences (for all their similarities) are important to understand. The idea of researcher control has a different valence in each: control is the key condition for validity in SBS, whereas in historiography, eliciting texts is looked upon with suspicion. Dataset- and document-archiving cultures overlap in the training and activities of professional archivists, but it is notable that SBS discussions of "data preservation and sharing" that reference ICPSR are conducted as if the Smithsonian and the American Philosophical Society document archives did not exist.

However much they may be grouped definitively in social science divisions of colleges and universities, anthropologists' practices with respect to their fieldnotes depart from and overlap with *both* of these research cultures. For example, like historians and other humanists, anthropologists tend to eschew controlled research conditions. They favor the kind of understanding that can be gleaned by participatory observation in "naturalistic," everyday settings: this is one of the reasons why their research periods tend to be lengthy (adapting The Supremes, you can't hurry life. . .). At the same time, like most social and behavioral scientists, anthropologists produce their own primary research records (fieldnotes, interview transcripts, video recordings).

Perhaps most anomalously, despite sociocultural anthropologists generally approving of the idea of archiving their notes, the practice of archiving is not normative in their subfield. Whereas other disciplinary subfields are comfortable with data sharing, sociocultural anthropologists have a long history of curating their field research materials privately, as a personal archive, shared selectively if at all during their lifetimes (Schmid 2008: 32). What is more, they have little in the way of professional protocols concerning depositing their data in public repositories, even at the ends of their careers. In these ways, they are rather like the many donors of personal papers whose trust archivists are at pains to cultivate and whose terms of access they negotiate (Leopold 2008).

In a later section of this chapter, I will consider in more detail anthropologists' resistance to sharing (an apparently odd penchant, considering their Maussian heritage). For now, consider that one kind of record generated by both science-oriented and interpretive sociocultural anthropologists—I will call them fieldnotes "in the narrow sense"—is anomalous *even* when compared with other kinds of qualitative social science records. By "fieldnotes in the narrow sense," I mean notes on conversations, events, and experiences—what the fieldworker sees, hears, is told, and is shown—in the form of handwritten and word-processed journals; diaries; letters and emails to colleagues, friends, and family; and the like—especially those not prompted by focused research routines (for example, premeditated interviewing).

Fieldnotes in the narrow sense can be usefully contrasted with interview tapes and transcripts, filled-out questionnaires and survey forms, and artifacts that anthropologists may "collect" during their research (everything from their hosts' writings to photocopies of archived documents). Other chapters in this volume illustrate how the forms and quantities of these other materials have changed over the past generation with the expansion of digital media. These are all important clues concerning the persons and agencies whose on- and offline activities we work to understand: in work on the politics and practices of research ethics regulation, I have found publicly available transcripts of presidential commission hearings, podcast and listserv discussions, and similar media to be indispensable. However, fieldnotes in the narrow sense—anthropologists' notoriously idiosyncratic inscriptions relating to their primary face-to-face fieldwork—are worth considering separately on account of their anomalousness compared with SBS datasets.

Contributors to *Fieldnotes* offered detailed examples of these kinds of notes, including their practical conditions of production, their unstandardized form and content, and, particularly, their amalgam of interpretive description, descriptive reflection, inherent specificity, and unavoidable, irremediable incompleteness (the last captured succinctly in the title of Jean Jackson's [1990] contribution to that volume: "I Am a Fieldnote"—a phrase, borrowed from one of her interviewees, that points to the importance of embodied memory in ethnographic sensemaking). These qualities render fieldnotes in the narrow sense incompatible with the critical SBS distinction between data "collection" and data "analysis" (that is, between "raw" or "primary" data and processed "findings" and the like). No matter what is done with them after they are written down, much of the substantive value of these particular "primary data" or "raw materials" is inextricable from their authors. (For this reason, as Nancy Lutkehaus [1990], Margery Wolf [1990], and other *Fieldnotes* authors illustrate, fieldnotes work very well as sources for histories of anthropology.)

Fieldnotes, Fieldnotes in the Narrow Sense, and Anthropological Practice

Fieldnotes remains a unique resource for fieldworkers. Most of the available literature on this aspect of field practice is written from a single authorial perspective and in a more or less prescriptive voice, but *Fieldnotes* distinctively offers multiple (indeed, conflicting) points of view, expressed through a variety of genres (memoir, history, ethnographic report) but all descriptively grounded and, not infrequently, analytically provocative. Over the past two decades, assigning it in graduate and undergraduate field methods courses, I have been impressed with the value of that variety for readers.

The collection's chapters were written in the middle and later 1980s amid a pervasive but still unconventional reflexivity concerning the anthropological project: in the wake of critical consciousness raising concerning the discipline's colonial contexts and gender biases in the 1960s and 1970s, our attention had most recently been directed to ethnographic writing, albeit overwhelmingly to the published end products of anthropological labor.

Our contemporary self-understanding, which was in formation during the final decades of the twentieth century, has it that "here" and "there" (or the observing/representing West and the observed/represented Rest) were conceptually segregated until critical demystification of the colonizing projects that enabled sociocultural anthropology rendered that segregation politically untenable and intellectually unconvincing. Consequently, anthropologists began to introduce explicit representations of the intellectual reciprocities of their field relationships into their published work, along with their material, sociable, and other (inter)dependencies (see, notably, Fabian 1983).

It is important to recognize just how countercultural those moves were in anthropology's SBS neighborhood, which, especially after World War II, inclined heavily toward objectivist natural-science research paradigms (see, for example, Steinmetz 2005): that is, toward paradigms in which reliable results depend on minimizing observer idiosyncrasies so that observed behavior can be understood as a function of research conditions that any investigator could in principle replicate. In the face of these inclinations, sociocultural anthropology's tenacious practical (if by no means consistently theory-driven) commitment to an alternative research model is remarkable.

Reliability—the SBS research standard—is contingent on investigator-controlled conditions that can theoretically be specified in advance (for example, sample surveys and experimental designs) and that enable rigorous hypothesis testing. Replacing reliability with realism, the value of anthropological fieldwork is understood to depend on the quality of a fieldworker's relationships with his or her hosts. It is also a function of the fieldworker's disciplined relinquishment of control over the investigation's location, pacing, and language: not infrequently, even the topical framing of a project is open to revision. Moving progressively "off the veranda" (Lederman 2013) from at least Malinowski's time—moving, that is, more definitively outside observer-controlled locations—sociocultural anthropology harbored at least implicit humanistic inclinations, even in the face of the high positivism of post–World War II SBS, when methods for mitigating "observer effects" and isolating variables for more precise study were innovated and elaborated, notably in social psychological experimentalism and sociological sample survey design (Steinmetz 2005). While sociocultural anthropologists participated in these trends (for one notable example, see the Human Relations Area Files website, http://hraf.yale.edu/about/), their commitment to realism tempered anthropological positivism throughout the twentieth century in ways I cannot elaborate here (but see Lederman 2005).

As their published work became more reflexive—integrating narrative accounts of ethnographers' practices, experiences, and field relationships—this practical undermining of standardized observer/observed relations and valorizing of openness to contingent discovery became increasingly visible.

It was always evident in their fieldnotes. Therefore it is no wonder that *Fieldnotes* contributed to these historical trends. Because of the practice-focused nature of their contributions, *Fieldnotes* authors undercut the fieldwork/homework distinction: they did not represent fieldnotes simply as products and indices of "the field" and "fieldwork." On the contrary, the contributions leave one with the impression that the activities of writing and reading fieldnotes do not clearly demarcate distinct reference frames and socio-moral relationalities. In other words, because *Fieldnotes* is centered on grounded description rather than on idealized prescription, it makes evident that the spaces of fieldwork (ethnographic research and its personal and professional enabling conditions) and of homework ("writing up," teaching, and the like and their personal and professional enabling conditions) blur even when anthropologists travel long distances to do their research.

For present purposes, my point is that both the obviousness of this way of describing anthropological practice and our intradisciplinary arguments over these issues set anthropology off from neighboring disciplines in the social and behavioral sciences. The work of translation on which "the making of anthropology" depends is about opening up, spreading out, and sorting through these hybrid experiences so as to conjure the objects of our specifically professional attention. At its core, that work involves decisions about where and how definitively to locate the boundaries between professional and personal meanings and practices: both ethnographers' field relationships—the source of their knowledge claims—and their fieldnotes are situated squarely on that shifting line.

Why Anthropologists Don't Share

In an earlier section, I noted sociocultural anthropologists' resistance to archiving their notes, certainly during their careers but also, not infrequently, after they retire. It is true that some have donated a portion of their research materials to university libraries, special repositories (such as the Tuzin Archive for Melanesian Anthropology at the University of California, San Diego), and the National Anthropological Archives. Over the years, the Smithsonian and other institutions have acquired large collections of anthropological papers: these resources are valued by indigenous scholars doing cultural heritage and land claims research, as well as by language revitalization activists (Leopold 2008; Schmid 2008); they are also valued by historians of anthropology. Nevertheless, anthropologists have a well-established convention of retaining their fieldnotes as a personal archive, a conventional reticence based in part on ethical principles: sociocultural anthropologists recognize a professional obligation to protect the confidentiality of what they learn by virtue of the privileged access to private and personal information that long-term field relationships make not only possible but inevitable. Ironies abound: for example, Robert Leopold (2008) describes some unintended consequences of this value once fieldnotes are archived.

Fieldnotes also made clear that there is no standard format or content to fieldnotes in the narrow sense. A quilting of personal and professional genres distinctive to each writer, serving multiple ends, fieldnotes are a mix of quoted and paraphrased speech inscribed in the original or as translations, descriptive interpretations of people and events, and reflexive commentary. This irregularity has persisted stubbornly in the face of copious practical advice in methods handbooks about how one might separate personal writing and interpretation from archivable description. Advocates of archiving are passionate about the importance of regularizing this distinction while also acknowledging the actual state of play. For example, in her contribution to the Committee on the Preservation of Anthropological Records (CoPAR) publications, Catherine Fowler (1995) counterposes "personal records" (correspondence, diaries, manuscripts) with "the raw material of observation" (or "basic data, the primary set of descriptive observations"); in the next breath, however, she admits that "Personal records, of course, may also contain synthesized (and sometimes primary) data" (64). She therefore advises that "a sound practice might be to keep notes separate from a field diary," in which one would record personal experience, initial analyses, and "details that might be important for interpretation but potentially damaging" (67). This is apparently sensible advice, but numerous examples in *Fieldnotes* suggest that having a separate field diary does not begin to address the roots of the archiving challenge posed by anthropological fieldnotes.

The American Anthropological Association's 2003 "Statement on the Confidentiality of Field Notes" digs deeper. It is informative that the statement doesn't explicitly reconcile its concern for the ethics of confidentiality with archiving advocates' concern for the ethics of preserving and making available "the raw material of observation." After asserting that "a researcher's fieldnotes should be considered privileged information as a matter of course," the statement characterizes fieldnotes as

> [A] hybrid of research ideas, research observations, general thoughts, and even a diary. They are works in progress and are often incomplete notations meant not only to clarify thoughts on situations but also to provide mental stimulation to help recall peripheral aspects of situations. To view them outside of the context of such is to view them in an incorrect light and distorts their true nature and utility. It is extremely important for researchers to be able to maintain the security of their thoughts and ideas, as well as the material gained through the confidence of the people studied or with whom they work. (American Anthropological Association 2003)

In other words, fieldnotes are not objectifiable as "data" collected or mined from external sources. To adapt historiographic categories, fieldnotes' qualities as primary sources (that is, firsthand transcriptions and paraphrases of their interlocutors' words and inscriptions of their own observations and experiences) are inextricable from their qualities as secondary sources (that is, products of scholarly interpretation, analysis, and reflexive scrutiny). Using SBS categories, these qualities render the distinction between data collection and data analysis theoretically inscrutable and difficult to apply in practice.[1] The statement's reference to the "security" of the researcher's thoughts, and material acquired in "confidence" from the people with whom they work, reminds us that fieldnotes are products of the relationships that their authors were able to form with the people with whom they interacted. The statement also alerts us to another difference between fieldnotes in the narrow sense and most "found" sources, digitally or otherwise mediated: fieldnotes are necessarily incomplete, because they work as mnemonic keys. However much anthropologists refer to their ethnographic writing as "based on" their notes, the anthropologist's memory holds the information necessary for making full use of them.

The point has broad relevance. That memory (or informal knowledge) is critical to a wide range of research beyond ethnographic fieldwork is at least indirectly acknowledged in the SBS literature concerning secondary data analysis.

Datasets Don't Speak for Themselves

As noted at the outset of this chapter, the phrase "secondary data analysis"—pervasive in writings on SBS archiving—most often refers to the use of pre-existing statistical data; in that context, in addition to referring to the study of datasets that other investigators have created, the term "secondary" can also qualify analyses of one's own data that were not anticipated in the original study design. Controversies concerning the secondary analysis of quantitative data will not concern me here (but see, for example, Goodwin 2012).

I will mention one key way in which documentary and database archiving cultures differ such that the former may be a better fit for anthropological fieldnotes. Discussion of secondary analysis of archived qualitative data is full of quarrels concerning the practical, ethical, and philosophical dimensions of providing secondary users with the metadata they may need to determine whether or how an archived dataset is suitable for their questions (see, for example, Bishop 2006, 2007; Cliggett 2013; Hammersley 1997, 2010; Irwin 2013; Irwin and Winterton 2011; Johnson and Bullock 2009; Mauthner and Parry 2009; Moore 2007).

Detailed proposals addressing this problem (such as Bishop 2006; Irwin and Winterton 2011) are meant to be helpful. But they lead one to conclude either that primary researchers would be burdened with crushing labor in the service of secondary users or that the metadata requested are hopelessly thin. No matter how detailed the contextual information provided is, secondary users are likely to need not so much something more as something else. The bottom line is that embodied experience *substantively* distinguishes primary field researchers from secondary users of research records, even when those records are not products of richly experiential long-term fieldwork: metadata can compensate for thin notes but is a poor proxy for living memory, which is not an archivable artifact (compare Bishop 2006: 12).

Here, once again, I am struck by the many linguistic and other disconnections between literatures on secondary data analysis/dataset archives and historiography/documentary archives. The historian's "primary source" documents are the SBS researcher's "pre-existing datasets": the very materials subject to "secondary data analysis" and at the center of arguments over the "metadata." Nevertheless, historians have never had anyone to fill them in on context. Setting oral history aside (rarely a first choice, as noted earlier), they work with whatever documentary and artifactual traces of the past have survived into the present. Because those traces were not produced for future scholars' purposes, there are no deliberately proffered metadata. How then does a user of such evidence cope?

Historians are detectives (see, for example, Ginzburg 1989): they rely on the skills of knowledgeable archivists, collegial advice (footnotes being the most formal and prominent kind), and their own cultivated ability to locate sources that answer their evolving questions. Following leads and being alert to the possibility of discovering clues that one had not anticipated are the creative challenges of historiography.

In conventional qualitative social science, "the use of documents in research" is special enough to deserve dedicated justification and guidance (see, for example, Gibson and Brown 2012). "Archives" referred to in this literature may have little in common with "archives" referred to in historiographic or humanities scholarship. To the extent that anthropologists have used fieldnotes, photographs, tapes, and papers of other ethnographers held in repositories such as the Smithsonian's National Anthropological Archives or university collections (see, for example, Dobrin and Bashkow 2006; Lutkehaus 1990; McDowell 1991), their purposes make a neat fit with typical research practice in historiography, literary studies, and the arts, all of which take the use of documents in research for granted (see, for example, Geselbracht 1986; Howell and Prevenier 2001).

Discussions about research using document archives and discussions about using database archives are parallel universes: the two rarely intersect (but see Hammersley 1997: 134; Mauthner and Parry 2009; also Stenhouse 1978). In contrast with SBS dataset archiving, traditions of humanist primary source preservation and research are centuries old, long predating digital media (Grafton 1999). As these archival traditions have, in recent years, been transformed by a proliferation of "digital humanities" initiatives (Hockney 2004), historians, anthropologists, and other humanistic scholars have renovated their rationales for valuing the original materialities of their sources (Association for Social Anthropology in Oceania 2013; Chassanoff 2013; Duff, Craig, and Cherry 2004).

While fieldnotes in the narrow sense may find a better home in documentary collections than in dataset archives, forces are at work that threaten to blur the difference I have been outlining.

Archived Fieldnotes and Human Research Ethics Regulations

As idiosyncratic amalgams of "research ideas, research observations, general thoughts, and even a diary," as "incomplete notations" to everyone but the persons whose memories complete them, and as "works in progress," fieldnotes in the narrow sense foil efforts to sort the public, archivable bits from the private ones. These qualities render the familiar distinction between primary (or "raw") data "collection" and secondary data "analysis" unintelligible. They are therefore a better match with the preservation and access conventions of historiographic document collections, whose archivists seek donations by or on behalf of historical actors, than they are with the conventions of repositories originally designed for quantitative datasets. Because their evocative qualities most completely engage ethnographic fieldwork's openness to surprise, fieldnotes in the narrow sense present an especially awkward fit as dataset-oriented digital archiving requirements become the funding norm.

They also align poorly with another powerful feature of contemporary social research environments, all of which have become subject over the past generation to human subject research (HSR) regulations that govern institutional review boards (IRBs, that is, research ethics committees). Heavily influenced by bioethics and the history of biomedical research scandals, IRBs' central concern is with the protection of research participants: their capacity for informed consent and their privacy. IRBs are only tangentially concerned with facilitating research: when it comes to research involving human participants, the advancement of knowledge and privacy protection are understood as conflicting values. The definition of "research," the object of regulation, is modeled on biomedical values, closely related to the SBS ideal (Lederman 2007).

This is evident in changes proposed a few years ago in the regulations. I will describe them briefly to suggest one more reason why anthropologists ought to approach the question of archiving fieldnotes with an awareness of the plurality of "digital worlds" and full range of alternatives available to us.

In July 2011, the *Federal Register* published an "advanced notice of proposed rulemaking" (ANPRM) that outlined plans for the first general overhaul of IRB regulations in forty years (Department of Health and Human Services 2011). Published notices concerning rulemaking are invitations to the public to comment on proposals before they are formalized.

These proposed regulatory revisions took aim at the expanding workloads with which IRBs have been coping and their related inability to devote adequate attention to the review of research activities posing "greater than minimal" risks, the category of risk requiring "full board" reviews of research plans. The ANPRM identified the cause as IRB overwork with a vast expansion in both the volume and diversity of research.

This document's creative centerpiece is a proposal to "excuse" from IRB review a class of research activities associated with a freshly distinguished kind of risk that it calls "informational": that is, the release of "personally identifiable information" (such as medical records, grades, or domestic behavior). The ANPRM notes that the vast majority of social research poses mostly informational risks (in contrast with biomedical and behavioral science experiments, which tend to pose "physical" or "psychological" risks as well). The key point here is that informational risks are understood to be posed not by the research process itself but only after data are collected. Excusal is to be contingent on the researcher putting in place a data protection plan to mitigate that risk before data analysis begins. Whereas, at present, one's research proposal must be approved by an IRB *before* one begins research, under the proposed regulations, one could begin research after registering it by means of a one-page form.

A quick reading of the ANPRM initially had historians, sociologists, and others elated. To some constitutional scholars and the American Association of University Professors, the prior review of research plans had always smacked of censorship (see Hamburger 2005), so this appeared to be a terrific move. This also appeared to be a boon to sociocultural anthropologists, who had long complained that responding to IRB questions concerning research designs, sampling strategies, and the like forced them to misrepresent fieldwork. Honest responses characterizing one's research plan as improvisational openness to serendipitous opportunities and informant-governed constraints always risk being branded incompetent (IRBs being guided by biomedical evaluative standards).

But a closer reading revealed significant problems. The ANPRM distinguishes between "data collection" and "data analysis." From a strictly regulatory perspective, "research" specifically refers to "data collection"—for example, distributing and then collecting "filled out" questionnaires, running an experiment, or (let's say) gathering online sources such as listserv threads. From a regulatory perspective, "data analysis" is not "research": it is what one does afterward.

Casting about for a model system for data management and security that could be used to minimize "informational" risk before data analysis begins, the proposed rules seize on the national standards governing the protection of health information defined by the 1996 Health Insurance Portability and Accountability Act (HIPAA). All research records posing "informational" risks by virtue of containing "personally identifiable private information" would be treated like medical records: they would need to be stripped of personal identifiers before analysis could commence.

Needless to say, this requirement would radically transform most anthropologists' use of all of their research materials: both hard-copy sources and the twenty-first-century digital kind. But consider what this means for fieldnotes in the narrow sense. Most anthropologists' fieldnotes would be rendered illegible if they were stripped of personally identifiable information pertaining to the people they consulted and observed in the course of fieldwork—a requirement not adequately addressed by the use of personal and place pseudonyms. Fieldnotes are, after all, also shot through with personally identifiable information about the anthropologist, whose research locations and circumstances are matters of public record. What is more, as mnemonic aids, even unredacted fieldnotes are the tip of the informational iceberg: the fieldworker's memory and that of his or her interlocutors would remain intact (or so one would hope).

These regulatory changes will most likely not come to pass as proposed: public commentary was almost unanimously against using HIPAA as a model for mitigating informational risk. Nevertheless, the proposals are significant as indicators of the dominance of a model of "research" incompatible with anthropological field practices.

Conclusion

Two trends stand out as especially salient with regard to archiving field-notes. The first of these is the expansion of digital media since 1990 and its cultural impacts. We are liberated with the advent of email, listservs, social networking, online conference webcasts, GPS, and the rest; at the same time, Bowker (2007) associates "databasing the world" with the rise of governmentality. Excitement about the research potential of data mining runs parallel with worries over information science innovations that enable just about any person—however anonymized—to be reidentified (see, for example, http://www.cs.utexas.edu/~shmat/shmat_cacm10.pdf). Recent controversies over the privacy implications of the donation of several years of Twitter archives to the Library of Congress (http://www.nytimes.com/2010/04/15/technology/15twitter.html) and joint academic/corporate manipulation of Facebook news feeds (http://www.nytimes.com/2014/06/30/technology/facebook-tinkers-with-users-emotions-in-news-feed-experiment-stirring-outcry.html) index the confused state of public discourse (see also Bourne 2014; Israel 2014) at the same time that privacy protection has become an increasingly central value both in law and in archiving scholarship, trumping other values (Kosseim 2007; Speck 2010).

Second, as Bowker's reference to governmentality implies, during this same period we have also witnessed the rise of "audit culture" and, within that, the expansion and intensification of biomedically inspired regulatory oversight of human research ethics. Here too, especially if we are focusing on social research, individual privacy protection trumps the preservation of a historical record and public access to information.

These forces will likely have an unpredictable impact on sociocultural anthropology over the next decades. I am by no means advocating a return to paper files. Nevertheless, it has to be said that their very disadvantages and inconveniences—their resistance to replication, their locatedness—are also strengths if privacy protection reigns. If preservation and access are in the foreground, then we need to remember that although we can still read paper records decades, centuries, even millennia after they were written, digital media—say, my five and a half inch floppy disks with DOS-based WordStar files from the 1980s—have, thus far, become unreadable remarkably quickly. Questions of media aside, the anthropological habit of curating fieldnotes privately has meant that the person to whom that information was entrusted directly was responsible for its care and ultimate disposition. Although that arrangement may disintegrate in the face of regulatory and funder pressures, its salient values can be preserved if we are aware of alternative archiving options (see, for example, Asher and Jahnke 2013).

My essential point is simple: sociocultural anthropologists should be aware of the differences between documentary and database archiving cultures (their similarities notwithstanding) and should also be aware of the larger forces that have tended to treat the SBS database model as a neutral standard. As a discipline, anthropology straddles the border, sharing research styles and interests with both cultures, but it relies most heavily on NSF, NIH, and other SBS funders, all of which presume database archiving. IRB oversight—another context that takes database archiving for granted as the standard—has likewise biased anthropologists' thinking about the long-term disposition of their research materials. Consequently, an active and explicit awareness of the fullest range of archiving options is prerequisite to keeping options that are less favored in these contexts wide open and their value clearly visible.

Acknowledgments

This chapter began as a talk presented as part of the American Anthropological Association annual meeting panel "eFieldnotes: Makings of Anthropology in a Digital World," organized by Roger Sanjek and Susan Tratner (Chicago, November 2013). I thank Roger and Susan for inviting me to participate; thanks also to Robert Leopold for his comments and corrections.

Note

1. The Human Relations Area Files (HRAF, http://hraf.yale.edu/) has arranged its elaborately searchable index and related tools for facilitating the comparative analysis of world cultures on "cultural materials." These have tended to be published ethnographic work and manuscripts, not collections of unpublished documents. It deserves a separate discussion, at the least, for what it reveals about the tendency of anthropologists to treat ethnographies as primary sources for comparative analysis and theory building (compare Cliggett 2013: 3).

Bibliography

American Anthropological Association. 2003. Statement on the Confidentiality of Field Notes. Accessed February 26, 2015. http://www.aaanet.org/stmts/field notes.htm.

Asher, Andrew, and Lori Jahnke. 2013. Curating the Ethnographic Moment. *Archive Journal* 3. Accessed February 26, 2015. http://www.archivejournal.net/issue/3/archivesremixed/curating-the-ethnographic-moment/.

Association for Social Anthropology in Oceania. 2013. ASAONET Archive: Old Fieldnotes/Journals. Accessed December 18–23, 2013. Available by request from ASAONET@listserv.uic.edu.

Bashkow, Ira. 2008. A Neo-Boasian Conception of Cultural Boundaries. *American Anthropologist* 106 (3): 443–458.

Bilton, Nick. 2014. Fare Thee Well, My Pen: The Demise of the Pen. *New York Times*, E2. Accessed February 26, 2015. http://www.nytimes.com/2014/07/24/fashion/the-demise-of-the-pen.html?_r = 1.

Bishop, Libby. 2006. A Proposal for Archiving Context for Secondary Analysis. *Methodological Innovations Online* 1 (2): 10–20.

———. 2007. A Reflexive Account of Reusing Qualitative Data: Beyond Primary/Secondary Dualism. In *The Secondary Analysis of Qualitative Data*. Vol. 3 of *Sage Secondary Data Analysis*, edited by John Goodwin, 141–163. London: Sage.

Bourne, Alden. 2014. Historians' Efforts to Research Civil War PTSD Thwarted by Privacy Law. Accessed February 26, 2015. http://nepr.net/news/2014/04/18/historians-efforts-to-research-civil-war-ptsd-thwarted-by-privacy-law/.

Bowker, Geoffrey. 2007. The Past and the Internet. In *Structures of Participation in Digital Culture*, edited by Joe Karaganis, 20–37. New York: Social Science Research Council.

Chassanoff, Alexandra. 2013. Historians and the Use of Primary Source Materials in the Digital Age. *The American Archivist* 76 (2): 458–480.

Cliggett, Lisa. 2013. Qualitative Data Archiving in the Digital Age. *The Qualitative Report* 18 (24): 1–11. Accessed February 26, 2015. http://www.nova.edu/ssss/QR/QR18/cliggett1.pdf.

Darnton, Robert. 1984. *The Great Cat Massacre*. New York: Basic.

Department of Health and Human Services. 2011. Human Subjects Research Protections: Enhancing Protections for Research Subjects and Reducing Burden, Delay, and Ambiguity for Investigators. *Federal Register* 76 (143): 44512–44531. Accessed February 26, 2015. http://www.gpo.gov/fdsys/pkg/FR-2011-07-26/pdf/2011-18792.pdf.

Dobrin, Lise, and Ira Bashkow. 2006. "Pigs for Dance Songs": Reo Fortune's Empathetic Ethnography of the Arapesh Roads. *Histories of Anthropology Annual* 2: 123–154.

Duff, Wendy, Barbara Craig, and Joan Cherry. 2004. Historians' Use of Archival Sources: Promises and Pitfalls of the Digital Age. *The Public Historian* 26 (20): 7–22.

Fabian, Johannes. 1983. *Time and the Other: How Anthropology Makes Its Object*. New York: Columbia University Press.

Fowler, Catherine. 1995. Ethical Considerations. In *Preserving the Anthropological Record*, edited by Sydel Silverman and Nancy Parezo, 63–72. 2nd edition. New York: Wenner-Gren Foundation for Anthropological Research.

Geselbracht, Raymond. 1986. The Origins of Restrictions on Access to Personal Papers at the Library of Congress and the National Archives. *The American Archivist* 49 (2): 142–162.

Gibson, William, and Andrew Brown. 2012. Using Documents in Research. In *The Secondary Analysis of Qualitative Data*. Vol. 3 of *Sage Secondary Data Analysis*, edited by John Goodwin, 205–225. London: Sage.

Ginzburg, Carlo. 1989. Clues: Roots of an Evidential Paradigm. In *Clues, Myths, and the Historical Method*, 96–125. Baltimore, Md.: Johns Hopkins University Press.

Goodwin, John, editor. 2012. *Sage Secondary Data Analysis*. 4 vols. London: Sage.

Grafton, Anthony. 1999. *The Footnote: A Curious History*. Cambridge, Mass.: Harvard University Press.

Hamburger, Philip. 2005. The New Censorship: Institutional Review Boards. *Supreme Court Review* (October 2004 Term): 271–354.

Hammersley, Martyn. 1997. Qualitative Data Archiving: Some Reflections on its Prospects and Problems. *Sociology* 31 (1): 131–142.

———. 2010. Can We Re-use Qualitative Data Via Secondary Analysis? Notes on Some Terminological and Substantive Issues. *Sociological Research Online* 15 (1): 5.

Heaton, Janet. 2004. What Is Secondary Analysis? In *Reworking Qualitative Data*, edited by Janet Heaton, 1–19. London: Sage. Accessed February 26, 2015. http://www.uk.sagepub.com/gray3e/study/chapter20/book%20chapters/What_is_Secondary_Analysis.pdf.

Hockney, Susan. 2004. The History of Humanities Computing. In *A Companion to Digital Humanities*, edited by Susan Schreibman, Ray Siemens, and John Unsworth, 3–19. Oxford: Blackwell.

Howell, Martha, and Walter Prevenier. 2001. *From Reliable Sources: An Introduction to Historical Methods*. Ithaca, N.Y.: Cornell University Press.

Irwin, Sarah. 2013. Qualitative Secondary Data Analysis: Ethics, Epistemology and Context. *Progress in Development Studies* 13 (4): 295–306.

———, and Mandy Winterton. 2011. Debates in Qualitative Secondary Analysis: Critical Reflections. Timescapes Working Paper Series No. 4. Accessed February 26, 2015. http://www.timescapes.leeds.ac.uk/assets/files/WP4-March-2011.pdf.

Israel, Mark. 2014. Gerry Adams Arrest: When Is It Right for Academics to Hand over Information to the Courts? *The Conversation*, May 6. Accessed February 26, 2015. http://theconversation.com/gerry-adams-arrest-when-is-it-right-for-academics-to-hand-over-information-to-the-courts-26209.

Jackson, Jean E. 1990. "I Am a Fieldnote": Fieldnotes as a Symbol of Professional Identity. In *Fieldnotes: The Makings of Anthropology*, edited by Roger Sanjek, 3–33. Ithaca, N.Y.: Cornell University Press.

Johnson, David, and Merry Bullock. 2009. The Ethics of Data Archiving: Issues From Four Perspectives. In *The Handbook of Social Research Ethics*, edited by Donna Mertens and Pauline Ginsberg, 214–228. London: Sage.

Kosseim, Patricia. 2007. Balance Between Privacy Protection and Information Flows. "Office of the Privacy Commissioner of Canada." Speeches. Accessed February 26, 2015. http://www.priv.gc.ca/media/sp-d/2007/sp-d_071126_pk_e.asp.

Lederman, Rena. 2005. Unchosen Ground: Cultivating Cross-Subfield Accents for a Public Voice. In *Unwrapping the Sacred Bundle: Reflections on the Disciplining of Anthropology*, edited by Dan Segal and Sylvia Yanagisako, 49–77. Durham, N.C.: Duke University Press.

———. 2007. Comparative "Research": A Modest Proposal Concerning the Object of Ethics Regulation. *PoLAR: The Political and Legal Anthropology Review* 30 (2): 305–327.

———. 2013. Ethics: Practices, Principles and Comparative Perspectives. In *The Handbook of Sociocultural Anthropology*, edited by James Carrier and Deborah Gewertz, 588–611. London: Bloomsbury.

Leopold, Robert. 2008. The Second Life of Ethnographic Fieldnotes. *Ateliers d'anthropologie* 32. Accessed January 27, 2014. http://ateliers.revues.org/3132

Lucas, Lydia. 1981. The Historian in the Archives: Limitations of Primary Source Materials. *Minnesota History* 47 (6): 227–232. Accessed February 26, 2015. http://collections.mnhs.org/MNHistoryMagazine/articles/47/v47i06p227-232.pdf.

Lutkehaus, Nancy. 1990. Refractions of Reality: On the Use of Other Ethnographers' Fieldnotes. In *Fieldnotes: The Makings of Anthropology*, edited by Roger Sanjek, 303–323. Ithaca, N.Y.: Cornell University Press.

Mauthner, Natasha, and Odette Parry. 2009. Qualitative Data Preservation and Sharing in the Social Sciences: On Whose Philosophical Terms? *Australian Journal of Social Issues* 44 (3): 291–307.

McDowell, Nancy. 1991. *The Mundugumor: From the Field Notes of Margaret Mead and Reo Fortune*. Washington, D.C.: Smithsonian Institution Press.

Moore, Niamh. 2007. (Re)Using Qualitative Data? In *Secondary Analysis of Qualitative Data*. Vol. 3 in *Sage Secondary Data Analysis*, edited by John Goodwin, 121–141. London: Sage.

Parezo, Nancy, Don Fowler, and Sydel Silverman. 2003. Preserving the Anthropological Record: A Decade of CoPAR Initiatives. *Current Anthropology* 44 (1): 111–116.

Parry, Odette, and Natasha Mauthner. 2004. Whose Data Are They Anyway? Practical, Legal and Ethical Issues in Archiving Qualitative Research Data. *Sociology* 38 (1): 139–152.

Sanjek, Roger, editor. 1990. *Fieldnotes: The Makings of Anthropology*. Ithaca, N.Y.: Cornell.

Schmid, Oona. 2008. Inside the National Anthropological Archives: An Interview with Robert Leopold. *Anthropology News* 49 (1): 32–33.

Silverman, Sydel, and Nancy Parezo, editors. 1995. *Preserving the Anthropological Record*. 2nd edition. New York: Wenner-Gren Foundation for Anthropological Research. Accessed February 26, 2015. http://copar.org/par/index.htm.

Speck, Jason. 2010. Protecting the Public Trust: An Archival Wake-Up Call. *Journal of Archival Organization* 8: 31–53.

Steinmetz, George, editor. 2005. *The Politics of Method in the Human Sciences: Positivism and Its Epistemological Others*. Durham, N.C.: Duke University Press.

Stenhouse, Lawrence. 1978. Case Study and Case Records: Towards a Contemporary History of Education. *British Educational Research Journal* 4 (2): 21–39.

Strathern, Marilyn. 1990. Negative Strategies in Melanesia. In *Localizing Strategies: Regional Traditions of Ethnographic Writing*, edited by Richard Fardon, 204–216. Edinburgh: Scottish Academic Press.

Tuzin, Donald. 1995. The Melanesian Archive. In *Preserving the Anthropological Record*, edited by Sydel Silverman and Nancy Parezo, 23–34. 2nd edition. New York: Wenner-Gren Foundation for Anthropological Research.

Winslow, Deborah. 2009. Fieldnotes . . . What Will Happen to Yours? *Anthropology News* 50 (6): 36.

Wolf, Margery. 1990. Chinanotes: Engendering Anthropology. In *Fieldnotes: The Makings of Anthropology*, edited by Roger Sanjek, 343–355. Ithaca, N.Y.: Cornell University Press.

Chapter 15

Digital Engagements: Fieldnotes and Queries for Anthropology Prompted by Iraqi Kurdistan in the Information Age

Diane E. King

What challenges for anthropology might be offered by the Information Age in the Kurdistan Region of Iraq? In this chapter, I will use the fieldnotes I have been writing since 1995 during trips and residential stints there, as well as attention paid by digital means from afar, to ask what this new age might mean for the craft of ethnographic anthropology.

On my first trip to Kurdistan in 1995, I did not bring a computer, because the area where I was working had lost municipal electricity in the 1991 Gulf War and had still not regained it. I was also concerned that, even if I were to bring my laptop for use in the few generator-powered settings that were available, I might lose or damage it. This tool of the budding information age was, on my graduate school budget, expensive, and I needed to preserve it for use during the next academic year's coursework. Although anthropologically reared completely in the computer (if not the Internet) age, when it came to fieldnote-taking, I did not at first proceed with confidence in my Middle East research.[1] Like decades of anthropologists before me, I did my initial note-taking in Kurdistan the old-fashioned way, by writing (often in cursive!) with a pen or pencil on paper. Most other anthropologists and ethnographers who wrote in Iraq and Kurdistan then used these age-old tools. At the very end of the second millennium, computers were the preserve of relief and development agencies, some government offices, and a few elites.

As I write this two decades later, however, millions of screens flicker in Kurdistan. Any computers I have brought to the field in recent years have represented a miniscule proportion of them, and only on the first of my ten Kurdistan research periods to date did I work without one. During my second stint there in 1997–1998, Iraqi Kurdistan was beginning to become the place that it is today, where many people stay up late gaming and using various chat venues to interact with others across the street or across the world and satellites beam in world (and other kinds of) affairs. Kurdistanis are not mere consumers but prodigious producers of digital information. They write novels, poetry, and news stories and, like digitally engaged people anywhere, use new technologies in creative, ever-changing ways. They opine among themselves as well as to the world.

What does the fact of a new information-rich environment mean for sociocultural anthropology, especially that most anthropological of practices, the gathering of fieldnotes? How can, or should, the new digital saturation and context of complex modern states shift an anthropologist's and anthropology's commitments and burdens? Whither our fieldnotes in an age of the protection of human subjects? This chapter will offer a rumination on such questions and issue a challenge to the profession regarding the preservation of anthropological knowledge.

First, I want to do a bit of an inventory in terms of the various methods I have used to gather fieldnotes during my ten research episodes in the Kurdistan Region of Iraq. Iraq is a state that imagined itself as "Arab" through the twentieth century, until it lost control of much of its Kurdish-majority region, which had a successful uprising in 1991 and became largely sovereign. I entered this newly sovereign zone four years later and began to take fieldnotes. I was operating in an environment of low levels of literacy, especially for females. Literacy rates have risen very significantly since then, as the area has remained relatively peaceful following more than a century of profound levels of violence, culminating in a series of mass attacks in the late 1980s that have been labeled genocide. The following period, of more than two decades now, has been largely politically stable.

Enter the anthropologist, taking notes. I was using very traditional data-gathering methods in the late 1990s, when other anthropologists were using more technically advanced methods. In the beginning, the main reason for this was that I had very little access to electricity. If I were to inventory my methods, I would describe something very much out of the first *Fieldnotes* volume (Sanjek 1990): I took scratchnotes or jottings on a little hand-held notepad, and then I used a larger notepad to write up those notes in more detail, almost always within a twenty-four hour period. I was staying with host families, whose members watched as I did this.

In 1997, I introduced a laptop into the equation, but not recordings, because although the area where I was working was politically stable, an overarching sense of political danger from the Saddam Hussein regime still influenced my data-gathering choices, and I felt that to record sound would be too threatening. Through 2002, for sit-down interviews, I still wrote physically on a legal pad. I have never stopped making jottings in small handheld notebooks. In the late 2000s, I started to use sound recording as a data-gathering method, both in the form of recorded interviews and by using quick voice memos in lieu of jottings. Now, in the 2010s, I increasingly acquire data that come to me without prompting, through new technologies. An interlocutor/friend sends me a "sticker" on Viber (see Figure 15.1), or someone in Kurdistan makes a comment on Facebook. A Kurdistani politician tweets. I have used a lot of photography and a bit of videography, which I view as a way to capture history; in other words, I assign it to the humanities and do not engage in it in a systematic fashion.

My presence in Kurdistan as a note-taker has occurred at a profound moment in the history of literacy and recorded history in Iraqi Kurdistan. I am operating at what I believe is the end of an age of colonial interventions in which outsiders described life in Kurdistan in much more detail, and in more enduring ways, than local people did. (Here I do not necessarily celebrate the fact that outsiders played this role, nor do I seek to denigrate it; I am simply pointing it out as a fact of history.) Local people are starting to take up the task in a vigorous way. Although they are taking it up in slightly different forms than we outsiders did, they are still describing and analyzing their own society in ways that they did not before.

At the same time, I want to use my experience and the historical moment to make a broader argument for anthropology: that we need to do more work than we are doing at present to determine what we want our fieldnotes to comprise and to mean in the long-term future, after we are gone but some of our notes remain and speak on our behalf and on behalf of those among whom we conduct research. Some of this work must constitute legal vigilance on behalf of our profession as we go about ethnography as members of modern states. I ask, how can we consider, and position, our fieldnotes so that they will be a valuable and valued part of a cacophony of voices emanating from our fieldsites, as is increasingly the case, rather

Figure 15.1. Viber "stickers" sent from a friend in Kurdistan to the author in the United States, 2014. The device is an iPhone 5. Photograph by Diane E. King.

than documents that represent rare colonial and postcolonial witness accounts, as in the first significant century of the existence of our discipline?

Fieldwork in the Kurdistan Region, Iraq

The period I have spent working in Iraq is very short—spanning a mere two decades. However, I cannot imagine a more profound set of changes converging on and in a place. For an ethnographer, the changes are of a technological nature (see Figure 15.2), of a political nature, and of a methodological nature:

Figure 15.2. Boys gaming in a computer shop in Zakho, Kurdistan, Iraq, 2002. The games were on the local computers' hard drives, not online. Photograph by Diane E. King.

Fieldnote, Friday 15 February 2002
[The friend whose home I was visiting, in the regional capital Hewler] showed me to the laptop computer in her bedroom, where I used the internet. She had a cable run from her brother's office several houses down, which has its own satellite linkup. She also has a mobile phone, which is a new thing since I was here last year.

As a note-taker, I used to be an oddity. I was an oddity for other reasons, such as being an American, but writing and generating material freely, even though I was documenting what I observed and experienced, seemed strange to some people, and they told me so. I was writing whatever I wanted to write on paper and on my computer, and for some, that was a new idea. Many female friends indicated that they especially found strange the idea of a woman sitting and writing whatever she wanted to write. People often made references to my computer, treating it almost as though it were a character in the drama of my everyday life as an American ethnographer in Kurdistan.

One thing that some people seemed to find striking was that I was not using writing as a means for study or memorization, which was common in Iraq, given that the educational system placed a great deal of emphasis on the memorization of texts. For many people, "writing" primarily meant copying a text or transcribing the words of an important religious or secular leader. Both the British-influenced modern education system, adapted and manipulated by the modern Iraqi state for its own purposes, and a much older system of Islamic education have encouraged such an approach to writing.

However, when I sat in a Kurdistani household and typed up my notes, I was writing in a less fettered way than most people around me were used to. My interlocutors do not normally see my notes, but they sometimes ask me about them, and I describe in general terms what I am writing. In the early years, I fielded many questions about what I was writing and why. Women, especially, seemed to have an ongoing sense that my writing activities were a little strange. "Remember that wedding we went to last night?" I would say. "Well, I'm writing down what I saw there."

As the years have gone by, I have found that people have found my activities much less curious. In fact it is now commonly said in Kurdistan that "there are now more writers than readers." There are now many Kurdistani writers, mainly writing in Kurdish, Arabic, or English. Much of what is written is autobiographical and activist, as people chronicle their experiences of injustice and suffering or lobby for political change. Just as similar shifts have occurred elsewhere (Messick 1993), the new writing is self-assured and diverse in comparison to older forms that tended to rely on appeals to authority, whether secular or religious. Much of it appears online. The age of digital subjectivities (Whitehead and Wesch 2012) is in full swing.

If we look at the history of written accounts of life in the Kurdistan Region and in Iraq as a whole, my fieldnotes are part of a body of work mostly written in English that began largely in the nineteenth century with European and European-descent travelers, missionaries, and colonizers (such as Bird 1891, Rich 1836). In the twentieth century, anthropological knowledge came to constitute a third category, as anthropologists such as Robert Fernea (1970 and other works) began to do ethnographic work there. In one case, a missionary, Dorothy Van Ess, produced an ethnography (1961) after spending a year at Columbia working with Margaret Mead. However, the body of work by anthropologists, including anthropologists' fieldnotes, now constitutes a blip on the screen. Massive amounts of information are now produced in and broadcast from Iraqi Kurdistan. Kurdistan's largest publisher is Aras Publishers, which was founded after the 1991 uprising despite opposition from Baghdad and during a double economic embargo that made production and distribution challenging. It mainly publishes in the Sorani dialect of Kurdish. On its website, it notes that it has published "850 books so far" (Aras Publishers 2014). It now makes all of its titles available online as free downloads. In the early years, its books were difficult to obtain outside of Iraqi Kurdistan. I knew one of its representatives, who personally carried paper copies of Aras books in his luggage as he traveled to a variety of Western countries with large Kurdish populations, where the books were gratefully purchased (including by me). As for journalism, Iraqi Kurdistan now has many journalists, several very successful news outlets that release their products in paper and electronically, and many smaller news outlets struggling to compete. In recent years, Rudaw .net has become the best-known journalistic website, releasing its stories in the two main Kurdish dialects, Arabic, and English. Numerous television stations, both local and satellite, serve both the local market and viewers abroad.[2]

A Note and a Query

In the spirit of "notes and queries," the title of the guide for anthropologists produced by the British Association for the Advancement of Science and, later, the Royal Anthropological Institute between the 1870s and the 1950s, I want to make one note about our notes and pose one query. I would like to note that the rise of the Information Age in Iraqi Kurdistan has taken place simultaneously with the rise of the modern state. The modern state began in the Middle East with the close of World War I. By "modern," I am specifically referring to a state that not only fits a basic Weberian definition of modern by claiming a monopoly on violence but also kept track of each of its citizens through legibility practices such as identity cards, provided an increasing number of services to them, and operated within a defined boundary recognized as an international border. However, in the Kurdistani mountains and the adjacent plains where Kurds are the majority, it can be argued that the states headquartered in Baghdad, Tehran,

Ankara, and Damascus never assumed full sovereignty in the twentieth century.

In my observation, however, the Kurdistan Regional Government (KRG) does now have sovereignty over most of the Iraqi portion of the Kurdish homeland. In 2014, its sovereignty was extended as the Islamic State advanced, the Iraqi military retreated, and Kurdish *peshmerga* forces filled the void. Disputed areas remain and, as of this writing, are being actively fought over. However, the KRG is now a complex, recognized government, and it and the population it governs are now very visible on the world stage (King 2014), even though, from the perspective of the world's other governments, they remain a part of "Iraq." So my fieldnotes have been produced in the milieu of a new state, and in time, if they survive and are evaluated in the future, I imagine they will be seen in that context: as documents produced in the early days of the Iraqi Kurdistani state.

Meanwhile, my fieldnotes have also been produced during a time of the intensification of the sovereignty of the American state in late capitalism. The American state exercises sovereignty over our fieldnotes in multiple ways, but I think the most consequential of those ways is through the laws and policies designed to protect human research subjects, as well as those designed to protect the university's economic interests. As an employee of the University of Kentucky with a research protocol approved by its institutional review board (IRB), I am required to follow strict practices of disclosure and consent when I gather structured data through research interviews and other focused interaction. My employer owns my fieldnotes, at least for the time being. The University of Kentucky's Data Retention & Ownership Policy (2011) states that the university owns scholarly data produced by its affiliates, that such data must be retained for five years (with certain exceptions), and that it must be immediately provided to the university administration upon request. None of my superiors have ever requested my notes, but if they did, I would be required to share them. My understanding is that the members of my university's administration are the only people who are allowed to see my fieldnotes at present. (Trained research assistants can also see them. I presently I do not have such an assistant, but a few years ago I was able to hire three students to digitize most of my handwritten notes and other physical research materials.) The administration's interest in the notes is not historical; it is interested in making sure that none of my research subjects are harmed as a result of my interaction with them and ensuring that the ownership of the data benefits the right parties in the eyes of the university.

Thus I operate within a paradox. I would like to see my notes as belonging to Kurdistanis. I would like to see them as telling part of Kurdistan's story. With many other anthropologists, I would like to think that the accounts I have recorded will have a longer lifespan than I do. However, they are owned by an institution that has claimed sovereign ownership of them (University of Kentucky Office of Research Integrity 2011) and that even implicitly retains the right to profit from them (University of Kentucky Provost and Vice President for Research 1993), but that has not expressed interest in or specified how it might or would allow them to constitute part of the record of early Kurdistan. Thus we are presented with a query: whither the fieldnotes produced by anthropologists presently operating in complex modern states?

A Call for Action Within the Profession of Anthropology

To get at this question, we must ask basic questions about curation. Curation questions must be addressed in light of another very important issue, that of the protection of human research subjects. I wholeheartedly support the spirit of the human subjects protection procedures of American universities; I am aware that they grew out of a concern that history could be repeated—most notably, the deceptive Tuskegee Syphilis Study of the mid-twentieth century in the United States, but also unspeakably egregious abuses by the Nazis and others conducting state-sponsored experiments. As a result, researchers working with live human beings are required to take specific measures to protect them from harm—a sign that, at least for now, the American legal system and the legal systems of other countries with similar requirements prioritize the safety of research subjects.

For researchers, however, this can be a mixed blessing. As we go about designing our research projects in the ways that we think will best speak to intellectual questions, we may wish for more freedoms than human subjects review boards grant us. Or, we may feel privileged to receive certain permissions, as I do: Although many researchers are required to use codes or pseudonyms in their fieldnotes, my own approved protocol allows me to use real names and identities as long as the notes are kept under lock and key and I protect the identities of research subjects (except for those who consent in writing) when I write up the research. As a fieldworker, I am grateful for this, because I would find it difficult to record fieldnotes using numbers or pseudonyms. I simply cannot keep that many identities in my head, and I value highly the fact that I know many of my interlocutors personally. Many are my friends and people I see on a continuing and regular basis, and treating them as numbers in my notes could slow down the process of recording notes and therefore reduce the notes' length and richness.

Having people's real names and other identifying features interspersed throughout my thousands of pages of fieldnotes, however, presents a problem of curation for the future. What will happen to my notes after I finish actively using them? Even if my employer now has the right to exercise control over those fieldnotes that I have created while I have been its employee, I will have full ownership of those notes when I retire from or leave the University of Kentucky. I already have full ownership of the fieldnotes I created while affiliated with several previous employers. My heirs will have full ownership of all of my notes (and other professional materials, my "papers," both physical and electronic) when I die.

To a great degree, issues of note preservation, curation, and access must be discussed in terms of specific time horizons. What will matter and apply one year from now differs vastly from what will matter and apply a century from now, after all of my research subjects and I are dead. What seems clear at the moment is that, at least in the near term, the issue of identification of individuals would have to be dealt with if my notes were to become available to a greater number of people than those of us at the University of Kentucky who are currently allowed to see and work with them. Redacting names and identifying features in a way that would preserve as much meaning as possible would be very time consuming. This is time that I simply do not have while I am actively practicing the profession. The time that I have budgeted for research and writing is already filled with gathering new data, analyzing it, and generating scholarly publications.

Another important issue is that public information is mixed in with private. For example, I make kinship charts in the field, noting who is related to whom and a few details about each individual. Most of the information on those charts, for example, the names of a person's claimed lineal male ascendants, is very public. Multiple interlocutors can and do readily provide that same information. However, I may also write some private information on the same sheet of paper.

As these brief examples illustrate (as do others mentioned by my co-authors in this volume), at this point in the history of anthropology and of the modern legal regimes in which anthropologists operate, issues of law and logistics and what appears on a leaf of paper or on a computer screen are extensive, and dealing with them fully is tedious. How many of the fieldnotes created by the thousands of people who have earned a Ph.D. in anthropology since the time of Boas have survived, and will survive, the continuing rise of the modern regulatory state? I think that remains to be seen. The state quite rightly wants to protect the people with whom anthropologists interact, but it seems to be much less concerned with protecting for future generations the knowledge about those people's lives that anthropologists have collected. In other words, its concerns about science and human rights seem to trump concerns about history.

Perhaps even more important for the profession of sociocultural anthropology is the question of how many of the fieldnotes created by these thousands of anthropologists will survive the lack of attention paid to curation by our discipline. During the academic year 2013–2014, the year that I started to write this chapter, I was a one-year faculty fellow in the Department of History at Ohio State University. Two other fellows and I were tasked with thinking for a year about state formation. Being surrounded by historians while thinking about a/the Kurdish state and states in general caused me to think a lot about documents. I spent much of my research energy that year working in archives, and I listened to my historian colleagues talk about documents. It seemed to me that my colleagues regarded documents in a way similar to the way in which we think of our interlocutors/informants. Historians' knowledge begins with a document and sociocultural anthropologists' begins with interlocution. For them, preservation is a given. Their enterprise is only possible because a person or a series of people in the past made a choice to preserve. Historians access a preserved document and create a scholarly publication through interacting with that document and the scholarly literature. We access a person or persons and create a scholarly publication through interacting with that person and the scholarly literature. As Sanjek puts it, we combine "rich ethnographic detail and cohesive supporting framework" into an "anthropological aesthetic" (2014: 41).

During that year, one colleague remarked to me that after a long day working with archival materials from the nineteenth century, he found himself about to utter to someone nearby a sentence in nineteenth-century English. He had started to take on the nineteenth-century community on which he was working as his own, he told me with a laugh. I thought about how my work, while involving a similar, if even more intense, type of personal immersion, also involves an additional step: the creation of written source texts, fieldnotes, which I derive from Kurdish verbal and behavioral material. I do not simply access texts; I interact, create texts from that interaction, and then access those texts later in a manner similar to the way in which a historian accesses an archive—except that for me, the archive is personal, even (as has been pointed out elsewhere in this volume) protected by my own professional organization as "confidential" (American Anthropological Association 2003).

From the point of view of one who has spent a year among historians, whose discipline and institutions depend on documents that are in many instances state owned and highly public and who are busy digitizing many of those documents so that historical source texts can be visible to billions of Internet users simultaneously, our practice of creating semiprivate fieldnotes seems almost bizarre. And yet, I do not know how we could operate any other way. Do I value the trust placed in me by numerous interlocutors, including interviewees who have told me things that in some instances could embarrass them or even get them killed (King 2009)? Absolutely. Their trust is nearly sacred to me. And yet more than one interlocutor/friend from Kurdistan has recently told me that I am writing Kurdistan's history. If I am helping to write its history along with the many other voices who are doing so, then I want as much of my version of this history to be preserved as possible.

So, I call for action: that the American Anthropological Association (AAA) and its relevant sections (especially the American Ethnological Society) take up the issue of fieldnote preservation in a serious way. The AAA and other institutions have already paid quite a bit of attention to curation and archiving. Efforts to showcase and preserve anthropological knowledge include the Registry of Anthropological Data Wiki, the Wenner-Gren Foundation for Anthropological Research Historical Archives Program, and others mentioned elsewhere in this volume and in the original *Fieldnotes* volume (Sanjek 1990). The profession has also paid increasing attention to the dilemmas and issues presented by the requirements for the protection of human subjects. I am very grateful for the work of Lise Dobrin and Rena Lederman of the Committee on Ethics of the AAA, who have made very specific recommendations to the U.S. federal government on behalf of the AAA and the profession of anthropology (Dobrin and Lederman 2011; Lederman, Chapter 14, this volume). They have called for a major rollback of policies that restrict anthropological note-taking and related activities. This is part of a significant conversation at the federal level that is ongoing.

What I hope the profession will do, led in the United States by the AAA and by equivalent organizations elsewhere, is to combine and expand on these two streams of effort. It is now impossible to divorce curation from human subjects protection. There are no easy answers. For me, a midcareer anthropologist with two decades of working in the same fieldsite behind me (as well as work in another site before that for my MA degree), the way forward is not clear. My notes, both physical and electronic, are currently under virtual and physical lock and key, which is where they should be for the moment. But where will they be in fifty years, and who will have access to them?

I do hope to be able to sort much of this out during my lifetime. As I do so, I would like my professional organization to offer guidance in a way that is much more substantive and visible than it has offered to date. I want us to develop some best practices that we do not yet have. According to the Bureau of Labor Statistics (2013), there were 6,560 anthropologists employed in the United States in 2013. Many more living people than that have earned a higher degree in anthropology. Rather than simply affirming for us and others that our notes are confidential, I want the AAA to think more deeply about the store of knowledge that our notes represent. I want it to see those notes as a kind of history and to then help us figure out how to make that history as accessible to future generations as possible and still honor our promises to our interlocutors.

This will take money and time, but it will be worth it—not simply to us, but to communities around the world who have generously allowed us to live among them and write about their lives. Fortunately, others outside anthropology have grappled with many of the issues that will inevitably arise, such as partial redactions, embargoes, and the like. On these issues, the Louie B. Nunn Center for Oral History at my own institution is a leader. The AAA could study the center's best practices and promote and educate its own constituency about those that it found appropriate.

Conclusion

Foucault noted in his article "What Is an Author?" that writing had come to be regarded as a way to ward off death. Once this became the case, it became linked to sacrifice. No longer did it provide immortality to its author (1977: 226). Ethnography differs from fiction, Foucault's main focus in that essay, in that it is supposed to give voice to real rather than made-up characters. However, ethnography shares with fiction a goal of illuminating the human condition. I think one of its major challenges in the present age is to find a way to justify itself and to make itself available while at the same time taking the focus off of itself as a fieldworker's product. It is produced in one modern state, but, in the case of scholars in (for example) the United States who do fieldwork abroad, it is housed and stored and owned in another. What a paradox: at the very historical moment when Kurdistanis assumed sovereignty and, partially as a consequence, started blogging, tweeting, Instagramming, and publicly expressing their opinions as never before, ethnography's future became encumbered by new forms of sovereignty emanating from protective state commitments on the other side of the world.

As an anthropologist who started in the twentieth and now works in the twenty-first century, I want to do all I can to give voice to my interlocutors. My work stands alongside that of Sana al-Khayyat's (1990) study of women's lives in Baghdad, and studies in Kurdistan by Leszek Dziegiel (1981), Andrea Fischer-Tahir (2009), and Robert Brenneman (2007) as the only in-depth ethnographic work carried out in Iraq while the Saddam Hussein regime was in power (1979–2003). I do not want to speak or to try to speak authoritatively but rather to let local people have their say as I record their remarks and observe their activities. I do want my fieldnotes to live on so that they can constitute one of the ways, along with the myriad other new and creative ways in which Iraqi Kurdistanis are now expressing themselves.

Acknowledgments

This piece grew out of a paper I presented at the American Anthropological Association annual meeting in Chicago in November 2013 as a part of the session "eFieldnotes: Makings of Anthropology in a Digital World," organized by Roger Sanjek and Susan Tratner. Lisa Cliggett suggested to Roger and Susan that I participate, and I am grateful to all three of them. I also thank the many people in and from the Kurdistan Region of Iraq who have spoken with me and shown me great hospitality, without whom this rumination on fieldnotes would not be possible.

Notes

1. On the other hand, during the ethnographic research in Malaysia that formed the basis of my MA thesis, I used a Tandy 102, one of the world's first laptops. By the standards of the present, its screen, memory, and battery life were minuscule, but using it to take fieldnotes in 1989 felt very progressive.

2. With few exceptions, Kurdistan has yet to produce its own "native" ethnographers. To my knowledge, Jasim Murad is the only Kurdish anthropologist from Iraq to complete a Ph.D., at UCLA in 1993 (Murad 1993). However, I expect this to change as Kurdistan's universities encourage study in the social sciences and as members of the Kurdish diaspora become more aware of sociocultural anthropology.

Bibliography

Al-Khayyat, Sana. 1990. *Honour and Shame: Women in Modern Iraq*. London: Saqi Books.

American Anthropological Association. 2003. Statement on the Confidentiality of Fieldnotes. Accessed February 28, 2015. http://www.aaanet.org/stmts/fieldnotes.htm.

Aras Publishers. 2014. Our Objectives. Accessed February 28, 2015. http://www.aras publishers.com/about/#our-objectives.

Bird, Isabella L. 1891. *Journeys in Persia and Kurdistan, Including a Summer in the Upper Karun Region and a Visit to the Nestorian Rayahs*. 2 vols. London: J. Murray.

Brenneman, Robert L. 2007. *As Strong as the Mountains: A Kurdish Cultural Journey*. Prospect Heights, Ill.: Waveland Press.

Bureau of Labor Statistics. 2013. Occupational Employment and Wages, May 2013: 19–3091 Anthropologists and Archeologists. United States Department of Labor. Acessed February 28, 2015. http://www.bls.gov/oes/current/oes193091.htm.

Dobrin, Lise, and Rena Lederman. 2011. Comments on Proposed Changes to the Common Rule (76 FR 44512). Accessed February 28, 2015. http://www.aaanet .org/issues/policy-advocacy/upload/Human-Subjects-Research.pdf.

Dziegiel, Leszek. 1981. *Rural Community of Contemporary Iraqi Kurdistan Facing Modernization*. Kraków: Agricultural Academy in Kraków, Institute of Tropical and Subtropical Agriculture and Forestry.

Fernea, Robert A. 1970. *Shaykh and Effendi: Changing Patterns of Authority Among the El Shabana of Southern Iraq*. Cambridge, Mass.: Harvard University Press.

Fischer-Tahir, Andrea. 2009. *Brave Men, Pretty Women? Gender and Symbolic Violence in Iraqi Kurdish Urban Society*. Berlin: Europäisches Zentrum für Kurdische Studien.

Foucault, Michel. 1977. What Is an Author? In *Language, Counter-Memory, Practice*, edited by D. F. Bouchard, 124–127. Ithaca, N.Y.: Cornell University Press.

King, Diane E. 2009. Fieldwork and Fear in Iraqi Kurdistan. In *Violence: Ethnographic Encounters*, edited by P. Ghassem-Fachandi, 51–69. Oxford: Berg.

———. 2014. *Kurdistan on the Global Stage: Kinship, Land, and Community in Iraq.* New Brunswick, N.J.: Rutgers University Press.

Messick, Brinkley. 1993. *The Calligraphic State: Textual Domination and History in a Muslim Society.* Berkeley: University of California Press.

Murad, Jasim Elias. 1993. The Sacred Poems of the Yazidis: An Anthropological Approach. Ph.D. diss., University of California, Los Angeles.

Rich, Claudius James. 1836. *Narrative of a Residence in Koordistan.* London: James Duncan.

Sanjek, Roger, editor. 1990. *Fieldnotes: The Makings of Anthropology.* Ithaca, N.Y.: Cornell University Press.

———. 2014. *Ethnography in Today's World: Color Full Before Color Blind.* Philadelphia: University of Pennsylvania Press.

University of Kentucky Office of Research Integrity. 2011. Data Retention & Ownership Policy. Accessed February 27, 2015. http://www.research.uky.edu/ori/data.htm.

University of Kentucky Provost and Vice President for Research. 1993. Intellectual Property Disposition and Administrative Regulation University of Kentucky. Accessed February 27, 2015. http://www.uky.edu/regs/files/ar/ar7-6.pdf.

Van Ess, Dorothy. 1961. *Fatima and Her Sisters.* New York: John Day.

Whitehead, Neil L., and Michael Wesch. 2012. *Human No More: Digital Subjectivities, Unhuman Subjects, and the End of Anthropology.* Boulder: University Press of Colorado.

Contributors

Jenna Burrell is Associate Professor at the School of Information, University of California, Berkeley.

Lisa Cliggett is Professor of Anthropology at the University of Kentucky.

Heather A. Horst is Associate Professor of Media and Communication at RMIT University in Melbourne, Australia.

Jean E. Jackson, Professor of Anthropology Emerita, Massachusetts Institute of Technology, began teaching at MIT in 1972.

Graham M. Jones is Associate Professor of Anthropology at the Massachusetts Institute of Technology.

William W. Kelly is Professor of Anthropology and Sumitomo Professor of Japanese Studies at Yale University.

Diane E. King is Associate Professor of Anthropology at the University of Kentucky.

Jordan Kraemer is Andrew W. Mellon Postdoctoral Fellow at the Center for the Humanities, Wesleyan University.

Rena Lederman is Professor of Anthropology at Princeton University.

Mary H. Moran is Professor of Anthropology and Africana and Latin American Studies at Colgate University.

Bonnie A. Nardi is Professor in the Department of Informatics at the School of Information and Computer Sciences, University of California, Irvine.

Roger Sanjek taught anthropology at Queens College, City University of New York, from 1972 to 2009.

Bambi B. Schieffelin is Collegiate Professor and Professor of Anthropology at New York University.

Mieke Schrooten is a Ph.D. student in the Department of Anthropology at the University of Leuven and Lecturer in the Department of Social Work at Odisee University College, Brussels.

Martin Slama is a researcher at the Institute for Social Anthropology, the Austrian Academy of Sciences.

Susan W. Tratner is Associate Professor in Business, Management, and Economics at SUNY Empire State College.

Index